Faculty Jurisdiction
of the Church of England

AUSTRALIA AND NEW ZEALAND
The Law Book Company Ltd.
Sydney : Melbourne : Perth

CANADA AND U.S.A.
The Carswell Company Ltd.
Agincourt, Ontario

INDIA
N. M. Tripathi Private Ltd.
Bombay
and
Eastern Law House Private Ltd.
Calcutta and Delhi
M.P.P. House
Bangalore

ISRAEL
Steimatzky's Agency Ltd.
Jerusalem : Tel Aviv : Haifa

MALAYSIA : SINGAPORE : BRUNEI
Malayan Law Journal (Pte.) Ltd.
Singapore and Kuala Lumpur

Faculty Jurisdiction
of the Church of England

by

G. H. Newsom, Q.C., M.A.
*A Bencher of Lincoln's Inn, Chancellor of the
Dioceses of London, Bath & Wells, and St. Albans*

LONDON
SWEET & MAXWELL
1988

Published in 1988 by
Sweet & Maxwell Limited of
11 New Fetter Lane, London.
Laserset by P.B. Computer Typesetting, Pickering, N. Yorks.
Printed by Page Brothers (Norwich) Ltd.

British Library Cataloguing in Publication Data

Newsom, G. H.
   Faculty Jurisdiction of the Church of England
   1.   Church of England. Consistory courts.
   Law
   I. Title
   262.9'83

ISBN 0–421–38760–2

All rights reserved.
No part of this publication may be
reproduced or transmitted, in any form
or by any means, electronic, mechanical, photocopying,
recording or otherwise, or stored in any retrieval
system of any nature without the written permission
of the copyright holder and the publisher, application
for which shall be made to the publisher

©
G. H. Newsom
1988

In memory of
The Venerable Basil Clark Snell, M.A.
Archdeacon of Bedford and later of St. Albans
to whose guidance and help in my early years
as Chancellor of the Diocese of St. Albans
I owe so much.

Chancellor

1. The bishop is not to sit with a chancellor in his Court (as being a thing either beneath him or beside him) no more than the King is to sit in the King's Bench when he has made a Lord Chief Justice.
2. The chancellor governed in the Church, who was a layman: and therefore 'tis false which they charge the bishops with, that they challenge sole jurisdiction: for the bishop can no more put out the chancellor than the chancellor the bishop. They were many of them made chancellors for their lives and he is the fittest man to govern, because divinity so overwhelms the rest.

Table Talk of John Selden Esq.

Printed for J. Wilkie of St. Paul's Churchyard (1777)

LEX TUA MEDITATIO MEA

The Vulgate, Psalm 119, verse 77.

Lambeth Palace London SE1 7JU

FOREWORD

The author of this book was my Chancellor at St. Albans where I discovered him to be an acknowledged expert in the subject upon which he now writes.

This subject is one of growing interest in an age in which conservation of both our natural and architectural heritage has become so important. As a result of the so-called "ecclesiastical exemption" the Church does not have to seek listed building consent in respect of churches in use. The original reason for that exemption was that by its faculty jurisdiction the Church maintained a strict control over the state of its churches, the control far stricter than was at that time maintained over secular buildings.

That control has continued but the faculty jurisdiction commission has now recommended improvements in the system. Some of these, being changes not requiring primary legislation, have been, or are about to be, made. Other changes are currently being considered by the General Synod.

This book is an attempt, and in my opinion a most successful attempt, to make knowledge of the system and how it works readily available to those concerned or interested. It will, no doubt, become required reading and a ready source of reference for Archdeacons and Church Wardens as well as Chancellors, Bishops and Archbishops.

Robert Cantuar.

Preface

Hitherto there has been no book dealing systematically and solely with the faculty jurisdiction. The law, and some of the practice, has had to be gleaned from scattered references in the larger general books on ecclesiastical law; the bulk of the practice has rested on oral tradition and has been subject to wide variations from one diocese to another. Such was the situation which I found when, with no previous professional experience of this subject, I started work as Chancellor of the Diocese of St. Albans in 1958. Such, too, is still the situation which confronts every new archdeacon and also every incumbent, churchwarden or other parish officer who needs, for the first time, to discover what steps he ought to take to obtain proper advice and due approval for work to be done to the church of which he is in charge, chattels appertaining to it, its churchyard or its curtilage. Much help is, of course, available from the Diocesan Registrar and his staff, and from the Diocesan Advisory Committee. But there is no compendious guide to the subject. Thus, when I came to give evidence to the recent Faculty Jurisdiction Commission, I found it most inconvenient that there was no single and authoritative statement of how the jurisdiction actually works or of what is the best current practice.

My purpose, therefore, is to provide a definitive account of the faculty jurisdiction, as exercised in 1988, including the changes made by the Faculty Jurisdiction (Amendment) Rules 1987, which will come into force on April 1, 1988.

For this purpose I have read the report of every ecclesiastical case that has appeared since 1950 in the Law Reports or Weekly Law Reports, as well as many earlier cases which set forth the enduring principles of this branch of the law. I have also drawn extensively on my own experience as chancellor of three dioceses for very many years and as the Chairman of the Rule Committee which made the recent Rules.

Before I became a chancellor I had supposed that his work was concerned with sterile disputes about controversial church equipment, such as candles or thuribles. It soon became apparent that, on the contrary, he is concerned to guide each parish in his diocese to do the very best it can for its church building and contents and for its churchyard or curtilage. The problems are multifarious and are as wide as the problems facing any trustee of an extensive, valuable and interesting property who is concerned that it shall be used, looked after and developed wisely. How the problems are solved by the church courts is no doubt sometimes different from the solution which would commend itself to a scrupulous private owner; that is because the consecrated church and churchyard are set apart by the act of consecration for perpetual sacred uses. But that makes the range of matters for consideration wider rather than narrower. Quite apart from routine cases about repairs and the like, there have been many modern cases, especially in the Diocese of London, where arrangements have been authorised for novel uses of consecrated buildings or land or church curtilages and a settled practice has developed in regard to them. Likewise there have been many cases about valuable goods appertaining to churches, especially organs and silver. In Chapter 4 I have sought to classify these physical subject-matters and to explain what is the law and the best modern practice in regard to each of them.

The faculty jurisdiction is of interest not only to congregations and the officers of the church, but to the public at large because it is concerned with buildings and things which are an important part of the aesthetic possessions of the nation. The church seeks, through the faculty jurisdiction, to look after its own, and its responsibility is recognised, by the state which excludes ecclesiastical buildings in use as such from listed building control. It is unlikely that this exemption will continue indefinitely unless all who are concerned with the faculty jurisdiction understand it and make sure that they use it adequately and efficiently. The intention of this book is to assist them in that large task, and I hope that a copy will be in use in every benefice and by every person who is concerned in the diocesan and central organisations which have responsibility in these matters.

G. H. NEWSOM

Bishop's Cannings,
Devizes

February 1988

Contents

Foreword	vii
Preface	ix
Table of Cases	xv
Table of Statutes	xxiii
Table of Measures	xxv
Table of Abbreviations	xxix

1.	**Introduction**	1
2.	**The Consistory Court, its Judge, Officers, Advisers and Jurisdiction**	7
	The court	7
	The chancellor	7
	The registrar	12
	The jurisdiction	15
	The archdeacon	23
	The diocesan advisory committee	32
	The parties to proceedings in the consistory court	43
3.	**Procedure in the Consistory Court**	52
	Introductory	52
	The petition	54
	Citation, notices and order nisi for faculty	58
	Appearance in opposition, pleadings and interlocutory orders	63
	Hearing	66
	Onus of proof	73
	The order	77
	Appeals	81

4. Fabric and Contents of the Church and Churchyard   83

The fabric of the church	83
Fixed equipment	103
Moveables	112
Reservation of the sacrament	130
Burial in church of cremated remains	133
Armorial bearings	134
Memorial tablets	135

5. Churchyards   139

Introductory	139
Burial rights	143
Re-ordering of churchyards	145
Introduction of new monuments	149
The Disused Burial Grounds Act 1884	153
The Open Spaces Act 1906	161
Reservation of gravespaces and the burial of ashes	163
Exhumation	165
The secular use of consecrated churchyards	168

6. Unconsecrated Buildings and Land   173

Buildings	173
Land	174

7. Enforcement, Costs and Fees   180

Enforcement	180
Costs and fees	184

Appendix A   189

Faculty Jurisdiction Measure 1964	191
Faculty Jurisdiction Rules 1967 as amended by the Faculty Jurisdiction Rules 1987	204

Appendix B		237
Forms of Delegation		239
Appendix C		249
The Ecclesiastical Exemption		251
Index		257

Table of Cases

All Saints', Leamington Priors, *Re* [1963] 1 W.L.R. 806; [1963] 2 All E.R. 1062 .... 129, 186
All Saints', Plymouth, *Re* [1980] 3 W.L.R. 876; (1980) 124 S.J. 741; [1981] Fam. 1, Exeter Consistory Ct. 91, 92
All Saints', Whistable, *Re* [1984] 1 W.L.R. 1164; (1984) 128 S.J. 720; (1985) 82 L.S.Gaz. 38, Commissary Ct. 118
Altofts Parish, *Re* (1941); unreported 132
Asher *v*. Calcraft (1887) 18 Q.B.D. 607 L.J.M.C. 57; 56 L.T. 490; 51 J.P. 598; 35 W.R. 651; 3 T.L.R. 485, D.C. 67
Att.-Gen. *v*. Howard United Reformed Church Trustees [1976] A.C. 363 .... 92, 251, 252
—— *v*. London Parochial Charities [1896] 1 Ch. 541 155
—— *v*. Ripon Cathedral (Dean & Chapter) [1945] 1 All E.R. 479; [1945] Ch. 239; 114 L.J.Ch. 257; 172 L.T. 350; 61 T.L.R. 327; 89 S.J. 235 19

Bermondsey Borough Council *v*. Mortimer [1926] P. 87 .... 156, 158, 162
Bideford Parish, *Re* [1900] P. 314 170
Bosworth and Gravesend Corporation, *Re* [1905] 1 K.B. 403 154
Boyce *v*. Paddington Borough Council [1903] 1 Ch. 109; [1903] 2 Ch. 556 .... 155, 157
Boyle deceased, *Re*; unreported 46
Brumfitt *v*. Roberts (1870) L.R. 5 C.P. 224; 1 Hop. & Colt. 387; 39 L.J.C.P. 95; 34 J.P. 376; 18 W.R. 678 109

Caister-on-Sea (Parish of), *Re*, Norfolk County Council *v*. Knights and Caister-on-Sea Joint Burial Committee [1958] 1 W.L.R. 309; 102 S.J. 197; [1958] 1 All E.R. 394 n.; *sub nom*. Norfolk County Council *v*. Knights, 122 J.P. 115 167
Capel St.Mary, Suffolk (Rector and Churchwardens) *v*. Packard [1927] P. 289; subsequent proceedings [1928] P. 69 107
Christ Church, Chislehurst, *Re* [1973] 1 W.L.R. 1317; 117 S.J. 647; [1974] 1 All E.R. 146, Consistory Ct. 71, 140, 176, 177, 178
Christ Church, Croydon, *Re* [1983] 1 W.L.R. 830; (1983) 127 S.J. 491, Commissary Ct. 88
Clifton *v*. Ridsdale (1876) 1 P.D. 315 113
Coleford Cemetery, *Re* [1984] 1 W.L.R. 1369; (1984) 128 S.J. 814; (1984) 81 L.S.Gaz. 3420 .... 139, 142, 170
Corke *v*. Rainger [1912] P. 69 .... 96, 161, 168

Davey *v*. Hinde [1901] P.95; [1903] P. 221 .... 43, 44
Dixon, *Re* [1892] P. 386; 56 J.P. 841; 8 T.L.R. 744 .... 144, 165, 166
Dupuis *v*. Ogbourne St. George Parishioners [1941] P. 119 .... 135, 136, 137

Ecclesiastical Commissioners for England and Wales, The *v*. Rowe (1880) 5 App.Cas. 736 .... 2, 100, 161, 168
Elphinstone *v*. Purchas (1870) L.R. 3A and E. 66; *sub nom*. Herbert *v*. Purchas (1872) L.R. & P.C. 301, P.C. 107

xv

Table of Cases

Escot Church, Re [1979] Fam. 125; [1979] 3 W.L.R. 339; (1979) 123 S.J. 487, Exeter Consistory Ct. 19, 117

Fagg v. Lee. See Lee v. Fagg.
Fallon v. Calvert [1960] 2 Q.B. 201; [1960] 2 W.L.R. 346; (1960) 104 S.J. 106; [1960] 1 All E.R. 281; 76 L.Q.R. 341, C.A. 69
Faulkner v. Litchfield and Stearn (1845) 1 Rob.Eccl. 184; 3 Not. Cas. 511; 5 L.T.O.S. 21; 9 Jur. 234; 163 E.R. 1007 .... 110, 111
Folkestone Parish (Parishioners) v. Woodward (1880) Trist. 177 73

Hansard v. St. Mathew, Bethnal Green Parishioners (1878) 4 P.D. 46; Trist. 74; sub nom. Re St. Mathew's, Bethnal Green, 42 J.P. 408 .... 43, 44

Jones v. National Coal Board [1957] 2 Q.B. 55; [1957] 2 W.L.R. 760; 101 S.J. 319; [1957] 2 All E.R. 155; [73 L.Q.R. 285; 21 M.L.R. 82], C.A. 69

Kensit v. St. Ethelburga, Bishopsgate Within (Rector) [1904] P. 80; 15 T.L.R. 549 45
Kerr, Re [1894] P. 284; 10 T.L.R. 352 .... 133, 145
Kino v. Rudkin (1887) 6 Ch.D. 160; 46 L.J.Ch. 807 68

Lapford (Devon) Parish Church, Re [1955] P. 205; [1954] 3 W.L.R. 748; 98 S.J. 866; sub nom. Re Lapford [1954] 3 All E.R. 484, C.A.; affirming [1954] P. 416; [1954] 2 W.L.R. 1105; 98 S.J. 375; [1954] 2 All E.R. 310 .... 116, 130, 131, 132
Lee v. Fagg (1874) L.R. 6 P.C. 38; 43 L.J.Eccl. 17; 30 L.T. 800; 38 J.P. 596; 22 W.R. 902, P.C.; affirming sub nom. Fagg v. Lee (1873) L.R. 4 A. & E. 135 .... 43, 45, 46, 47
—— v. Hawtrey [1898] P. 63 .... 1, 2, 16
Liddell v. Westerton (1857) Brod. & F. 117; (1857) 2 L.T.O.S. 54 .. 110, 111, 112
Little Gaddesden Churchyard, Re, ex p. Cuthbertson [1933] P. 150; sub nom. Cuthbertson v. Little Gaddsden Parishioners 77 S.J. 268 ...... 21, 150, 151
London County Council v. Dundas [1904] P. 1; 19 T.L.R. 670 .. 64, 79, 155, 160
—— v. Greenwich Corporation [1929] 1 Ch. 305; 98 L.J.Ch. 49; 140 L.T. 456; 93 J.P. 123; 45 T.L.R. 144; 27 L.G.R. 282 155

Mackonochie v. Penzance (Lord) (1881) 6 App.Cas. 424; 50 L.J.Q.B. 611; 44 L.T. 479; 45 J.P. 584; sub nom. Maconochie v. Penzance (Lord) 29 W.R. 633, H.L.; affirming sub nom. Martin v. Mackonochie (1879) 4 Q.B.D. 697, C.A. 19
Maidman v. Malpas (1884) 1 Hag.Com. 125; 161 E.R. 526 143
Martin v. Mackonochie (1867) 36 L.J.Eccl. 25; (1868) L.R. 2 P.C. 365 113
Matheson, Re [1958] 1 W.L.R. 246; 102 S.J. 161; [1958] 1 All E.R. 202 166

National Employers Mutual General Insurance Association v. Jones [1987] 3 W.L.R. 901 180
Nicholl v. Llantwit Major Parish Council [1924] 2 Ch. 214; 93 L.J.Ch. 602; 131 L.T. 634; 68 S.J. 778 154
Nickalls v. Briscoe [1892] P. 269 .... 2, 17
Noble v. Reast [1904] P. 34 .... 45, 46, 47

Oxford (Bishop) v. Henly [1907] P. 88; 23 T.L.R. 152; subsequent proceedings [1909] P. 319 130

Paddington B.C. v. Attorney-General [1906] A.C. 1; 75 L.J.Ch. 4; 93 L.T. 673; 70 J.P. 41; 54 W.R. 317; 22 T.L.R. 55; 50 S.J. 41; 4 L.G.R. 19, H.L.; reversing *sub nom.* Boyce v. Paddington B.C. [1903] 2 Ch. 556, C.A. 141, 155, 156, 157, 158
Peek v. Trower (1881) 7 P.D. 21; 45 J.P. 797 73
Perivale Faculty, the, *Re* [1966] P. 332 .... 164, 165
Phillips v. Halliday [1891] A.C. 228; 61 L.J.Q.B. 210; 64 L.T. 745; 55 J.P. 741, H.L.; affirming *sub nom.* Halliday v. Phillips (1889) 23 Q.B.D. 48, C.A. 109
Plumstead District Board of Works v. Ecclesiastical Commissioners for England [1891] 2 Q.B. 361; 64 L.T. 830; 55 J.P. 791; 39 W.R. 700, P.C. . 175
Ponsford and Newport District School Board, *Re* [1894] 1 Ch. 454; 63 L.J.Ch. 278; 42 W.R. 358; 10 T.L.R. 207; 38 S.J. 199; 7 R. 622; *sub nom.* Ponsford v. Newport District School Board, 70 L.T. 502, C.A. .. 154, 155

R. v. Daily Herald (Editor, Printers and Publishers of), *ex p.* Norwich (Bishop); R. v. Empire News, Editor, Printers and Publishers of v. Norwich (Bishop) [1932] 2 K.B. 402; 101 L.J.K.B. 305; 146 L.T. 485; 48 T.L.R. 253; 76 S.J. 165, P.C. 184
—— v. Harris [1927] 2 K.B. 587 69
—— v. St. Edmundsbury and Ipswich Diocese (Chancellor of), *ex p.* White [1948] 1 K.B. 195; 177 L.T. 488; 63 T.L.R. 523; 91 S.J. 369; [1947] 2 All E.R. 170; [63 L.Q.R. 208], C.A.; affirming [1947] K.B. 263 20
—— v. Sharpe (1845) Dea. & Bell C.C. 160 166
—— v. Tregear [1967] 2 Q.B. 574; [1967] 2 W.L.R. 1414; 131 J.P. 314; 111 S.J. 175; [1967] 1 All E.R. 989; 51 Cr.App.R. 280, C.A. 69
—— v. Tristram [1901] 2 K.B. 141; [1902] 1 K.B. 816; 71 L.J.K.B. 418; 86 L.T. 515; 50 W.R. 477; 18 T.L.R. 406, C.A. 11, 45
Redland Bricks v. Morris [1970] A.C. 652; [1969] 2 W.L.R. 1437; 113 S.J. 405; [1969] 2 All E.R. 576, H.L.; reversing *sub nom.* Morris v. Redland Bricks [1907] 1 W.L.R. 967; 111 S.J. 373; [1967] 3 All E.R. 1, C.A. 79

St. Agnes', Toxteth Park, *Re* [1985] 1 W.L.R. 641; (1985) 129 S.J. 218; (1985) 82 L.S.Gaz. 1249 .... 80, 81, 123
St. Andrew's Church, Backwell, *Re* (1982); unreported 45, 50, 65, 93, 94, 95, 96, 97, 161, 167, 186
St. Andrew's, Dearnley, *Re* [1981] Fam. 50; [1981] 2 W.L.R. 37; (1980) 124 S.J. 774, Manchester Consistory Ct. 33, 58, 113, 129
St. Andrew's, Heddington, *Re* [1977] 3 W.L.R. 286; (1976) 121 S.J. 286; [1978] Fam. 121, Salisbury Consistory Ct. 11, 67, 124
St. Andrew's, Thornhaugh, *Re* [1976] Fam. 230; [1976] 2 W.L.R. 123; (1975) 120 S.J. 80; [1976] 1 All E.R. 154 .... 123, 138, 147
St. Anne's Church, Kew, *Re* [1977] Fam. 12, Southwark Consistory Ct. 93, 97, 98, 161, 167
St. Augustine's Brinksway, *Re* [1963] P. 364; [1963] 3 W.L.R. 338; [1963] 3 All E.R. 389 115
St. Botolph Without Aldgate (Vicar and Churchwardens) v. St. Botolph Without Aldgate (Parishioners) [1892] P. 161; subsequent proceedings [1892] P. 173 .... 2, 17, 44, 161, 167, 168
St. Botolph, Aldersgate Without (Vicar) v. St. Botolph, Aldersgate Without (Parishioners) [1900] P. 69 .... 159, 160
St. Cuthbert's, Doveridge, *Re* [1983] 1 W.L.R. 845; (1983) 127 S.J. 491, Const. Ct. 61
St. Dunstan's, Stepney, *Re* [1937] P. 199; 53 T.L.R. 905 .... 156, 163

St. Edburga's, Abberton, *Re* [1962] P. 10; [1961] 3 W.L.R. 87; 105 S.J. 572; [1961] 2 All E.R. 429; reversing *sub nom.* St. James's, Bishampton, *Re*, St. Edburga's, Abberton, *Re* [1961] 1 W.L.R. 257; 105 S.J. 132; [1961] 2 All E.R. 11 .... 46, 82

St. Edward the Confessor, Mottingham, *Re* [1983] 1 W.L.R. 364; (1982) 126 S.J. 835, Consistory Ct. 116

St. Gabriel, Fenchurch Street (Rector and Churchwardens) *v.* City of London Real Property Ltd. [1896] P. 95 .... 161, 168, 170

St. George's, Birmingham, *Re* [1960] 1 W.L.R. 1069; 104 S.J. 827; [1960] 3 All E.R. 185 .... 87, 92, 185

St. George's, Oakdale, *Re* [1976] Fam. 210; [1975] 3 W.L.R. 804; *sub nom.* St. George's Church, Oakdale, *Re*, 119 S.J. 808; [1975] 2 All E.R. 870, Consistory Ct. 1, 140, 176, 177, 178

St. George's, Southall, *Re* [1952] 1 All E.R. 323 129

St. Gregory's, Tredington, *Re* [1972] Fam. 236; [1971] 2 W.L.R. 796; (1970) 115 S.J. 284; [1971] 3 All E.R. 269 .... 1, 27, 53, 82, 86, 106, 121, 122, 123, 124, 127, 143, 180, 185

St. Helen's, Brant Broughton, *Re* [1974] Fam. 16; [1973] 3 W.L.R. 228; (1972) 117 S.J. 581; [1973] 3 All E.R. 386, Arches Ct. of Canterbury 82, 122, 123, 124, 186

St. James, Bishampton, *Re. See* St. Edburga's, Abberton, *Re.*

St. James', Heywood, *Re* [1982] 1 W.L.R. 1289; (1982) 126 S.J. 671; (1982) 79 L.S.Gaz. 1444, Consistory Ct. 145

St. James the Less, Bethnal Green (Vicar) *v.* Parishioners of Same [1899] P. 55 160

St. John The Evangelist, Clevedon (Vicar and Churchwardens) *v.* All Having Interest [1909] P. 6 107

St. John the Evangelist, Ford End, *Re* [1984] 1 W.L.R. 1194; (1984) 128 S.J. 736; (1984) 81 L.S.Gaz. 3173 .... 88, 89

St. John's, Chelsea, *Re* [1962] 1 W.L.R. 706; 106 S.J. 314; [1962] 2 All E.R. 850; [26 Conv. 307] 1, 2, 27, 58, 88, 96, 102, 141, 153, 161, 167, 171, 176, 185

St. John's Church, Bishop's Hatfield, *Re* [1967] P. 113; [1966] 2 W.L.R. 705; 110 S.J. 246; [1966] 2 All E.R. 403 .... 140, 176, 177, 178

St. John's, Hampstead, *Re* [1939] P. 281; 160 L.T. 641; 55 T.L.R. 585; 83 S.J. 342 158

St. John-in-Bedwardine, Worcester, *Re* [1962] P. 20; [1961] 3 All E.R. 216; *sub nom.* St. John-in-Bredwardine, Worcester, *Re* [1961] 3 W.L.R. 69; 105 S.J. 572 .... 78, 183

St. Luke's, Cheetham, *Re* [1977] Fam. 144; [1977] 3 W.L.R. 969; (1977) 121 S.J. 828; [1978] 1 All E.R. 1118, Consistory Ct. 88, 92, 113

St. Luke's, Chelsea, *Re* [1976] Fam. 295; [1975] 3 W.L.R. 564; 119 S.J. 726; [1976] 1 All E.R. 609, Consistory Ct. 27, 44, 46, 58, 62, 64, 71, 98, 142, 155, 156, 158, 162, 163

——, *Re* (No. 2) [1976] Fam. 318; [1976] 3 W.L.R. 364; 120 S.J. 569, London Consistory Ct. 82

——, (Rector and Churchwardens) *v.* Wheeler [1904] P. 257; *sub nom.* St. Luke's, Chelsea, 20 T.L.R. 422 110

St. Margaret's, Fartham, *Re* (1981) 125 S.J. 441; [1981] 1 W.L.R. 1129, Arches Ct. 135

St. Margaret's, Lothbury (Rector and Churchwardens) *v.* London County Council [1909] P. 310; 25 T.L.R. 734 .... 155, 160

St. Mark's Church, Lincoln, *Re* [1956] P. 336; [1956] 3 W.L.R. 147; 100 S.J. 438; [1956] 2 All E.R. 579; affirming [1956] P. 166; [1955] 3 W.L.R. 844; 99 S.J. 835; [1955] 2 All E.R. 699; [1955] C.L.Y. 891 .... 158, 159, 160

St. Mark's, Haydock, *Re* [1981] 1 W.L.R. 1164, Consistory Ct. 151, 153, 185
——, *Re* (No. 2) [1981] 1 W.L.R. 1167, Consistory Ct. 152
St. Martin's, Ashton-upon-Mersey, *Re* [1981] 1 W.L.R. 1288, Constistory
   Ct. 104, 105
St. Martin's-in-the-Fields, *Re* (1972); unreported 122
St. Mary, Aldermary, *Re* [1985] Fam. 101; [1985] 3 W.L.R. 396; (1985) 129
   S.J. 557; [1985] 2 All E.R. 445; (1985) 82 L.S.Gaz. 3083, Consistory
   Ct. 55, 101, 172
St. Mary, Baldock, *Re*; unreported 95
St. Mary le Bow, *Re* [1984] 1 W.L.R. 1363; (1984) 128 S.J. 850; (1985) 82
   L.S.Gaz. 278 .... 27, 122, 123, 124, 185
St. Mary Magdalene, Altofits, *Re* [1958] P. 172 n. 132
St. Mary Magdalene, Paddington, *Re* [1980] Fam. 99; [1980] 3 W.L.R. 243;
   (1979) 124 S.J. 309; [1980] 1 All E.R. 279, Consistory Ct. . 1, 140, 176, 177,
                                                                                                                              178
St. Mary, Northolt (Vicar and Churchwardens) *v.* Parishioners of St.
   Mary's, Northolt [1920] P. 97 122
St. Mary of Charity, Faversham, *Re* [1986] Fam. 143; [1985] 3 W.L.R. 924;
   (1985) 129 S.J. 793; [1986] 1 All E.R. 993 .... 19, 117, 123
St. Mary The Virgin, Ilmington, *Re* [1962] P. 147; [1962] 2 W.L.R. 572; 106
   S.J. 115; [1962] 1 All E.R. 560 137
St. Mary the Virgin, Selling, *Re* [1980] 1 W.L.R. 1545; (1980) 124 S.J. 726,
   Commissary Ct. 114, 137
St. Mary the Virgin, West Moors, *Re* [1963] P. 390; [1963] 2 W.L.R. 1334; 107
   S.J. 537; [1962] 1 All E.R. 560 115
St. Mary the Virgin, Woodkirk, *Re* [1969] 1 W.L.R. 1867; 113 S.J. 977; *sub
   nom*. Morley Borough Council *v.* St. Mary the Virgin, Woodkirk
   (Vicar and Churchwardens) [1969] 3 All E.R. 952 .... 27, 96, 141, 153,
                                                                                                                167, 170, 171, 186
St. Mary, Tyne Dock, *Re* [1954] P. 369; [1954] 2 W.L.R. 1129; 98 S.J. 374;
   [1954] 2 All E.R. 339 .... 107, 114, 115, 116, 129, 132, 181
——, *Re* (No. 2) [1958] P. 156; [1957] 3 W.L.R. 945; 101 S.J. 922; *sub nom.* Re
   St. Mary's Tyne Dock (No. 2) [1958] 1 All E.R. 1 .... 78, 79, 107, 115,
                                                                                                                116, 130, 132, 181, 186
St. Mary's, Balham, *Re* [1978] 1 All E.R. 993 .... 26, 29, 80, 103, 181, 182
St. Mary's, Banbury, *Re* [1987] Fam. 136; [1987] 3 W.L.R. 717; [1986] Pam.
   24; [1985] 3 W.L.R. 924; (1985) 129 S.J. 793; [1985] 2 All E.R. 611;
   (1985) 82 L.S.Gaz. 3530 .... 74, 82, 109, 112, 118, 119, 186, 254
St. Mary's, Barnes, *Re* [1982] 1 W.L.R. 531; [1982] 1 All E.R. 456, Consistory
   Ct. 11
St. Mary's, Barton-upon-Humber, *Re* [1987] Fam. 41; [1986] 3 W.L.R.
   906 .... 28, 80, 103, 123, 124, 180
St. Mary's, Broadwater, *Re* [1976] Fam. 222 .... 123, 137, 138
St. Mary's, Fawkham, *Re* [1981] 1 W.L.R. 1171; (1980) 125 S.J. 355, Ct. of
   Arches 149, 151, 186
St. Mary's, Gilston, *Re* [1967] P. 125; [1966] 2 W.l.R. 697; 110 S.J. 246; [1966]
   2 All E.R. 408 .... 122, 185
St. Mary's, Lancaster, *Re* [1980] 1 W.L.R. 657; (1979) 124 S.J. 428, Blackburn
   Consistory Ct. 104, 105
St. Mary's, Luton, *Re* [1968] P. 47; [1966] 3 W.L.R. 1171; 100 S.J. 600; [1966] 3
   All E.R. 638; [1966] C.L.Y. 4218; affirming [1967] P. 151; [1966] 3
   W.L.R. 532 .... 48, 64, 93, 98, 160, 186
St. Mary's, Warwick, *Re* [1981] 3 W.L.R. 781; (1981) 125 S.J. 775; [1981] Fam.
   170, Consistory Ct. 123, 126, 127
St. Mary's, Westwell, *Re* [1968] 1 W.L.R. 513; (1968) 112 S.J. 292; [1968] 1 All
   E.R. 631 .... 122, 185

Table of Cases

St. Mathew's, Wimbledon, *Re* [1985] 3 All E.R. 670, Consistory Ct. 133
St. Michael and All Angels, Great Torrington, *Re* [1985] Fam. 81; [1985] 2 W.L.R. 857; (1985) 129 S.J. 187; [1985] 1 All E.R. 993; (1985) 82 L.S.Gaz. 1249, Ecclesiastical Ct. 27, 73, 77, 82, 113, 114, 181, 186
St. Michael and All Angels, Bishopwearmouth, *Re*, Bishopwearmouth (Rector and Churchwardens) *v.* Adey [1958] 1 W.L.R. 1183; 102 S.J. 862; *sub nom.* Bishopwearmouth (Rector and Churchwardens) *v.* Adey [1958] 3 All E.R. 441 .... 130, 132
St. Michael The Archangel, Brantham *and* St. Peter United with St. Mary at Quay, Ipswich, *Re* [1962] 1 W.L.R. 1067; [1962] 3 All E.R. 609 59
St. Nicholas, Acons *v.* London County Council [1928] A.C. 469; 97 L.J.P.C. 113; 139 L.T. 530; 92 J.P. 185; 44 T.L.R. 656; 26 L.G.R. 583, P.C. 155, 159, 160
St. Nicholas, Baddesley Ensor, *Re* [1983] Fam. 1; [1982] 3 W.L.R. 631; (1982) 126 S.J. 591; [1982] 2 All E.R. 351; (1982) 79 L.S.Gaz. 1412, Consistory Ct. 143
St. Nicholas, Brokenhurst, *Re* [1978] Fam. 157; [1978] 3 W.L.R. 96; (1977) 122 S.J. 456; [1977] 3 All E.R. 1027, Winchester Consistory Ct. 135
St. Nicholas, Cole Abbey, *Re*, St. Benet Fink, Churchyard [1893] P. 58 159
St. Nicholas, Plumstead, *Re* [1961] 1 W.L.R. 916; 105 S.J. 493; [1961] 1 All E.R. 298; [105 S.J. 222] 116, 132, 133
St. Paul, Hanging Heaton, *Re* [1968] 1 W.L.R. 1210; (1966) 112 S.J. 582 .... 143, 144, 150, 151
St. Paul's Church, Battersea, *Re* [1954] 1 W.L.R. 920; 98 S.J. 440; [1954] 2 All E.R. 595 135
St. Paul's, Covent Garden, *Re* [1974] Fam. 1; [1973] 1 W.L.R. 464; (1972) 117 S.J. 265, Consistory Ct. 45, 100, 161, 169
St. Peter and St. Paul, Leckhampton, *Re* [1968] P. 495; [1968] 2 W.L.R. 1551; (1968) 112 S.J. 460; *sub nom.* St. Peter and St. Paul, *Re*; Leckhampton (Rector and Churchwardens) *v.* Barnard [1967] 3 All E.R. 1057 131, 133
St. Peter, Kineton, *Re* [1967] 1 W.L.R. 347 .... 149, 150
St. Peter, Roydon, *Re* [1969] 1 W.L.R. 1849; 113 S.J. 977; [1969] 2 All E.R. 1233 .... 99, 113, 118, 120
St. Peter, St. Helier, Morden, *Re* [1951] P. 303; [1951] 1 T.L.R. 1033; 95 S.J. 401; [1951] 2 All E.R. 53 .... 115, 116
St. Peter the Great, Chichester, *Re* [1961] 1 W.L.R. 907; 105 S.J. 368; [1961] 2 All E.R. 513 .... 158, 170
St. Peter, Vere Street, *Re*; unreported 102
St. Peter's, Bushey Heath, *Re* [1971] 1 W.L.R. 357; (1970) 115 S.J. 186; [1971] 2 All E.R. 704 .... 139, 140, 177, 179
St. Peter's, Folkestone, *Re* [1982] 1 W.L.R. 1283; (1982) 126 S.J. 671, Commissary Ct. 134, 135
St. Saviour's Church, Walthamstow, *Re* [1951] P. 147; [1956] W.N. 457; 66 T.L.R. (Pt. 2) 666; 94 S.J. 613; [1950] 2 All E.R. 812 .... 117, 129
St. Stephen's, Walbrook, *Re* [1987] Fam. 146; [1986] 3 W.L.R. 790; (1986) 130 S.J. 821; [1986] 2 All E.R. 705; (1986) 83 L.S.Gaz. 3591 .... 27, 73, 74, 76, 82, 111, 112, 114, 119, 186
St. Thomas, Lymington, *Re* [1980] Fam. 89; [1980] 2 W.L.R. 267; (1979) 124 S.J. 167; [1980] 2 All E.R. 84, Winchester Consistory Ct. 93, 97, 98, 161, 167
Salsbury *v.* Woodland [1970] 1 Q.B. 324; [1969] 3 W.L.R. 29; 113 S.J. 327; [1969] 3 All E.R. 863, C.A. 71
Sargent, *Re* (1890) 15 P.D. 168 164
South Creake (Parish of), *Re* [1959] 1 W.L.R. 427; 103 S.J. 329; [1959] 1 All E.R. 197 137

Talbot, *Re* [1901] P. 1	166
Watford Parish Church; unreported	95
West Camel Church, *Re*; Yatton Church, *Re* [1979] Fam. 79; [1979] 2 W.L.R. 501; (1978) 123 S.J. 270; [1979] 2 All E.R. 652, Bath and Wells Consistory Ct.	7, 106, 108, 186
West Tarring (Rector and Churchwardens), *Re* [1954] 1 W.L.R. 923n.; 98 S.J. 440; *sub nom.* West Tarring Parish Church, *Re* [1954] 2 All E.R. 591	135
Westerton *v.* Liddell (1857) Moo.Spec.Rep. 133	113
Williams *v.* Williams (1882) 20 Ch.D. 659	166
Woldingham Churchyard, *Re* [1957] 1 W.L.R. 811; 101 S.J. 535; [1957] 2 All E.R. 323	29, 78, 79, 143, 149, 153, 181, 182, 185

Table of Statutes

1708	Parochial Libraries Act (7 Anne, c. 14) ... 16, 125, 126		1906	Open Spaces Act (6 Edw. 7, c. 25) 161, 163	
	s. 1	125		s. 6	161
	ss. 2–9	125		s. 10	161, 162
	s. 4	126		s. 11	162, 195
	s. 10 .... 125, 126, 196			(1)	162
1829	Ecclesiastical Courts Act (10 Geo. 4, c. 53)	155		(2)	162
1832	Ecclesiastical Courts (Contempt) Act (2 & 3 Will. 4, c. 93)	183		(3)	162
				(4)	162
			1913	Ancient Monuments Consolidation and Amendment Act (3 & 4 Geo. 5, c. 32)	4, 18
1857	Burial Act (20 & 21 Vict. c. 81)—				
	s. 25	166		s. 22	4, 18
1860	Ecclesiastical Courts Jurisdiction Act (23 & 24 Vict. c. 32)—		1916	Larceny Act (6 & 7 Geo. 5, c. 50)—	
				s. 26	140
	s. 2	67		s. 46 (3)	140
	s. 3	67	1925	Administration of Estates Act (15 & 16 Geo. 5, c. 23)	147
1870	Gun Licence Act (33 & 34 Vict. c. 57)—				
	s. 7	140		Criminal Justice Act (15 & 16 Geo. 5, c. 86)—	
1879	Public Health (Internments) Act (42 & 43 Vict. c. 31) 165, 198			s. 41	11, 67
			1935	London County Council (General Powers) Act (25 & 26 Geo. 5, c. 33)—	
1881	Metropolitan Open Spaces Act (44 & 45 Vict. c. 34) 154, 161				
				s. 42	156, 162
	s. 4	157		s. 51	156, 162
	s. 5	157	1936	Public Health Act (26 Geo. 5 & 1 Edw. 8, c. 49)	91
1884	Disused Burial Grounds Act (47 & 48 Vict. c. 72) 27, 62, 95, 153, 158, 163				
			1939	London Building Acts (Amendment) Act (2 & 3 Geo. 6, c. 97)—	
	s. 3 .... 57, 98, 141, 148, 154, 155, 157, 159, 160, 162, 163, 169, 172, 177				
				s. 62 (2)	90
1885	Metropolitan Board of Works (Various Powers) Act (48 & 49 Vict. c. 50)	155	1954	Landlord and Tenant Act (2 & 3 Eliz. 2, c. 56)	100
				City of London (Various Powers) Act (2 & 3 Eliz. c. 27)—	
1887	Open Spaces Act (50 & 51 Vict. c. 32)	158			
	s. 4	98, 154		s. 4	163, 169
1889	Interpretation Act (52 & 53 Vict. c. 63)—		1971	Criminal Damage Act (c. 48)	181
	s. 26	218			

xxiii

1971	Town and Country Planning Act (c. 78) 4, 75, 141, 254		1979	Sale of Goods Act—*cont.*	
	s. 54	4		s. 25 (1)	180
	(1)	251		Ancient Monuments and Archaeological Areas Act (c. 46)—	
	(9)	253			
	s. 55	4, 252		s. 61 (8)	252
	(1)	251	1984	Building Act (c. 55)—	
	s. 56	4		s. 77	90, 195
	(1)	252, 253		s. 78	90, 195
	(3)	254		s. 79	91, 195
	s. 58 (1)	251, 252		s. 131	90
	(2)	253		Sched. 6	90, 195
	s. 58AA	253	1986	Housing and Planning Act (c. 63)	4
	(1)	253			
	(2)	253		s. 40	252
	(3)	254		Sched. 9, Pt. I	252
	s. 287	254		para. 1	253
1979	Sale of Goods Act (c. 54)—			(1)	251
	s. 22	180		para. 5	253

Table of Measures

[References in bold type are to Appendix A where text is set out in full]

1921	Parochial Church Councils (Powers) Measure (11 & 12 Geo. 5, No. 1)	83
1925	Interpretation Measure (15 & 16 Geo. 5, No. 1)	205, 218
	s. 3	87, 174
1938	Faculty Jurisdiction Measure (1 & 2 Geo. 6, No. 6)	32, 33, 78, 79, 192, 203
	s. 1	47
	s. 3(1)	78
1955	Inspection of Churches Measure (3 & 4 Eliz. 2, No. 1)	5, 18, 25, 83, 85, 86
	s. 1	33
	(1)	83
	(2)(*b*)	83
	(*c*)	34, 83
	(*d*)	83
	s. 2	83
1956	Parochial Church Councils (Powers) Measure (4 & 5 Eliz. 2, No. 3)—	
	s. 4	47, 152
	(1)(ii)	83, 84
	(*c*)	144
1962	Ecclesiastical Fees Measure (10 & 11 Eliz. 2, No. 1)	185
1963	Ecclesiastical Jurisdiction Measure (No. 1)	7, 15, 16, 20, 43, 70, 126, 155, 183
	s. 1(1)	7
	s. 2(1)	7
	(2)	8
	(3)	8
	(4)	8

1963	Ecclesiastical Jurisdiction Measure—*cont*.	
	s. 2(4)—*cont*.	
	(*a*)	7
	(*b*)	8
	(5)	8
	s. 4(1)	10
	(2)	10
	s. 6	15
	(1)(*b*)(ii)	126
	s. 7(1)(*b*)	81
	(2)(*a*)	81
	s. 8	20, 82
	s. 10(1)	81
	(2)	81
	(3)	81
	s. 11	20, 82
	s. 12	10
	s. 13(2)	10
	s. 27	10
	s. 45(3)	76, 111
	s. 46	7, 10
	(1)	10
	s. 60	48, 81, 184, 210
	(1)	65
	s. 61	81, 184, 187
	(2)	184
	s. 80	11, 67
	s. 81	65
	(1)	68, 69
	(2)	68, 183
	(3)	68, 184
	s. 83(1)	9
	(2)(*d*)	9
1964	Faculty Jurisdiction Measure (No. 5)	5, 33, 70, 79, 87, 111, 126, 176, 183, **191**, 203, 204, 205
	s. 1	148, **192**
	s. 2	53, 56, 57, 66, 87, 88, **193**, 207, 217
	(*a*)	216

xxv

1964 Faculty Jurisdiction
Measure—*cont.*
  s. 2—*cont.*
    (1) 72, 88, 211, 214
      (i) 88, 209
      (ii) 62, 89, 213
      (iii) 89
      (iv) .. 67, 212, 213, 232, 233
        (*a*) 89
        (*b*) 89, 90
    (2) 88
    (3) 62
      (i) 88
      (ii) 90
    (4) 90, 91, 92
      (iii) 91
      (iv) 91
  s. 3 .... 46, 97, 138, 146, 147, 153, **195**
    (2) 147
    (4) 146, 147
  s. 4 .... 1, **196**, 211, 217
    (1) 126
    (2) 126
  s. 5 .... 20, 56, 84, 181, 183, 184, **196**
    (1) 78, 183
    (2) 78
  s. 6 .... 2, 23, 52, 173, 174, 175, **197**
    (1) 173
    (2) 173
    (3) 173
  s. 7 .. 1, 23, 140, 173, 175, 176, **198**
    (1) 174, 175
    (2) 175
  s. 8 .... 165, **198**
  s. 9 .... 27, 64, , 182, 183, **198**
    (1) 47
    (2) 47, 217, 233
    (3) 27
  s. 10 .... 84, **199**
    (*a*) 28, 29, 80
    (*b*) 29, 79
    (*c*) 29, 80, 184
  s. 11 .... 184, **199**
  s. 12 .... 22, 33, 58, **200**, 216, 217, 220, 223, 225
    (1) 26, 205, 206, 223
    (2) 206
    (3) 207, 216, 224
    (4) 207
    (7) 205, 206, 223
  s. 13 .... 33, **201**

1964 Faculty Jurisdiction
Measure—*cont.*
  s. 13—*cont.*
    (1) 25, 34
    (2) 33
      (*a*) 42, 70
  s. 14 .... **202**
  Sched. **204**
Holy Table Measure (No. 4)—
  s. 1 110
1965 Prayer Book (Alternative and Other Services) Measure (No. 1) 133
1968 Pastoral Measure (No. 1)—
  s. 49 106
1969 Synodical Government Measure (No. 2) 30
1974 Church of England (Worship and Doctrine) Measure (No. 3)—
  s. 6 (3) 111
  Sched. 2 111
1975 Ecclesiastical Offices (Age Limit) Measure (No. 2)—
  s. 1 (3) 24
    (4) (*d*) 24
  s. 3 (1) 24
1976 Church of England (Miscellaneous Provisions) Measure (No. 3)—
  s. 6 (1) (2) 143
Ecclesiastical Judges and Legal Officers Measure (No. 2) 9, 14
  s. 1 (1) 8
    (3) 8
  s. 2 9
  s. 4 (1) 12, 14
    (2) 12
    (3) 13
    (4) 12
  s. 5 14
    (1) 13
    (2) 13
    (3) 13
    (4) 13
    (5) 13
    (6) 13
    (7) 13
  s. 6 (1) 13
  s. 9 (2) 8, 13

1983	Pastoral Measure (No. 1) 92, 100, 141, 171	1983	Pastoral Measure—*cont.* s. 56—*cont.*	
	s. 30 95		(3) 100, 169	
	s. 56 (2) 100, 169	1986	Ecclesiastical Fees Measure (No. 2)	185

Abbreviations

C.C.C.	Central Council for Churches
D.A.C.	Diocesan Advisory Committee
D.B.G.A. 1884	Disused Burial Grounds Act 1884
E.J.M. 1963	Ecclesiastical Jurisdiction Measure 1963
F.J.C.	Report of the Faculty Jurisdiction Commission 1984
F.J.M. 1938	Faculty Jurisdiction Measure 1938
F.J.M. 1964	Faculty Jurisdiction Measure 1964
F.J.R. 1967	Faculty Jurisdiction Rules 1967 as amended by Faculty Jurisdiction (Amendment) Rules 1987
F.J.(A.)R. 1987	Faculty Jurisdiction (Amendment) Rules
P.C.C.	Parochial Church Council

1. Introduction

A building becomes subject to the faculty jurisdiction of the consistory court of the diocese when the bishop of the diocese signs a sentence "by which he separates and sets apart the building from all profane and common uses whatsoever, dedicates the same to the service of Almighty God for the performance therein of divine offices, and consecrates the same for the celebration of such offices."[1] In consequence of the sentence "the building, and with it the land on which it stands, becomes consecrated land, held to sacred uses and subject to the jurisdiction of this [*i.e. the consistory*] court."[2] In respect of a churchyard the sentence "refers to the interment of the remains of the dead instead of to the performance of divine offices; but its other material wording is the same and its legal effect is equally to set the land apart as land held on sacred uses and to subject it to the court's jurisdiction."[3]

Consecration either as a church or as a churchyard thus founds the faculty jurisdiction. It has always extended also to chattels appertaining to a consecrated church or to a consecrated churchyard.[4] Further, it has always extended to unconsecrated churchyard, that is, to land surrounding and ancillary to a consecrated church,[5] and this part of the jurisdiction was expressly confirmed by section 7 of the F.J.M. 1964, so far as any such land could correctly be described as curtilage of the church. Finally, there are two express statutory extensions of the jurisdiction, *i.e.* to parochial libraries[6] and to any unconsecrated buildings licensed

---

[1] *Re St. John's, Chelsea* [1962] 1 W.L.R. 706 at 708.
[2] *Ibid.*
[3] *Ibid.*
[4] *Lee v. Hawtrey* [1898] P. 63 at 74. Cf. *Re St. Gregory's, Tredington* [1972] Fam. 236 at 240.
[5] *Re St. George's Oakdale* [1976] Fam. 210 at 214; see also *Re St. Mary Magdalene Paddington* [1980] Fam. 99.
[6] F.J.M. 1964, s.4.

for public worship which are brought within the jurisdiction of the court by an order of the bishop.[7]

The freehold of a church or churchyard is normally in the incumbent (the fee simple being in abeyance)[8] and the chattels of a church are vested in the churchwardens. Incumbents and churchwardens change often and there is an obvious need for supervision by a paramount authority over what they do in respect of the land and goods temporarily vested in them. The consistory court of a diocese, of which the chancellor of the diocese is the judge, with its registry and permanent records operating in accordance with the English doctrine of precedent, provides this enduring and consistent supervision on behalf of the ordinary, the bishop of the diocese. "The final control of the church and chancel and of the churchyard is vested in the chancellor, as ordinary for this purpose."[9]

The effect of land, buildings or goods being under the jurisdiction of the ordinary is that "no material alteration" can be made in any of them "except under the authority of a faculty decreed by the Ecclesiastical Courts, obtainable... only after the parishioners, as being interested therein, have been cited."[10]

As Lord Penzance, Dean of Arches, pointed out in *Nickalls* v. *Briscoe*[11] "The sacred edifice has a future as well as a past. It belongs not to any one generation, nor are its interests and condition the exclusive care of those who inhabit the parish at any one period of time." The chancellor, in exercising the jurisdiction, must therefore look to the permanent interest of the parishioners, for whose benefit the church and churchyard are held; further, he must not allow any change which conflicts with the sacred uses imposed by consecration.[12] While these essential

---

[7] F.J.M. 1964, s.6. It is thought that while such an order is in force the jurisdiction extends to the chattels appertaining to the building.

[8] The title of the incumbent is analogous to that of a tenant for life: see *per* Lord Selborne, L.C. in *The Ecclesiastical Commissioners for England and Wales* v. *Rowe* (1880) 5 App.Cas. 736 at 744. His estate is therefore correctly described as one of freehold, since a life estate is one of freehold.

[9] *Per* Dr. Tristram Ch. in *The Vicar and One of the Churchwardens of St. Botolph without Aldgate* v. *The Parishioners of the Same* [1892] P.161 at 167. The same learned judge mentioned in *Lee* v. *Hawtrey* [1898] P.63 at 74 that the consistory court has had this jurisdiction "from shortly after the Conquest up to the present day."

[10] *Lee* v. *Hawtrey* [1898] P.63 at 74.

[11] [1892] P. 269 at 283.

[12] *Re St. John's, Chelsea* [1962] 1 W.L.R. 706.

conditions are paramount, his task is not different in kind from that of the judge of the Chancery Division who enforces and administers a trust and grants facilities to the persons in whom the trust property is vested. While opposed causes have to be heard in open court, those which are unopposed are normally dealt with in the less formal atmosphere of chambers. The latter procedure is very convenient, especially where difficult and complicated matters of property are to be adjusted in the interests of all concerned. It is no part of the duty of a court, supervising a secular trust or exercising the faculty jurisdiction, to block all change. On the contrary, development is essential to life, and insights and aesthetic tastes vary as the years pass. In a church, change is essential as liturgical patterns and understandings evolve. Few old churches look, or should look, today as they did in the seventeenth or eighteenth centuries. Rather too many do look as they looked at the end of the nineteenth century, since public opinion, which is intensely conservative, has been brought more to bear on those responsible for churches than it used to be. However, considerable evolution has occurred in many places, especially since 1950.

The faculty jurisdiction has been exercised with different emphasis and different vigour at different periods of history. In a valuable article,[13] Dr. John Addy has considered the activities of the consistory court of the diocese of Chester from 1660 to 1760 and has shown that the court then dealt with the multifarious subject-matter concerned with the physical state of the churches and such things as rights to pews. In the nineteenth century, with the controversies which followed the Oxford Movement, many cases in the Law Reports were concerned with particular items of church furnishings which were alleged or held to be objectionable on doctrinal grounds. Towards the end of that century too there was a series of cases in the London consistory court in which the eminent judge Dr. Tristram wrestled with the problems of churchyards in the crowded area of the city. On the other hand, it seems that in the nineteenth century the ecclesiastical courts did not insist very strongly on the need for a faculty whenever any "material alteration" was made to a church or its contents. Thus it appears

---

[13] In *Churchscape*, the Annual Review of the Council for the Care of Churches (1982) p. 7.

from the Appendix to the Charge of George Moberly, D.C.L., Bishop of Salisbury, issued in 1882, that since his visitation of 1879 only 18 faculties had been granted in the diocese, seven of them in Wiltshire and 11 in Dorset. Indeed in the years 1880 and 1882, none at all were granted in Wiltshire. On the other hand he listed 20 churches "and probably others" which had been "restored or enlarged" in those years, only five of which were in parishes named as having had faculties. In the body of the Charge, some 11,000 words in length, there is no reference whatever to the physical care of churches. There is no reason to suppose that, around 1880, the administration of the diocese of Salisbury was unusually slack. But a great deal of work, including "restoration" of many churches, must have been done without the chancellor being concerned: the words "and probably others" are significant.

It is therefore not altogether surprising that the secular authorities had doubts at the beginning of the twentieth century whether church buildings, some of which are among the glories of England, were always being looked after and cherished adequately. In the Bill which became the Ancient Monuments Consolidation and Amendment Act 1913, it was therefore proposed that churches should be within the legislation under which ancient monuments were to be protected. Archbishop Davidson, however, gave assurances in the House of Lords that the church would look after its own buildings, and "an ecclesiastical building which is for the time being used for ecclesiastical purposes" was therefore excluded from the definition of "monument" in the Act as finally passed.[14] This exclusion has been maintained in later ancient monuments legislation. Further, under the Town and Country Planning Act 1971 there is a similar provision exempting "an ecclesiastical building which is for the time being used for ecclesiastical purposes" from the need for "listed building consent."[15] These provisions are collectively known as the "ecclesiastical exemption." The relevant law is more fully stated at p. 253. It is of great importance to the church that this exemption should be maintained. For listed buildings are controlled by the secular

---

[14] Ancient Monuments Consolidation and Amendment Act 1913, s.22.
[15] See ss.54, 55 and 56. The government has recently acquired powers, under the Housing and Planning Act 1986, by order to modify s.56, subject to negative resolution in either House of Parliament.

local authorities, who are necessarily more concerned with conservation than with development. Moreover the control applies to things affixed to the inside of a listed building as well as to its exterior: if the exemption were taken away much current liturgical re-arrangement of the inside of churches would be subjected to secular control.

Following Archbishop Davidson's assurances, the consistory courts began to take a more active interest in what was done to churches, and at the same time there began to be, in most dioceses, a Diocesan Advisory Committee for the care of churches (commonly known as the D.A.C.), charged with giving aesthetic and technical and historical advice to those who were contemplating work upon a church. These committees became statutory in 1938 and are now governed by the F.J.M. 1964. Thus the jurisdiction, having in previous centuries been negative, became directed towards ensuring that the best possible expert advice should be taken by the officers of the parishes both from the D.A.C. and also from the church architect whom each church has had to have since the Inspection of Churches Measure 1955. It is implicit in the Report of the Faculty Jurisdiction Commission, which appeared early in 1984, that the proposed new legislation arising from the report will be designed to make sure that the public interest in churches as part of the aesthetic possessions of the nation is properly attended to by the consistory courts. Thus any attempt to take away the ecclesiastical exemption can, it is hoped, be repelled. It is therefore necessary that the faculty jurisdiction shall be efficiently enforced under the new arrangements, lest Parliament think it necessary to secure the public interest in churches by removing or modifying the ecclesiastical exemption.

Hitherto, although the jurisdiction has been of late far more energetically applied than seems to have been the case a century ago, there are wide differences between dioceses, as is shown by the statistics set out in Table III of Appendix III to the Report of the Faculty Jurisdiction Commission. It is to be hoped that over the next few years the new arrangements will result in greater uniformity.

To sum up, the task of the ecclesiastical courts in exercising the faculty jurisdiction is to ensure that the sacred uses are protected, that the parishioners are duly consulted, that the wider aesthetic interests of the public are considered, but remembering always that a church is a place of worship and not a museum. The courts must also ensure that those who in their generation have care of each church obtain and follow the best available aesthetic and technical advice. And they must authorise and supervise changes as times change. These various objectives are not always obviously consistent; the task of the chancellor is to weigh them all and to reach a just conclusion in each case. He is not an ecclesiastical civil servant but a judge.

2. The Consistory Court, its Judge, Officers, Advisers and Jurisdiction

The court

Since 1963 there is for each diocese "a court of the bishop thereof (to be called the consistory court of the diocese or, in the case of the court for the diocese of Canterbury, the commissary court thereof),"[1] which has the original jurisdiction conferred upon it by the E.J.M. 1963.

The chancellor

In exercising the faculty jurisdiction, the consistory court of the diocese is presided over by a single judge "who shall be styled the chancellor of the diocese or, in the case of the diocese of Canterbury, the commissary general..."[2] The chancellor or commissary general is appointed by the bishop of the diocese by letters patent.[3] He is *oculus episcopi*, and he ranks in the diocese second only to the bishop, saving the precedence of the dean within the cathedral.

Tenure

A chancellor is entitled to resign his office by an instrument under his hand addressed to, and served on, the bishop of the diocese,[4] and he may be removed by the bishop if the upper house of convocation of the relevant province resolves "that he

---

[1] E.J.M. 1963, s.1(1). In this book "consistory court" includes the commissary court.
[2] Ibid., s.2(1). But see below, pp. 10, 11, as to the anomalous power of a diocesan bishop to act in a limited class of cases as judge under s.46 of the Measure of 1963.
[3] Ibid., s.2(1). In this book "the chancellor" includes the commissary general.
[4] Ibid., s.2(4)(a).

is incapable of acting or unfit to act."[5] But otherwise a chancellor whose appointment has been confirmed by the capitular body of the cathedral church of the diocese holds office until he attains the age of 75 years, or without limit of time in the case of a chancellor who was appointed on or before April 24, 1976.[6] If his appointment is not so confirmed, it ceases to have effect upon the termination of a vacancy in the see[7]: in the latter case the age limit seems not to apply, since the provisions of section 1(1) of the Ecclesiastical Judges and Legal Officers Measures 1976 are expressed to modify section 2(4) of the E.J.M. 1963, but are silent as to those of section 2(3) of that Measure. Each Measure contains a provision entitling a chancellor who retires at 75 or loses office upon the ending of a vacancy in the see to finish the cases already depending before him.[8] A person who is invited to accept office as chancellor would be well advised to refuse unless he can be assured that his appointment will be confirmed. A judge should be completely independent; one whose tenure depends upon that of a particular bishop will tend to become a lion under the throne.

Qualification

Before appointing a layman as chancellor the bishop must satisfy himself that the candidate is a communicant: the person appointed must be at least 30 years of age and must either be a barrister of at least seven years standing or a person who has held high judicial office.[9] The person appointed must, before entering upon the execution of his office, take and subscribe the oath of allegiance and the judicial oath and (if he is a layman) must also make a declaration assenting to the 39 articles, the Book of Common Prayer and the Ordinal. The oath must be taken before the diocesan bishop in the presence of the registrar, or in open court in the presence of the registrar, and the latter must in either case make a record of what is done.[10]

[5] E.J.M., s.2(4)(b).
[6] Ibid., s.2(3) and (4), and Ecclesiastical Judges and Legal Officers Measure 1976, ss.1(1) and (3) and 9(2).
[7] Ibid., s.2(3).
[8] Ibid., s.2(3) and Ecclesiastical Judges and Legal Officers Measure 1976, s.1(1).
[9] Ibid., s.2(2).
[10] Ibid., s.2(5).

The vicar general

Nothing in the Measure of 1963 affects the "mode of appointment, office, and duties of vicars general of ... dioceses"[11]; in practice the letters patent constituting a chancellor always constitute him also as the vicar general. This is an office existing at common law and in holding it the chancellor has powers and duties of a largely undefined character which are additional to those which he has in the, now statutory, office of chancellor; for example, paragraph 3 of Canon C18 recognises that the diocesan bishop may exercise his jurisdiction as ordinary by his vicar general, and it is as vicar general that the chancellor grants marriage licences. Beyond these specific items there is a wide and undefined field of matters in which he can act for the bishop. There is no provision in the Measure of 1963, nor in that of 1976, as to the length of the tenure of a vicar general, and it seems that, since the offices of chancellor and vicar general are distinct from one another a person once duly appointed as vicar general is not subject as such to being required to retire at the age of 75 or to losing his office (if unconfirmed) on the termination of a vacancy in the see.

Any judge of the consistory court who was appointed to his office before the commencement of the Measure of 1963 continues in his office as if he had been appointed under that Measure and the terms and conditions of his existing appointment continue unaffected.[12]

Number of chancellorships

The House of Bishops of the General Synod has power to make regulations as to the maximum number of chancellorships which any one person may hold.[13]

The official principal

The chancellor of a diocese is also, by virtue of his office

---

[11] E.J.M. 1963, s.83(2)(d).
[12] Ibid., s.83(1).
[13] Ecclesiastical Judges and Legal Officers Measure 1976, s.2; this power has not been exercised.

as such, the official principal of the bishop of that diocese[14]: it is not clear what additional powers or status, if any, this provision confers upon him.

Deputy chancellors

In the event of the illness or temporary incapacity of a chancellor the bishop of the diocese may appoint a fit and proper person to act as deputy chancellor during such illness or incapacity, and the person appointed then has all the powers, and is to perform all the duties, of the chancellor.[15] This provision is not at all well drafted: it appears to contemplate that a deputy chancellor shall act for all purposes, so that it is not as clear as it ought to be that a deputy can be appointed to deal only with a particular case which it is inconvenient or otherwise improper or unsuitable for the chancellor himself to handle.[16] A deputy chancellor needs no specific qualifications beyond being "fit and proper,"[17] but he is required to take the same oaths as a chancellor.[18]

Acting chancellor during vacancy: no power to appoint

There seems to be nothing to enable a bishop to appoint a person to act as chancellor while the chancellorship itself is vacant and, since the consistory court is now statutory, and the chancellor is in faculty matters its sole judge,[19] the court itself appears to be immobilised during such a vacancy. On the other hand it is expressly provided that the court can continue to function during a vacancy in the see.[20]

Reservation to bishop in patent of chancellor

The proviso to section 46(1) of the E.J.M. 1963 continues the anomalous rule that a diocesan bishop can hear causes of faculty

---

[14] E.J.M. 1963, s.13(2).
[15] Ibid. s.4(1).
[16] In fact this is fairly often done: in the criminal jurisdiction of the consistory court there is an express power: E.J.M. 1963, s.27.
[17] Ibid., s.4(1).
[18] Ibid., s.4(2).
[19] Ibid., s.46. But see below as to the power in some circumstances of a diocesan bishop to sit in these cases.
[20] Ibid., s.12.

either alone or with the chancellor "if, and insofar as, provision ... is made in the letters patent by which the chancellor of the diocese is appointed." That a reservation of this sort could be made was recognised by the Court of Appeal in *R. v. Tristram*.[21] In most dioceses there is no such reservation, but in at least one diocese it still existed until recently and caused much inconvenience. It was condemned by Garth Moore Ch. as "antiquated and regrettable" in *Re St. Mary's, Barnes*.[22] It would be expedient that no further patent should be issued in this form and a person invited to be chancellor should make sure that it is not included in his patent.

Place of hearing

The chancellor can exercise his powers wherever he is, but when a hearing is necessary, the court is to be held "in any place convenient to the court ... due regard being paid to the convenience of the parties and witnesses": E.J.M. 1963, s.80. In practice hearings in chambers are almost always held in the diocesan registry: many, but not all, hearings in open court are held at the church in respect of which the proceedings arise. This arrangement sometimes has obvious conveniences for the parties and the witnesses: it also enables the chancellor to see in three dimensions what are the surroundings in which the problem in question arises. Further, the churchwardens can protect the court from interference. Canon E1, paragraph 4, requires them to maintain order and decency in the church and the churchyard "especially during the time of divine service," but not only then.

By section 41 of the Criminal Justice Act 1925 it is an offence punishable by fine, to take any photograph or make any sketch (or to attempt to do so) of the chancellor or of any witness with a view to publication, or to publish such photograph or sketch. This provision applies not only during the sitting of the court, but if the persons photographed are entering or leaving the precincts of the court.[23]

---

[21] [1902] 1 K.B. 816.
[22] [1982] 1 W.L.R. 531 at 532.
[23] *Re St. Andrew's, Heddington* [1978] Fam. 121 at 124, 125.

Style and robes

The chancellor is addressed in court as "Worshipful Sir" or as "Sir" *simpliciter*. Most chancellors, whether of the rank of Queen's Counsel or not, when sitting in court wear the robes of that rank. It is a frequent practice of at least one chancellor to sit in academic robes. When it is necessary to refer to the court itself, it is styled "this venerable court."

The mace and the seal

In most dioceses the chancellor is provided with a mace, which is the symbol of the authority of the court and is placed in front of him during a hearing. It is carried before him by an officer known as the apparitor, who is appointed by the chancellor. This office has no remuneration and is usually held by a member of the staff of the diocesan registrar. In all the dioceses there is a seal which is used to authenticate the formal acts of the chancellor. Its form is a matter to be settled in each diocese: in some it is expressed on its face to be the seal of the vicar general. In directing that a faculty is to be issued it is sometimes convenient for the chancellor to make an order that the faculty shall "pass the seal." The registrar has custody of the seal and should never use it without the authority of the chancellor for doing so.

The registrar

Office and tenure

The Ecclesiastical Judges and Legal Officers Measure 1976, s.4(1) provides that for every diocese there shall be an office the holder of which shall be known as the registrar of the diocese, and the holder of that office shall also be the legal adviser to the bishop of the diocese. Under section 4(2), the registrar of a diocese is to perform the functions laid by any enactment or canon "on such registrar or on the registrar of the consistory court of the diocese ... " The office of registrar of a diocese may be held by two persons jointly.[24] The registrar is appointed by

---

[24] Ecclesiastical Judges and Legal Officers Measure 1976, s.4(4).

the bishop of the diocese who, before making the appointment, is required to "consult the bishop's council and the standing committee of the diocesan synod."[25] The House of Bishops of the General Synod has power to make regulations as to the maximum number of registrarships which any one person may hold.[26] A registrar vacates office on attaining the age of 70 years; but this provision does not apply to a registrar who was in office on April 24, 1976.[27] Regulations may similarly apply a lower age limit for retirement.[28] The appointment of a registrar may be terminated either by an instrument in writing under his hand addressed to the bishop of the diocese and served on him or by a like instrument under the hand of the bishop of the diocese, addressed to and served on the registrar: in either case the instrument is to specify the date of termination, which must be at least 12 months after that of the service of the instrument. But this power can only be exercised by the bishop with the consent of the archbishop of the province.[29] Further, these arrangements do not apply to a registrar in office on April 24, 1976.[30] There are various transitional provisions for bringing to an end the practice, adopted formerly in some dioceses, of a registrar and the bishop's legal secretary being different persons. A registrar is required to take the same oaths as a chancellor and, (if a layman) also to make the same declaration. There is no statutory provision on this subject, but it is required by Canon G4, paragraph 3. Paragraph 2 of that Canon provides that a person to be appointed registrar must be a solicitor of the Supreme Court "learned in the ecclesiastical laws and the laws of the realm," and the bishop must satisfy himself that the person in question is a communicant.

Rule 11A of the F.J.R. 1967 provides that the chancellor shall have power to appoint another practising solicitor to sit as clerk of the court at a hearing in place of the registrar if the chancellor thinks that the registrar ought not to do so "by reason of the fact that the registrar has acted for any of the parties or has otherwise been personally connected with the proceedings..."

---

[25] Ecclesiastical Judges and Legal Officers Measure 1976, s.4(3).
[26] Ibid., s.5(1), (2). This power has not been exercised.
[27] Ibid., ss.5(3), 6(1) and 9(2).
[28] Ibid., s.5(3), (4). This power has not been exercised.
[29] Ibid., s.5(5), (6) and (7).
[30] Ibid., ss.6(1) and 9(2).

Appointment

Though the existence of the registrar of the diocese and of the consistory court is recognised in a number of enactments, the Measure of 1976 is the only legislation directly affecting his appointment and tenure. In the past some bishops have purported to grant estates of freehold to their diocesan registrars. Such an appointment may well have been innocuous and was perhaps permissible when the registrar was not the same person as the legal secretary of the bishop or his legal adviser. For the registrar is an independent judicial officer. But it would certainly be objectionable now for any such appointment to be made. For under section 4(1) of the Measure of 1976, the registrar of a diocese must always be the legal adviser of the bishop. The offices are now inseparable. A bishop cannot be expected to have a person as his legal adviser unless he has confidence in him, and he should be able to free himself quickly of a legal adviser in whom he has lost confidence, or in whom, being the appointee of the bishop's predecessor, he has never had any such confidence. It is therefore respectfully submitted that, while the provisions as to notice in section 5 of the Measure of 1976 are useful as an ultimate resort, a bishop will always be wise to appoint a registrar under a contract specifying a much shorter period of notice. There does not appear to be any legislation which would prevent that being done and it would be as well if the diocesan board of finance were a party to any such contract, since it is likely to have to provide some at least of the money towards the registrar's remuneration. The position of the registrar is, of course, quite different in this respect from that of a chancellor, who is a judge and so must always be wholly independent of his bishop (who can, indeed, be a litigant before him).[31]

Deputy or acting registrar

There appears to be no provision of any measure or canon regulating the appointment of a deputy registrar, but it is convenient that there should be someone to take charge when

---

[31] See *Halsbury's Laws of England* (4th ed.) Vol. 14, para. 1275 and cases therein cited.

the registrar is, for example, indisposed or unavailable at the hearing of a particular case. In the experience of the author the appointment of a regular deputy registrar is usually made by the diocesan bishop, but that of a deputy registrar for the purposes of a particular case is made by the chancellor. There is a recognised power[32] for the bishop temporarily to appoint an acting registrar when there is no registrar, and it will often be prudent that a person who is being considered for the definitive appointment shall, at the outset, be appointed as acting registrar until he and the bishop and chancellor are all satisfied that he should hold the substantive office.

Duties

The duties of a diocesan registrar as registrar of the consistory court are in general the same as those of the registrar or clerk of any other court. He must maintain the necessary staff to enable the court to function and to keep its records. He must be available to sit with the chancellor in court or chambers, to swear the witnesses, to mark the exhibits, to keep a note of the proceedings, and generally to lend all possible assistance to the chancellor as the judge. A number of specific duties are laid on him by the F.J.R. 1967, and these will be noticed later.

The jurisdiction

Scope

In this book we are concerned only with the faculty jurisdiction and not with any of the other jurisdictions conferred on a consistory court by the E.J.M. 1963.

The relevant provision is in section 6 of that Measure, the material words being as follows:

"(1) Subject to the provisions of the following subsection the consistory court of a diocese has original jurisdiction to hear and determine— ...
  (b) a cause of faculty for authorising
    (i) any act relating to land within the diocese, or to anything on or in such land, being an act for the doing of which the decree of a faculty is requisite;

---

[32] *Halsbury's Laws of England* (4th ed.) Vol. 14, para. 1281, note 3. This power is often exercised.

(ii) the sale of books comprised in a library... to which the Parochial Libraries Act 1708, applies;...
(2) Nothing contained in the foregoing subsection shall extend, or be construed as extending, the jurisdiction of the consistory court in faculty matters to any land or to anything or on in such land in respect of which such court had no jurisdiction immediately before the passing of this Measure."

The effect of these provisions is to leave the scope of the faculty jurisdiction exactly where it was on July 31, 1963, the day on which the Measure received the Royal Assent, subject of course to any subsequent legislation.

This jurisdiction has a long history. Thus in *Lee* v. *Hawtrey*[33] Dr. Tristram Ch. said:

"... the fabric of our parish churches, and the pews, fittings, and vaults therein, and the parish churchyard, with the vaults, graves, and bodies interred therein, have been under the protection and exclusive jurisdiction of the ecclesiastical courts of this country from shortly after the Conquest up to the present day, so much so that no material alteration can be made either in a church or churchyard, or any human remains removed from any vault or grave in either, except under the authority of a faculty decreed by the Ecclesiastical Court, obtainable ... only after the parishioners, as being interested therein, have been cited...".

This passage does not in terms cover the movable ornaments and other goods which are in, or appertain to, the church. Such goods have always been vested in the churchwardens, as is recognised by paragraph 5 of Canon E1. Under paragraph 3 of Canon F13 the minister and churchwardens have a duty "if any alterations, additions, renewals, or repairs are proposed to be made in the fabric, ornaments or furniture of the church, to obtain the faculty or licence of the ordinary before proceeding to execute the same."[34] The faculty jurisdiction therefore covers all the goods appertaining to the church, as well as its fabric and

---

[33] [1898] P. 63 at 74.
[34] This paragraph recognises the archdeacon's certificate as an alternative to a faculty in certain cases.

any fittings annexed to the realty, and also the churchyard. In short, as Dr. Tristram Ch. said in the *St. Botolph* case: "The final control of the church and chancel and of the churchyard is vested in the chancellor, as ordinary for this purpose."[35]

The reason for the jurisdiction was stated by Lord Penzance, Dean of Arches, in *Nickalls* v. *Briscoe*[36]:

> "... the sacred edifice has a future as well a past. It belongs not to any one generation, nor are its interests and condition the exclusive care of those who inhabit the parish at any one period of time. It is in entire conformity with this aspect of the parish church that the law has forbidden any structural alterations to be made in it, save those which are approved by a disinterested authority in the person of the Ordinary, whose deputed discretion and judgment we are here to exercise to-day."

These passages and provisions show the essential features of the faculty jurisdiction to be as follows:

(1) the jurisdiction protects the building and the churchyard and everything in them, movable or immovable;
(2) the existing parishioners have to be consulted and must always be cited;
(3) the judgment is that of the ordinary, the disinterested authority, who looks to the future as well as to the present and to the past.

Exercise of jurisdiction at different periods

Different aspects of the jurisdiction have received emphasis at different periods. A useful piece of research in the records of the consistory court of the diocese of Chester[37] has shown that court concerning itself in the seventeenth and eighteenth centuries mainly with pews, galleries and organs. In the nineteenth and early twentieth centuries, the Law Reports abound with cases about fittings and chattels inside churches, mainly from the

---

[35] [1892] P.161 at 167.
[36] [1892] P.269 at 283.
[37] See the article by Dr. John Addy in *Churchscape* (1982), the annual publication of the Council for the Care of Churches, at pp. 7 *et seq.*

point of view that some of these objects might be thought to be idolatrous or otherwise illegal. Especially in London there were in the nineteenth century also numerous cases about churchyards and burial rights. From about 1912 a great change has come over the jurisdiction. For in the Bill which became the Ancient Monuments Consolidation and Amendment Act 1913 it was proposed to include churches, along with other sorts of ancient monument, thus implying that the Government thought that they were not then being looked after properly. "An ecclesiastical building which is for the time being used for ecclesiastical purposes" is, however, excepted from the definition of "monument" in that Act in the form in which it was passed, consequent upon an assurance given by Archbishop Davidson in the House of Lords that the church would in future look after its own.[38] This promise has been honoured by the much more thorough enforcement of the faculty jurisdiction over all church buildings and their contents and churchyards, accompanied by the provision of means for ensuring both that defects of repair now come to light under the Inspection of Churches Measure 1955 and that the court, in exercising this jurisdiction, has at its disposal adequate sources of aesthetic and technical advice through the D.A.C. and the C.C.C. Reinforced by archdeacons taking very seriously the part of their duty of visitation which is concerned with the material property of the church, the exercise of the jurisdiction is now far more comprehensive and better informed than it has ever been.

The much greater interest which has recently been expressed by the community as a whole in the care of churches as part of the national heritage is entirely to be welcomed, and it is the business of the ecclesiastical courts to see that due attention is paid to informed opinions on aesthetic matters which are sincerely held. At the same time the court must not give the effect to such opinions as are motivated merely by a blind desire to conserve things inherited from the past at the expense of the present and future of the church building and its use as a vehicle of worship and the teaching of the church. The changes introduced into the practice of the consistory court by the F.J.R. 1987 are designed to give more opportunities to informed critics from outside the parish to comment on proposals which they

---

[38] Ancient Monuments Consolidation and Amendment Act 1913, s.22.

think will affect adversely the aesthetic appearance of a church, while yet to leave the decision of each question firmly in the hands of Her Majesty's ecclesiastical courts, where it has always been.

Relation to secular courts

The law applied by the ecclesiastical courts is part of the law of England and the reports of relevant cases in either jurisdiction are cited in the courts exercising the other jurisdiction.

In *Att.-Gen.* v. *Dean and Chapter of Ripon Cathedral*[39] Uthwatt J. said:

> "Ecclesiastical law is part of the law of the land: (*Mackonochie* v. *Lord Penzance* (1881) 6 App.Cas. 424 at 446). The law is one but jurisdiction as to its enforcement is divided between the ecclesiastical courts and the temporal courts. When a matter of general law arises incidentally for consideration in a case before an ecclesiastical court, that court is bound to ascertain the general law and order itself accordingly; and where a matter depending on ecclesiastical law finds a place in a cause properly before the temporal courts those courts similarly will ascertain for themselves the ecclesiastical law and apply it as part of the law they administer. Each court ascertains the law by reason and argument—not by evidence—... The unity and coherence of the law is not affected by the division of jurisdiction as to its enforcement."[40]

The two jurisdictions thus exist side by side in courts which all exercise their powers as the judges of the Sovereign. But whereas the ultimate Court of Appeal in temporal matters is the House of Lords, the ultimate Court of Appeal in ecclesiastical causes had until 1963 been the Privy Council. Since then, in causes involving doctrine, ritual or ceremonial, the final authority is a commission of review appointed under the Great Seal and consisting of three Lords of Appeal and two Lords Spiritual.

---

[39] [1945] Ch. 239 at 245.
[40] Thus the ecclesiastical court decides any question of title to property which arises in cases before it: *Re St. Mary of Charity, Faversham* [1986] Fam. 143 and *Re Escot Church* [1979] Fam. 125.

In all other sorts of cases, the final authority is still the Privy Council (E.J.M. 1963, ss.8 and 11).

However the ecclesiastical courts, while not subject to any process of appeal to the temporal courts, are subject to the control of those of the temporal courts which now make orders replacing the old prerogative writs, to the extent, but only to the extent, that prohibition will issue to an ecclesiastical court which entertains a matter not within its jurisdiction, and perhaps also mandamus to such a court if it refuses to deal with a matter which is within its jurisdiction. But certiorari can never issue to an ecclesiastical court and the only way in which its errors can be corrected is by appeal under the E.J.M. 1963.[41]

Cases not dealt with by the court itself

Although the faculty jurisdiction extends to the whole of the church, its contents, the land on which it stands and its churchyard, there are certain defined categories of operation in respect of which the court does not interfere in practice.

(1) De minimis The first category is that of matters *de minimis*. This category is best not further defined and should be left to the practical commonsense of the archdeacon and the local church officers. The sanction against excessive use of this facility is that anything serious will be likely to be noticed by the archdeacon on his next inspection, and if what has been done is excessive he will either require those officers to apply for a confirmatory faculty, or will himself petition for a faculty to undo the work, with unpleasant consequences as to costs and expenses in either case.[42] A prudent incumbent or churchwarden will therefore always consult the archdeacon before seeking to do anything except ordinary annual maintenance under the *de minimis* rule.

(2) Tombstones The second category is the introduction of tombstones into a churchyard. Here the incumbent acts as the delegate of the chancellor. In some dioceses there is an express instrument of delegation defining the sorts of tombstone which an incumbent is authorised to allow. A specimen of such an

---

[41] *R. v. St. Edmundsbury and Ipswich Diocese (Chancellor of), ex p. White* [1947] K.B. 263; [1948] 1 K.B. 195.

[42] As to confirmatory faculties see p. 80. As to a petition to undo the work see F.J.M. 1964, s.5 and pp. 77 *et seq.*

instrument is provided in Appendix B. This form of instrument allows the same powers to the rural dean during a vacancy in the living. That he should have these powers is very important, because it has been found in practice that unsatisfactory stones are far too often introduced when there is no incumbent. In the absence of an express instrument of delegation, there is an implied power for the incumbent to allow the introduction of reasonable monuments; this power is, of course, suspended by the express terms of the instrument. It is very desirable that diocesan regulations should provide for any consent of an incumbent to be given in duplicate on a prescribed form, one copy of which he should retain when he gives the other to the applicant. In the absence of such an arrangement disputes only too frequently arise as to precisely what has been authorised. This subject is very fully dealt with in the Churchyard Handbook issued by the C.C.C., a copy of which should be in every church vestry at the expense of the P.C.C. Permission to introduce a particular monument given by an incumbent is not irrevocable: it operates only until further order made by the chancellor. If the decision of the incumbent is challenged, the matter must be dealt with by faculty and the chancellor is completely free whether or not to grand the faculty.[43]

(3) **Cases dealt with by archdeacon** The third category of case within the faculty jurisdiction but not dealt with in practice by faculty consists of those cases which are dealt with by the archdeacon.

There are many cases in which particular items of furnishing or arrangements of furnishings of a church are in question and where it is convenient to allow them to be used for, say, six months, so that the parishioners can form a view as to what they will look like if introduced permanently. It is usual to allow the archdeacon to authorise experimental user for a limited period. Of course, if any parishioner is unwilling to see the particular arrangement even tried he will petition for a faculty to remove the item in question, or to undo the proposed arrangement, and it will then be open to those who support the experiment to lodge a cross-petition for leave to do what is proposed. Of

---

[43] *Re Little Gaddesden Churchyard, ex p. Cuthbertson* [1933] P. 150 at 152.

course it seldom comes to this; the informal temporary permission of the archdeacon is normally accepted.

There are provisions in section 12 of the F.J.M. 1964 under which an archdeacon can, with the approval of the D.A.C., grant a certificate which stands in place of a faculty for certain sorts of repairs and redecoration of a church or its contents, assuming the application to be made by the incumbent and churchwardens. These arrangements are statutory and therefore inflexible. They never had any advantages except that the fees in respect of an archdeacon's certificate were less than those for a faculty. But now that no fees are charged for most applications made by incumbents and churchwardens in most dioceses the procedure under section 12 is tending to become obsolete.

On the other hand the author has always held the view that, since it is accepted that there is, and always has been, power for the chancellor to delegate functions of the court to an incumbent in respect of churchyard monuments, it is not logically objectionable for him to request his archdeacons to act for him in defined classes of less important cases where a faculty is in strictness required. This he does by instrument of delegation (a specimen of which is set out in Appendix B) which is revocable at his discretion and so can be reframed from time to time in consultation with his archdeacons. This system works well and is far more flexible than the statutory system. Every such instrument of delegation must of course make adequate provision for the applicants to consult the D.A.C. and obtain its approval before the archdeacon exercises his powers. With well organised registries this procedure is in fact not much more expeditious, nor does it make much less work, than using a faculty; but it is in many small cases a convenience to all concerned to have this degree of delegation and informality. For such a system to be possible at all relations of great confidence must exist between the chancellor and the archdeacons. It is essential that such relations should be formed, cultivated and cherished; otherwise the faculty jurisdiction itself will not work as it can and should do.

Extensions of jurisdiction

The faculty jurisdiction is in its essence confined to consecrated land and buildings and their contents. Indeed it is often said that the result of consecration is to bring a building and its contents within the jurisdiction of the consistory court. But there are two provisions extending the jurisdiction outside this primary scope.

The first is section 6 of the F.J.M. 1964, under which a diocesan bishop may make an order that a building which he has licensed for public worship shall be subject to the jurisdiction. The order, when made, brings not only the building within the jurisdiction of the court but also all "its furnishings and contents." An order of this sort is often desirable, especially to protect the contents from being reorganised in an undesirable way, or unsuitable contents introduced, or valuables (especially the communion silver) sold for inadequate reasons.

The second provision is to be found in section 7 of the same Measure, which is expressed to be "for avoidance of doubt" and declares that "where consecrated land forms, or is part of, the curtilage of a church within the jurisdiction of a court that court has the same jurisdiction over such land as over the church."

It is doubtful how far, if at all, this enactment was necessary; but at least it clarifies the position of church curtilage. The meaning of curtilage and the scope of the ancient jurisdiction over unconsecrated churchyards is discussed more fully in a later section.

The archdeacon

His office, tenure and duties in general

The office of archdeacon is of great antiquity and much curious learning about it is to be found in the older textbooks, as for example Sir Robert Phillimore's *Ecclesiastical Law* ((1873), Vol. I, pp. 236 *et seq.*). In the nineteenth century the archdeacon usually held a benefice, but modern legislation by Measure has so much increased the burden of the duties of an archdeacon that he should now be regarded as holding an office which demands practically all his time. His work in connection with the faculty jurisdiction is extremely important, but it is only a fairly small part of his total duties.

An archdeacon is normally appointed by the bishop of the diocese (though apparently there are still a few lay patrons of archdeaconries[44]), and his office is one of freehold subject to the requirement that he shall vacate it on his seventieth birthday,[45] unless he was already in office on August 1, 1975,[46] or unless the bishop continues him in office for a further period not exceeding one year.[47] He cannot be appointed until he has been six years in priest's orders.[48]

Some, though by no means all, of the duties of his office are prescribed by Canon C22. It lays down that within his archdeaconry he exercises his jurisdiction as an ordinary jurisdiction.[49] That is to say, when he exercises the jurisdiction of the archdeacon he acts in his own right and not as the delegate of the bishop. In so doing, he is entitled to act either in person or by a commissary to whom he has formally committed authority to act.[50] But in so far as he has duties which cannot be said to involve the exercise of his ordinary jurisdiction, as is the case with much that he does in connection with the faculty jurisdiction, he cannot appoint a commissary to act for him.

The archdeacon is to act within his archdeaconry "under the bishop," whom he is to assist "in his pastoral care and office": in particular the archdeacon is to see that all who hold ecclesiastical office "perform their duties with diligence," and he is to bring to the attention of the bishop "what calls for correction or merits praise."[51] His office as defined by the Canon is thus essentially a disciplinary one, though in many matters, of which the faculty jurisdiction is only one, he is concerned with much more than the mere enforcement of discipline. Archdeacons are members of most diocesan committees, and they hold a key position in the administration of the diocese. But the Canon also charges the archdeacon with supervising the care of the property of the church in his archdeaconry, in that it specifically requires him to hold annual visitations:

---

[44] *Halsbury's Laws of England*, (4th ed.) Vol. 14, para. 497.
[45] Ecclesiastical Offices (Age Limit) Measure 1975, s.1(3).
[46] *Ibid.*, s.1(4)(*d*).
[47] *Ibid.*, s.3(1).
[48] Canon C22, para. 1.
[49] *Ibid.*, para. 2.
[50] *Ibid.*, para. 3.
[51] *Ibid.*, para. 4.

"and he shall also survey in person or by deputy all churches, chancels, and churchyards and give direction for the amendment of all defects in the walls, fabric, ornaments, and furniture of the same, and in particular shall exercise the powers conferred on him by the Inspection of Churches Measure 1955[52]: he shall also, on receiving directions of the bishop, induct any priest who has been instituted to a benefice into possession of the temporalities of the same."[53]

Duties in relation to the faculty jurisdiction

(1) General It follows from his position as protector of church property that the archdeacon has a great part in the enforcement of the faculty jurisdiction. Indeed in his own archdeaconry he is altogether the most important person concerned with it. Unlike the chancellor, whose office is judicial and covers the whole diocese, so that he is comparatively remote, the archdeacon is closely acquainted with all the parishes in his archdeaconry; he knows all his churches and the persons who actually look after them. It is essential to the working of the faculty jurisdiction that incumbents and parish officers shall turn first to the archdeacon when they are beginning to consider any project which, if pursued, will need to be authorised by a faculty, that is to say any project whatever for physical work to the church, its contents or the land surrounding it. An informal talk on the telephone at, or even before, the outset, will ensure that the project starts in the right way, and that the right advice is obtained early enough to be effective. Archdeacons on the one side, and parish officers on the other, should consider discussions with one another as the normal procedure and should hold them frequently. This part of his work gives many pastoral opportunities to an archdeacon.

(2) The archdeacon as a member of the D.A.C. Every archdeacon is *ex officio* a member of the D.A.C.,[54] so that he can explain to the parish officers who consult him the likely attitude of the committee to what they want to do. Thus, when the case

---

[52] His powers under this Measure are, briefly, to force an inspection of any church if it has not been inspected for five years.
[53] Canon C22, para. 5.
[54] F.J.M. 1964, s.13(1). As to the committee, see below, pp. 32 *et seq.*

reaches the committee after such consultations, it is likely to be presented properly. Moreover, the archdeacon will be in a good position to explain to the committee each problem from his archdeaconry that comes before it. In the other direction, all archdeacons have ready access to the chancellor (usually by telephone) and can obtain his advice about the management of any pending case. Thus the archdeacon is at the central point from which it is easy to communicate with all concerned in every faculty case, so that the business can be made to flow smoothly and there shall be no misunderstandings. These propositions are not to be found in any earlier textbook; there seems indeed to be no manual of instructions for an archdeacon. But they form the core of the practice followed and advocated by the author in all his dioceses for very many years. It is essential that the chancellor should be on easy and understanding terms with all his archdeacons and they with him. He and they should meet at least once a year even if there is no specific problem to be discussed. If these suggestions are followed, the jurisdiction should work easily, and a few well chosen words on the telephone can save a ream of correspondence.

(3) Intervention in proceedings The archdeacon is deemed to have an interest as such for the purposes of any proceeding for obtaining a faculty in respect of any parish in his archdeaconry.[55] That is to say, he is a competent party, either as a petitioner or as a party opponent, in any cause of faculty arising in his archdeaconry. Thus, if some work is done without authority in one of his churches, he can petition for authority to undo it. Likewise he can petition to remove an object which has been placed without authority in any such church or churchyard.[56] Alternatively, cases fairly often arise where no qualified person enters appearance against a petition, but where the chancellor considers that the case needs to be argued fully in order to enable him to come to the right decision. For example, cases in which a parish wishes to dispose of valuable silver are often not

---

[55] F.J.M. 1964, s.9(1).
[56] In these cases the court has the powers given to it by s.5 of the Measure of 1964 to provide for the costs and expenses of undoing the illegal work. This section is discussed further below. For an example of such a petition by an archdeacon, see *Re St. Mary's, Balham* [1978] 1 All E.R. 993.

opposed locally, but they need full argument.[57] Again, in some cases the D.A.C. has doubts about or objections to a petition. Since the committee is not itself normally entitled to enter appearance, the archdeacon should do so to explain its point of view to the court. Or a case may arise where it is doubtful whether an unopposed petition can lawfully be granted, perhaps because the proposed work would be a breach of the D.B.G.A. 1884, or because it would involve an illegitimate use of consecrated land or of a church under the rules laid down in *Re St. John's Church, Chelsea*.[58] In any of these cases the chancellor should invite the archdeacon to enter appearance and either oppose the petition or put the petitioners to proof of their case.[59]

Where an archdeacon intervenes in proceedings in exercise of his powers under section 9 of the F.J.M. 1964, he is to be indemnified against his proper costs, or any costs awarded against him, by the diocesan board of finance, provided that the board has approved the intervention in writing.[60] This proviso can give rise to trouble in practice, since not all boards of finance appreciate the need for giving this assistance to the administration of justice in the court of their respective bishops. In the diocese of London the possible difficulty was dealt with some years ago by an understanding between Bishop Stopford, the chancellor and the London diocesan fund[61] that if the chancellor were to invite intervention and the board were to be unwilling to approve it, the bishop in person should decide what was to be done. In fact this issue is of little but academic interest, since the court usually orders the other party to pay the costs of the archdeacon in any such circumstances.

(4) **Acting archdeacons** Cases sometimes arise where an archdeaconry is vacant when an intervention is needed or where the archdeacon is "incapacitated by absence or illness

---

[57] See *Re St. Gregory's, Tredington* [1972] Fam. 236 at 239. This passage was made more emphatic by the judgment of the Court of Ecclesiastical Causes reserved: *Re St. Michael and All Angels, Great Torrington* [1985] Fam. 81 at 91.
[58] [1962] 1 W.L.R. 705. This decision was approved by the Appellate Court in the Northern Province in *Re St. Mary the Virgin, Woodkirk* [1969] 1 W.L.R. 1867, but it has not yet been considered by the Court of Arches.
[59] For examples of such a case see *Re. St. Luke's, Chelsea* [1976] Fam. 295, *Re St. Mary le Bow* [1984] 1 W.L.R. 1363 and *Re St. Stephen's, Walbrook* [1987] Fam. 146.
[60] F.J.M. 1964, s.9(3): see also F.J.R. 1967, r. 11 and Appendix, Form No. 12.
[61] The local name for the diocesan board of finance.

from exercising or fulfilling the rights and duties conferred or imposed upon him by this Measure."[62] In that event "such other person as the bishop shall appoint in that behalf in writing shall have power to act in the place of the archdeacon for the purposes of this Measure in any particular case." The bishop has the same power to appoint an acting archdeacon if the archdeacon is "in the opinion of the bishop for any other reason unable or unwilling to act." It can easily happen, in the course of the desptach of diocesan business, that an archdeacon has become so much involved with a particular project which needs a faculty as to make it reasonable for the bishop to form the opinion that the archdeacon is "unable" to act as a party opponent in the proceedings for a faculty in respect of that project. Indeed in such a case the archdeacon himself is, more than likely, "unwilling" so to act. This power enables the bishop to provide the court with a substitute who can approach the case dispassionately and thus assist the court in doing justice. The same provisions in respect of costs apply to an acting archdeacon as to the archdeacon himself. There is no requirement that an acting archdeacon shall be a clergyman. Indeed it is an advantage, especially where the real issue in the case is one of law, to appoint a solicitor with a knowledge of ecclesiastical law (though of course not the registrar). The author has on occasion found this device most helpful.[63]

(5) Supervision by archdeacon Under section 10(*a*) of the F.J.M. 1964 the consistory court may decree the issue of a faculty "subject to a condition requiring the work authorised thereby or any part thereof to be carried out under the supervision of the archdeacon or of any other person nominated by the court in that behalf..." Orders of this sort are sometimes made where a project has been the subject of controversy between the petitioners and the D.A.C., and the court is of the opinion that the petition should be granted but that the committee is entitled to be reassured by independent supervision that what has been allowed will be properly carried out. If the archdeacon is to supervise he will in fact probably arrange for some professional

---

[62] This phrase of course covers more than intervening in litigation, *e.g.* it applies to an archdeacon's powers and duties as an *ex officio* member of the D.A.C.
[63] In *Re St. Mary's, Barton-upon-Humber* [1987] Fam. 41, Goodman Ch. had the assistance of an acting archdeacon.

assistance, perhaps from another member of the committee. The court has power under section 10(c) to order that costs and expenses of the archdeacon be paid by any other party to the proceedings. But for some reason it does not provide for the costs and expenses of any other person appointed to supervise under section 10(a). The preferable order therefore is that the archdeacon shall supervise; then if he needs professional assistance he will engage it and will recoup himself under section 10(c).

(6) Faculty for archdeacon to do work in default of local action A faculty is merely a licence to the petitioner to have a given piece of work done, as distinct from an order upon him to do it. Cases may arise where the court, when it grants a faculty to an incumbent and churchwardens, wishes to ensure that the work is in fact done. In such cases the court is given power by section 10(b) of the F.J.M. 1964 to direct that, in default of the incumbent and churchwardens carrying out the work authorised by the faculty within a certain time, a further faculty shall issue to the archdeacon authorising him to do the work. His costs and expenses may be ordered to be paid by any other party under section 10(c). The author has no personal experience of an order under section 10(b) but it is in line with the practice laid down by the consistory court of the diocese of Southwark in *Re Woldingham Churchyard*,[64] which is generally recognised as authoritative.

(7) Meeting in parish under archdeacon's presidency Circumstances sometimes arise where a proposal is put forward from a parish, perhaps only by a majority of the P.C.C., when it seems likely that if a petition is presented and pressed there will be formal opposition and a hearing will become inevitable. In such a case it is frequently convenient for the chancellor to invite the archdeacon to go to the parish and see all the parties with a view to making sure that each side understands the point of view of the other and to lay the foundations for an agreed solution. Similarly, a local meeting with the archdeacon presiding can sometimes be very helpful in resolving a difference of opinion between the parish and the D.A.C. In cases of these sorts the

---

[64] [1957] 1 W.L.R. 811. For a similar case in the same court, see *Re St. Mary's, Balham* [1978] 1 All E.R. 993.

archdeacon is in a position of advantage as chairman. The local incumbent has understandably identified himself with the proposals under discussion and he is in a difficulty if he has to take the chair: the archdeacon is independent of any group in the parish. Again if the difference is between the parish and the D.A.C., the protagonist for the committee is likely to be the relevant specialist, and the archdeacon, though a member of the committee, is in a good position to understand both points of view. Devices of this sort have, in the author's experience, often made possible the reconciliation of differences before they reach the point where a hearing is necessary. An archdeacon's meeting can be much less formal than a hearing, and if it is called at the right moment it can be very beneficial to all concerned. Such a meeting can normally be arranged without difficulty. But if, for any reason, it is necessary to summon such a meeting in due form, it should usually be possible to arrange for a third of the lay members of the P.C.C. to make a written representation to the archdeacon under rule 18(2) of the Church Representation Rules, made under the Synodical Government Measure 1969.

(8) Delegated powers There is also a good deal of work which the archdeacon can do as the delegate of the chancellor to ease the dispatch of business in connection with the faculty jurisdiction. While the statutory procedure by way of archdeacon's certificate has in many dioceses fallen into disuse, it has long been the practice in the author's dioceses for certain matters within the jurisdiction to be dealt with by the archdeacon at the request and with the authority of the chancellor. Such a delegation may be either special or general. Cases arise quite frequently where there is some point of important detail which can only be dealt with adequately by someone who has seen the *locus in quo*. For example, it may be settled that a memorial of a particular design is to be allowed, but there is a difficulty as to its position. Or, a petitioner may have asked for leave to put a particular sort of tombstone into a churchyard, being one which would not comply with the normal regulations, and he may argue that in the part of the churchyard concerned there are already many tombstones of that sort. In such a case the chancellor may very well ask the archdeacon to visit and make the decision. There are also many cases, of no great importance in themselves but clearly within the jurisdiction of the court, in which the archdeacon can help; many of them can be delegated to him by a general instrument of delegation. There are some cases so small as to be only just above the level of cases needing no formal authorisation as being *de minimis*: these can be left by the instrument to the archdeacon alone. In the rest of the cases delegated to him, the instrument should make it clear that the powers of the archdeacon are not to be exercised without his having discussed the case with the D.A.C. (or its appropriate sub-committee or officer) and obtained the approval of the committee. In every case the decision should be given in writing and a copy lodged in the registry with copies of the plans, specifications and so forth which define the work which it has authorised. The exact form of the instrument of delegation is a matter for decision in each diocese. It should be discussed between the chancellor and the archdeacons and if in any way it needs amendment after practical experience it should be amended. These arrangements, which are extremely valuable in practice, as enabling relatively simple matters to be handled with the minimum of formality or friction, are dependent upon there existing between the chancellor and each archdeacon, and between the chancellor and the archdeacons collectively, relations of understanding and complete confidence. These relations are of the essence of the harmonious operation of the faculty jurisdiction and the cultivation of them is worth much labour and care.

The older legislation which set up the jurisdiction of the archdeacon to issue certificates was unsatisfactory. The legal boundaries of the power to issue certificates were rigid. Moreover, the jurisdiction was in a sense a rival to that of the chancellor in that the certificate is absolute and binding and there is no process of appeal from it. The system of informal delegation is much more satisfactory because it provides a clear chain of authority from the chancellor to the archdeacon and defines its scope. The instrument of delegation normally provides that he must satisfy himself that there is unanimous support for the proposals in the parish; if, by any chance, he makes a mistake in that respect his decision is not final and binding. But it is always open to a petitioner to apply to the consistory court for a faculty to have the work undone. In the author's experience this has in fact never happened, but the theoretical possibility is a safeguard against a blurring of authority. The form of instrument of delegation in use at the time of writing in the diocese of Bath and Wells is set out in Appendix B, as is also the form in which in that diocese the archdeacons give permissions. In other dioceses other forms may well be found convenient. It is a matter for local decision.

The diocesan advisory committee

Terms of reference and appointment

The F.J.M. 1938 was the first which required there to be an advisory committee in each diocese, but such committees had grown up informally in most dioceses in the years following the First World War. They were, indeed, part of the arrangements for enabling the church to fulfil the promise made by Archbishop Davidson in the House of Lords in 1912 that the church would look after its own buildings properly if they were not brought into the ancient monuments legislation.[65] Most of the daily work of the consistory court concerns proposals which have to be considered either aesthetically or technically, and it is on these sorts of subject that it is so valuable for the judge to have skilled and independent advice. It is indeed difficult to understand how the courts can have done their work before they had this assistance.

Further, long before any such case reaches the court those who run the affairs of the parish will benefit by having, in addition to any architect or other professional adviser whom they may instruct, the services of a skilled and continuous body accustomed to the sorts of questions which arise in looking after and adding to churches and their contents.

The committees are now an integral part of the arrangements for executing the faculty jurisdiction. In each diocese the bishop, the chancellor, the archdeacons and the registrar must give close attention to organising the smooth flow of business to, in and from the committee. In this they need the active co-operation of the committee itself, its officers and of the diocesan board of finance.

---

[65] See also Appendix C.

The committees now operate under section 13 of the F.J.M. 1964.[66] All members of the committee give their services free, as their offering to the church; but a good deal of expense arises in the proper execution of their duties. It was one of the weaknesses of the Measures of 1938 and 1964 that neither made any express provision on this subject. Though many diocesan boards of finance provided adequately for these commitees in their dioceses, some did not. As late as 1987 the author learned of one diocese where only £250 a year was provided (which hardly covered the postage of the secretary) at a time when in two of his own dioceses each committee was provided for at a cost of several thousand pounds a year.

Under section 13(2) of the F.J.M. 1964, the functions of the committee in each diocese are as follows:

(1) To advise the archdeacon before the issue of an archdeacon's certificate under section 12 (and, inferentially, if he is exercising powers delegated to him by the chancellor).
(2) "If required to do so" the committee is to advise
  (a) the judge;
  (b) intending applicants for faculties;
  (c) persons building new churches or converting buildings for the purpose of churches or erecting buildings or converting existing buildings with the intention that they shall be licensed for public worship; and
  (d) persons owning or responsible for the upkeep of unconsecrated buildings licensed for public worship.

Of these functions (c) stands by itself in never being concerned with the faculty jurisdiction. Of the buildings mentioned in paragraph (d) some will probably have been brought within the jurisdiction by an order under section 6 of the Measure of 1964 and they are accordingly assimilated to ordinary churches. It is mainly with paragraphs (a) and (b) that we are concerned.

Under section 1 of the Inspection of Churches Measure 1955 the diocesan synod of each diocese is required to make a scheme

---

[66] For some general observations on the D.A.C. see, *per* Spafford Ch. in *Re St. Andrew's, Dearnley* [1981] Fam. 50 at 54, 55.

for the inspection of every church at least once in every five years. Section 1(2)(c) requires these schemes to "provide for the appointment of an architect or architects approved by the advisory committee..." to inspect the churches and to report. The "church architect," *i.e.* the architect appointed under this measure, is an important person in the exercise of the faculty jurisdiction, as the court and the D.A.C. tend to rely on him. So the approval of his appointment is a valuable service which the committee must render.

Subsection (1) of section 13 of the F.J.M. 1964 requires a D.A.C. to exist in every diocese and that it shall include the archdeacons of all the archdeaconries within the diocese. The bishop is, by writing, to appoint the rest of the members. It is thus, to a greater extent than other permanent committees of the diocese, the bishop's own committee. Further, the bishop has power to appoint one of the members to be chairman. The term of office of a member is five years and care is needed to ensure that this provision is observed, which it often is not. Dr. Runcie, as Bishop of St. Albans, re-formed his committee for the lustrum beginning on January 1, 1979, and his successor did so again as from January 1, 1984. This distinguished example deserves to be followed; otherwise a muddle ensues. Copies of the written documents of appointment should be filed with the diocesan secretary, and he should be made responsible to the bishop to see that they are brought to the attention of the bishop at least three months before the end of a lustrum. This is particularly important when there has been a change of bishop. All appointments at other times should be expressed to expire at the end of a current lustrum. By section 13(1) all members are eligible for reappointment.

The appointment of the chairman of the committee is one requiring very serious consideration and consultation. However, he need not be a specialist and perhaps it is better that he should not be. Further, he may equally well be a clergyman or a layman and he does not necessarily have to be young. The bishop should always discuss the appointment with the archdeacons, who are *ex officio* members of the committee and are central to the whole administration, and also with the chancellor, who will need to rely on the chairman as a close and trusted colleague over a period of years, continuity being of great importance.

The secretariat

The secretary of the committee is not provided for by the legislation. The arrangements for the secretary and the secretariat vary from one diocese to another and are a matter for local arrangement. The author is in no doubt that the most satisfactory arrangement is for the diocesan secretary to be the secretary. The committee should usually be housed in the diocesan office and should be provided with staff by the diocesan board of finance. The diocesan secretary is then responsible for the committee and it is for him, in consultation with the chairman of the diocesan board of finance, to allot the necessary staff. If any part of the arrangements needs to be altered or commented on, the bishop or the chancellor or the chairman of the D.A.C. can deal direct with the chairman of the diocesan board of finance and with the diocesan secretary.

Some diocesan secretaries happen to be interested in problems of the sort with which the committee deals; others do not. A diocesan secretary, however much interested, is unlikely to have time to supervise the daily work of the committee. One who is not interested should not attempt to do so.

Thus in any event there should be a deputy secretary or clerk to the committee, under the diocesan secretary. This person must of course be interested in the work of the committee and it is he who will actually organise its daily business. For convenience, we refer in this book to the committee's secretariat collectively rather than to the secretary or the clerk. A well run committee has a great deal of correspondence, mainly with intending applicants for faculties. They need and seek advice and the earlier they obtain it the better. The secretariat must keep in close touch with each of them, must find out exactly what each one has in mind and must refer them to anyone who can help either to define what they want to do or to get skilled advice as to how to do it. Whenever there is a problem or a hitch, the secretariat should discuss it with the relevant archdeacon, and also, if the problem is in any sense a legal one, with the registrar. The secretariat may well feel the need, even at an early stage of the case, to visit the parish so as to see the places and things in question and talk to the local people. In doing this they should be careful to keep the archdeacon informed. It is often best that he and they should go together, and the purpose must be to present a well thought out agenda to the committee, and to give it all the background information which it needs, preferably in a written statement circulated in advance of the meeting, or to some extent by oral presentation at the meeting.

The secretariat should also be alert to see whether a case that is coming forward for consideration is important enough to be considered by the committee itself or whether it could usefully be dealt with more summarily.

The standing committee used for this purpose is an essential piece of machinery if the main committee is not to be overburdened with unimportant cases. The most satisfactory form of standing committee in the author's opinion is that which has long operated in the diocese of St. Albans, *i.e.* that in respect of any given case the standing committee consists of the chairman of the committee, the relevant archdeacon and the relevant expert. The secretariat sees that each of them has any necessary papers and information; the deliberations of the standing committee are informal, often taking place by telephone without there being an actual meeting. This body has power to act, as if it were the committee itself, in any case in which the whole of the standing committee dealing with it agrees that it is proper to be disposed of by the standing committee. If any member of the standing committee thinks that it would be better to send the case to the main committee, it goes there. All the decisions of the standing committee are reported to the next meeting of the main committee and are mentioned in its written agenda. A very large number of cases lend themselves to this summary procedure, including most cases of building work, where a full specification made by a responsible architect has been supplied and can readily be considered and adopted. This system has worked without difficulty for many years: it enables the committee itself to have more time for full discussion of the more important cases. The standing committee is, however, dependent upon having an alert and active secretariat in daily touch with the business of the advisory committee, even if the officers concerned have also other duties in the diocesan office.

Where the committee or standing committee has reached a conclusion, it is for the secretariat to convey it to the applicants and also if a petition has already been lodged, to the registrar. In a fair number of cases the conclusion of the committee is that further discussion is needed. It is then for the secretariat, always in collaboration with the archdeacon, to organise these discussions. Consultation is far the most important thing that the committee does, for if, from the beginning, the committee is engaged in discussion with the parish, the latter is advised as to what specific plans to propose at a stage at which the project is still flexible. Thus the applicants save the expense of preparing plans which will be criticised adversely and so to some extent may be wasted. After the plans are crystallised, the committee reaches a conclusion about them and then it can often be too late.

This consultative process is followed by the committee's recommendation to the chancellor; the secretariat should communicate that recommendation, within 48 hours, to the registry and to the applicants. Thereafter the secretariat is *functus officio* except in so far as it is again expressly consulted by the chancellor, the registrar, the archdeacon or the applicants. Their most important function at this late stage is to prepare, for approval by the committee, the draft of any formal report in the proceedings which may be called for by the chancellor and to organise the instruction and production of any judge's witnesses whom the chancellor may wish to call at the hearing.

Though the secretariat occupies a relatively junior place in the organisation of the faculty jurisdiction, it is an important one. An active, imaginative and efficient secretariat contributes greatly to the facility and lack of friction with which the cases eventually come to a decision.

The members of the committee

Except in the minor cases suitable to be handled summarily by a standing committee, the committee operates collectively as a body of experts and other useful members. This concept is important: otherwise there is a danger that in serious matters the committee will defer too much to the particular specialist member who may be exercised with a particular case. The specialists in other disciplines and the members who are not specialists at all have much to contribute to every case.

Persons appointed as specialist members should cover all the main sorts of discipline which arise in the business of the committee; but those who serve in respect of some of the disciplines which are needed only occasionally should be consultants rather than full members of the committee. This means that, if they wish, they can have agenda and minutes of the committee, to keep them in touch, but they will not be expected to attend meetings unless their own subject is going to arise or unless they wish to do so for some other reason. In some of the rarer disciplines, indeed, it may well be more convenient to have a consultant away from the diocese who will normally report to the committee in writing. Of the disciplines most often concerned, there is much the most work for architects, of whom every committee should have at least three. Then come organ advisers: they are constantly in demand and their work is very delicate since they are concerned with what is usually the most valuable single object in any church. Further, they are dealing with a subject in which far too many people in parishes have views which are as strong as they are ill-informed. Normally at least two organ advisers are needed. Then come the heating and electrical experts, whose problems to some extent overlap; for these two disciplines together there should be at least two members. Next come specialists in bells. Each committee should have at least one. Then there are advisers on archaeology, including the problems of old tombstones and the general matter of historical perspective. This subject needs one member: probably one of the lay members who can also help with advice on churchyard clearances. Silver, pictures, embroidery, carpets, fabrics, antique furniture and stained glass all need to be looked after. This can be done to some extent by members who are experts in other fields and to some extent by consultants and to some extent by non-specialist members who wish to take them up.

There are in every diocese both experienced parish priests and experienced laymen, each with good taste. Two or three of them are an important ingredient in an advisory committee. They can interpret the specialist to the parishes, and can help the specialist to be realistic. Sometimes members of this sort develop a specialised experience while they are members of the committee itself, for example as being the member who knows about churchyard problems or about reordering the interior of churches. But their primary function is as giving voice to the ideas of the ordinary informed churchman.

Finally, there are the archdeacons all of whom are *ex officio* members of the committee. As stated above, they are central to the working of the whole system. But as members of the committee they have also another function in that an archdeacon knows about the parish from which a case comes, its local problems and its puzzlements, in a way that no other member of the committee does. This local knowledge, coupled with the commonsense of the non-expert members, is essential to the mixture of knowledge, thought and feeling which the committee's conclusions must seek to synthesise.

All members of the committee should automatically be indemnified by the diocesan board of finance against their reasonable expenses of attending meetings of the committee, visits to parishes and correspondence, unless they positively elect not to be paid. This is an important matter, lest the committee become the preserve only of the well-to-do.

The advice of the committee

In the great majority of the cases which come before it, the committee has full plans and specifications; its task is then simple. For these are cases which have probably been discussed already between the applicants and their architects, the archdeacon and the secretariat, raising no particular aesthetic question. Most cases raise no questions of policy either, since it is generally fairly obvious in which way the discretion of the court should be exercised, for example, cases concerned with repairs to buildings, routine building operations, repairs or renewals to heating, lighting or bells or the introduction of new chattels of no great significance. What is needed in all such cases is that the committee should subject the plans and specifications to technical scrutiny so as to advise the parish and the chancellor whether they are technically satisfactory, or, if they are not, what adjustments are desirable. This work is of great importance; for the parish and its own builders, architects, heating engineers and the like profit by an independent critique of the documents which they have submitted. The chancellor moreover depends on the expert evidence that is put before him. A case of this kind, with an identified set of plans and specifications recommended by the committee, can normally be initialled by the chancellor without more ado.

The problems of the committee are quite different where there are questions of policy or discretion. For example, reordering of the interior of a church presents a number of different possibilities. Here the committee should as usual be consulted while the scheme is still fluid; for in that event it is easy to adjust such plans as may have been framed. Again, if the proposal is that a parish shall be allowed to sell one of its valuables, for example, a flagon, the decision is essentially one for the discretion of the court exercised upon full information. It is useless for the committee to resolve, especially by a majority, that it is either in favour of or against the proposed sale. That is to place itself in the position of the court. What the committee is called upon to do in such a case is to inform the court of the value and intrinsic and historical interest of the object which it is proposed to sell, and to provide informed facts bearing on the alleged special reason for sale. For instance, it may be argued that work must be done to the church and that the parochial church council cannot afford it. Then what is wanted is that the committee should make an assessment of the proposed work and its needfulness. They need not go into the parish accounts: the chancellor will require these to be produced to him.

The third class of case is where the parish proposes to do something, usually not particularly worthy from an aesthetic or technical point of view, and proposes to argue that pastoral need makes it desirable. Here again the committee should be wary of trying to adjudicate. What it should do is to assess the proposed works, technically and aesthetically. Then it will probably advise against them for technical and aesthetic reasons, which it should formulate and minute. It should also alert the chancellor to the existence of the alleged pastoral reasons for allowing the work (if it knows them) leaving to the chancellor to perform his duty of deciding whether to uphold the aesthetic objections or to allow the alleged grounds to prevail. He will of course consult the archdeacon as well as eliciting evidence from the responsible parties to the parish, especially the churchwardens who are the bishop's officers and as such are entitled to give hearsay evidence as to opinion in the parish.

Then there are many cases in which the relevant considerations are almost purely aesthetic, for example new stained glass windows. Here the committee should produce a critique of the design and should indicate whether, on purely aesthetic grounds, the proposal is one to be recommended.

In some of these cases a hearing is going to be needed and in those cases the chancellor will usually ask for a formal written report from the committee, which will become evidence in the proceedings. He is likely also to ask the committee to nominate someone to give such evidence at the hearing, usually as a judge's witness.

The committee has no power to "approve" anything except the proposed issue of an archdeacon's certificate (or an act of the archdeacon under his delegated powers). It should beware of using this verb in any other sort of case, since it is calculated to mislead an applicant for a faculty. The phrases "recommends to the chancellor of the diocese that the proposals be approved," or "commends the proposals" to him should be used. A less enthusiastic form is to say "does not think it necessary to object" to the proposals, or "does not think it necessary to advise the chancellor against approving them." The active negative should be "does not feel able to recommend the chancellor to approve" or even "advises the chancellor not to approve." In any such case the reasons for the committee's view should be formulated, minuted and communicated both to the applicants and to the registrar, or in a really important case direct to the chancellor himself. The court cannot reject a petition for a faculty without an oral hearing (or, in a few cases, the exchange of written representations under F.J.R. 1967, rule 6A); the committee should in such cases always be prepared to provide a witness or witnesses to give evidence in public to support its advice that a petition be rejected.

It is important for the court to know precisely what documents the committee has considered; the committee should therefore have a rubber stamp and place it on every such document so as to identify it. In some dioceses a more elaborate stamp is used which both identifies the document considered and states that the proposals therein contained are recommended or not. Another diocese uses a letter for this purpose by reference to stamped documents. In every case where the committee recommends proposals it should state in writing to the applicants that a faculty will be needed and should supply a petition form if there is not already a petition. The committee's resolutions should be passed not only to the applicants but also to the registrar.

The chancellor always pays great attention to the advice of the committee, but he is not bound by it and in a few cases he will decide to grant a petition which the committee has not recommended. But he is unwise to do so without consultation with the archdeacon, and often also with the chairman of the committee. To grant an unrecommended petition does not require a hearing, though to refuse it does so. When the chancellor grants such a petition he should always let the committee know, sometimes direct or sometimes through the archdeacon, his reasons for doing so. Such reasons may be of many sorts, but they should not simply be that, without hearing the case, he prefers his own aesthetic taste to that of the committee.

It is important that the committee should not by delays put itself in the position of barring the applicant from access to the court. It should always be made clear to the applicant that he is at liberty at any time to present his petition, which will then proceed to a decision. In such a case the chancellor is likely to call for the advice of the committee under section 13(2)(a) of the F.J.M. 1964 and rule 10(2) of the F.J.R. 1967; but he will then be in control of the proceedings and can determine their speed. Some committees have at some times allowed themselves to get into the wrong position on these matters, which is undesirable in principle and has the incidental disadvantage of impairing the goodwill which those in charge of parishes ought to feel towards the committee and its officers. If such delays appear to be arising, the archdeacon should inform the registrar so that the court may act. It is a good working rule that if any case appears more than twice on the agenda of the committee the archdeacon and registrar should enquire about it.

Very occasionally there arises in the committee a case of such outstanding aesthetic importance that the committee itself wishes to have further advice from the C.C.C., the body set up by the General Synod, *inter alia*, to co-ordinate the activities of diocesan advisory committees. This step always leads to delay and if the committee is taking it, the secretariat should notify both the registrar and the applicants. There are also some cases in which the chancellor himself, having had his committee's advice, wishes to have also that of the C.C.C. under rule 10(2) of the F.J.R. 1967. In such a case the registrar should notify both the secretariat and the applicants.

The parties to proceedings in the consistory court

The faculty jurisdiction, now exercised by the consistory court created by the E.J.M. 1963, derives from the civil jurisdiction of the former consistory court, not from its criminal jurisdiction. In the latter, proceedings were *ad publicam vindictam*. They were open "to any person whom the Ordinary may think fit to allow to promote his office."[67] That is to say, proceedings could only be started with the leave of the court, but with that leave anyone might be prosecutor. In the civil jurisdiction, however, no leave was needed, but the suit was only open to those "who have a personal interest in it." This distinction is not unimportant, for "the preservation of the peace in the church generally, as well as in particular parishes, may in great measure be dependent upon it."[68] For:

> "it would be a great evil if... the inhabitant of a parish in Cornwall could interfere in matters relating to the fabric of a church in Northumberland, in which he has no private interest, as to which he has sustained no civil injury and as to which he may be acting in opposition to the wishes of the parishioners and incumbent."[69]

The test therefore is whether the proposed party "has a personal interest." This phrase was slightly elaborated by Dr. Tristram in *Hansard* v. *Parishioners of St. Matthew, Bethnal Green*[70] when he said that "... to entitle a person to oppose the granting of a faculty he must shew some interest in the subject-matter of the application." In another case the phrase used by the same learned judge was "... a present interest, or the possibility of an interest in the subject-matter of the suit...."[71] How these

---

[67] *Fagg* v. *Lee* (1873) 4 A. & E. 135 at 150, *per* Sir Robert Phillimore, Dean of Arches. This decision was upheld by the Privy Council: *Lee* v. *Fagg* (1874) L.R. 6 P.C. 38.
[68] *Ibid.*
[69] *Ibid.*
[70] (1878) 4 P.D. 46 at 54.
[71] *Davey* v. *Hinde* [1901] P. 95 at 108.

phrases are to be interpreted depends to some extent on what the subject-matter of the application is. Thus in *Hansard's* case[72] the proposal was to build a mortuary in a churchyard[73] and the court held that two gentlemen, neither of whom was resident in the parish, were entitled to oppose the petition on the ground that they were freeholders of houses in the immediate vicinity of the church to which the mortuary might have been injurious on sanitary grounds. It is much more doubtful whether a non-resident freeholder, as distinct from his resident tenants, would be a qualified party in respect of a case about furnishing or ornaments, which can hardly affect the neighbouring freeholds. Of course, as was indicated in *Hansard's* case, the qualification offered in most cases is that the party is a resident parishioner or a ratepayer. But there are other sorts of qualification, for example the owner of a family vault, wherever resident, will be entitled to oppose a petition to interfere with the vault,[74] and in a case for the exhumation and removal of bones the grandson of one of those whose bones were in question was entitled to be heard, though he was not a parishioner in any sense.[74a] Again, in a case where the freehold of a churchyard was vested in the local authority, the authority was entitled as freeholder to petition for leave to erect an obelisk in the churchyard, and the members of the committee which had been formed to organise this operation and to pay for it were also admitted as ancillary to the freeholder.[75] On the other hand:

> "It is not the law that anyone can confer upon himself a sufficient interest to be a litigant in the consistory court merely by deciding that he wants to do something to a church or churchyard in the diocese."[76]

In the usual case of an intending donor of a chattel to a church, it is therefore doubtful whether the donor is, as such, entitled to petition, unless he is qualified as a parishioner or is joined with, or supported by, some person who would be a competent petitioner or party opponent. The incumbent and the

---

[72] (1878) 4 P.D. 46.
[73] This was of course before the D.B.G.A. 1884.
[74] *Hansard's* case, above n. 72, at 54.
[74a] *Vicar and One of the Churchwardens of St. Botolph without Aldgate v. The Parishioners of the same* [1892] P. 161 at 166, 172.
[75] *Re St. Luke's, Chelsea* [1976] P. 295 at 305E.
[76] *Ibid.* at 305D.

churchwardens or the parochial church council will normally be co-petitioners with the donor if they are all willing to accept the gift: but if they refuse, the petition would still be well constituted if any resident parishioner were to join as petitioner. Again, in a recent case the (civil) parish council was admitted as a party opponent, it is thought rightly, because it wished to argue that the proposed building would affect the amenities of the village and relationships within it and would necessitate "desecrating" the churchyard[77] in which the local electors were interested as parishioners.

Though the test is in its origin proprietary, it seems to be generally recognised that a person resident in the parish is qualified even if the proposals do not affect his property. The test in such a case appears to be whether the person is a "rateable occupier."[78] If so, it does not matter that he acquired that position purely in order to qualify himself to be a litigant in the consistory court,[79] or that he qualified in respect of one room in which he was a weekly tenant, where he never slept and to which he went only occasionally.[80] On the other hand, in the dioceses of each of the archbishops it has been held that their respective legal secretaries are not competent petitioners in civil suits for the removal of allegedly illegal ornaments.[81] One of the most tenuous cases of personal

---

[77] *Re St. Andrew's Church, Backwell*: this case is unfortunately unreported. It arose in 1982 in the consistory court of the diocese of Bath and Wells. This opponent was ordered to pay half the costs of the petitioners.
[78] *Davey* v. *Hinde* [1901] P. 95 at 111, *per* Dr. Tristram Ch. On this basis Moss Bross. Ltd. was allowed to appear as a party opponent in *Re St. Paul's, Covent Garden* [1974] Fam. 1.
[79] *Kensit* v. *Rector and Churchwardens of St. Ethelburga, Bishopsgate Within* [1904] P. 80 at 101, 102, where the petitioners were tenants in rateable occupation of a small office in a house in the parish. See also *Davey* v. *Hinde* [1901] P. 95 at 112.
[80] *Davey* v. *Hinde* [1903] P. 221 at 229–231. Other stages of this much litigated case are reported at [1901] P. 95 and (as *R.* v. *Tristram*) [1901] 2 K.B. 141 and [1902] 1 K.B. 816.
[81] *Fagg* v. *Lee* (1873) L.R. 4 A. & E. 135; (1874) L.R. 6 P.C. 38, and *Noble* v. *Reast* [1904] P. 34. In the former case the Privy Council declined to take cognisance of any description of Mr. Lee other than that he was of Number 2 Broad Sanctuary, Westminster. Mr. Lee did not allege that he had any interest in the subject-matter of the suit. In the latter case the petitioner expressly described himself as secretary to the Archbishop of York, but with no more success.

interest was in *Re St. James's, Bishampton*[82] where the Minister of Aviation petitioned for leave to put on the church tower a mast nearly 13 feet high with a warning light on top of it. Boydell Ch. held that the Minister had a "sufficient personal interest," apparently on the ground that he was in charge of an airfield (in another parish), which was vested in the Crown and from which aircraft came and went on their lawful errands and that the church tower constituted a danger to aviation. The learned chancellor observed that it is not uncommon for a faculty to be granted to persons not otherwise qualified who wished to instal memorial tablets in churches. No doubt such a person usually has the support of the incumbent, churchwardens, parochial church council or a resident parishioner (each of whom certainly has *locus standi*); but as mentioned above in connection with *Re St. Luke's, Chelsea*, it seems that in the absence of such support a mere volunteer cannot launch such a petition. On the other hand it is clear that, in regard to a grave in a churchyard, the close relatives of the deceased and his executors who arranged his burial have a sufficient interest to support a petition for a tombstone: further, the title to the tombstone apparently devolves on the heirs at law of the person commemorated and they must have a sufficient interest to enable them to appear in proceedings about the tombstone.[83]

These principles left two considerable gaps. First, persons who are so much associated with the church as to be on its

---

[82] [1961] 1 W.L.R. 257. In this case the petition was granted. In the associated case of *Re St. Edburga's, Abberton* [1962] P. 10 the chancellor decided that the minister had *locus standi*, but dismissed the petition on the merits. The Court of Arches reversed his decision but the learned dean made it clear that he was expressing no approval or disapproval of the decision about *locus standi*, which was not challenged in the Court of Arches. In the *Abberton* case counsel who had appeared as *amicus curiae* in the Court below was apparently allowed to represent the Bishop of Worcester in the Court of Arches. The Bishop had entered appearance, without objection by the appellants, since the date of the judgment in the court below. It is not clear how the Bishop came to have the *locus standi* to appear at all in view of *Fagg* v. *Lee* and *Noble* v. *Reast*.

[83] See F.J.M. 1964, s.3. The law on the subject of title to tombstones is unsatisfactory and requires to be reformed. In the London consistory court in the autumn of 1982 a petitioner in the United States of America was held to be entitled to petition for authority to remove a tombstone and re-erect it in Canada. This was on the basis that she was a surviving co-parcener entitled under the law applicable in 1923, the year of the death of the testator, to any realty of which he died intestate. *Re Boyle deceased* (unreported).

electoral roll but who live in another parish were excluded. This was remedied by the F.J.M. 1964, s.9(1) which provides that "... any person who is entered on the electoral roll of the parish concerned but who does not reside therein..." is to be deemed "to have an interest as though he were a parishioner of that parish." In this context the word "parishioner" presumably means a person resident within the parish.

The other lacuna is as to enforcement, as witness *Lee* v. *Fagg* and *Noble* v. *Reast*.[84] This lacuna also is remedied by section 9(1) of the Measure of 1964,[85] which provides that "For the purposes of any proceedings for obtaining a faculty the archdeacon of the archdeaconry in which the parish concerned is situate shall be deemed to have an interest as such," and section 9(2) has provisions under which the bishop can appoint someone to act if the archdeaconry is vacant or the archdeacon is unable or unwilling to act.

The incumbent is always interested in any case arising in his parish, since the freehold of the church and churchyard is vested in him. Likewise the churchwardens are always interested in cases about the chattels of a parish since such chattels are vested in them. Moreover, it seems that they are, and always have been, in any event interested in all cases in their parish as the officers of the bishop responsible, among other things, for seeing that the law is enforced in the parish.

The P.C.C. is the creature of modern legislation, which does not appear to make any direct provision as to the *locus standi* of such council. But the Parochial Church Councils (Powers) Measure 1956, s.4 throws upon the council the care, maintenance, preservation and insurance of the fabric of the church and the goods and ornaments thereof. It has similar liabilities in respect of the churchyard. Hence, anything that is proposed to be done to, or in respect of, a church or its contents or its churchyard must have some financial implications for the council, and it appears therefore that the council is always a competent party, either for or against a petition.

The most usual practice is for the incumbent and churchwardens to be petitioners though the P.P.C. is also quite often a petitioner. But whenever undertakings to the court

---

[84] [1904] P. 34.
[85] Similar provision was made for the first time in the F.J.M. 1938, s.1.

are necessary they should always be given by the P.C.C. which endures, being a body corporate, and not by the incumbent and churchwardens who individually are transient. Their undertakings could probably not be enforced against anyone but themselves.[86]

It also appears that there are some cases in which the diocesan board of finance is a competent party as being the freeholder of some unconsecrated churchyards or church curtilages. Further, in some cases where the court is allowing valuables vested in churchwardens to be sold it orders the proceeds of sale to be held by the board as trustee. In such a case it is convenient to join the board as a party so that it can give undertakings to the court about the fund.

The persons and bodies mentioned in the foregoing paragraphs are qualified to become parties to faculty proceedings either as petitioners or as parties opponent. But under F.J.R. 1967, rule 5A, various other persons and bodies can become parties opponent, though not petitioners.

Sub-rule (1) of rule 5A, which came into force on April 1, 1988, provides that "any interested person" who wishes to object to a proposed faculty shall be entitled, during the period of citation or within seven days thereafter, to give a notice of objection as there provided "and he shall thereupon be treated as a party opponent for all purposes including any order for costs which may be made by the judge pursuant to section 60 of the Ecclesiastical Jurisdiction Measure 1963."

Sub-rule (2) defines "interested person" as meaning various categories set out in paragraphs (*a*) to (*f*) of that sub-rule.

Paragraph (*a*) covers persons resident in the parish or entered on the electoral roll of it, although not resident therein. Paragraph (*b*) covers the relevant archdeacon, and paragraph (*f*) covers "any other person appearing to the registrar to have a lawful interest in the subject matter of the petition." None of these provisions goes beyond what was already the law as described above; but the other three paragraphs are new.

Under paragraph (*c*) "the local planning authority for the area in which the church or place of worship is situated" becomes an interested person. The "local planning authority" is not

---

[86] Arrangements to bring in the P.C.C. were made in *Re St. Mary's, Luton* [1967] P. 151.

defined, but presumably it means the body which would give planning permission or listed building consent for the proposed project if such permission or consent is or were to be necessary, *i.e.* the district council or its local equivalent. Since there are no provisions requiring service or notice of the citation or proceedings on any of these bodies the judge and the registrar should be alert to see if in any given case the local planning authority is likely to be interested and should call to its attention the fact that the case is starting and that the authority is entitled to lodge a notice of objection, with the consequent liability for costs. In practice it is likely that such an interest will have emerged during the previous consultations with the archdeacon and the D.A.C.

Paragraph (*d*) enables notice of objection to be lodged by "any statutory amenity society." This phrase is defined by rule 2(1) as meaning "the Ancient Monuments Society, the Council for British Archaeology, the Georgian Group, the Society for the Protection of Ancient Buildings, the Victorian Society and such other body as may be designated by the Dean of the Arches as a statutory amenity society either generally or for the purpose of any class of application for faculty."

The five national bodies enumerated already have various privileges in the administration of the planning law. They have considerable expertise and their evidence or comments can well be very useful to the consistory court. Previously, this help could only be given by them through nominated witnesses. The intention is now that any of these bodies shall be able to take part, as a party, in faculty proceedings with all the rights and liabilities of any other party. The Dean's power of designation will enable him to keep the list of statutory amenity societies in line with the list used in planning matters. This power has not so far been exercised. It is to be expected that arrangements will be made in each diocese for the D.A.C. to be informed of any likely interest of any statutory amenity society through one of its members who is also a member of the relevant society or through the secretariat of the D.A.C. itself. Conversely, arrangements are to be made for the agenda of each D.A.C. meeting to be sent to the statutory amenity societies in good time before the meeting, so that the relevant society is alerted to get in touch with the registrar in any case where the society is likely to wish to take part in the proceedings or, indeed, to offer advice. The co-operation and goodwill of these bodies is of importance to the harmonious working of the faculty jurisdiction, and the court should ensure that any such body which wishes to appear in a given case is able to do so, provided that it declares its interest in good time.

Finally, paragraph (e) includes as an interested person "any other body designated by the judge for the purpose of the petition." The most obvious sort of body which could be designated under this provision is a responsible local amenity society. Previously any such body had to find one or more parishioners willing to incur the risks and expense of entering objection and then work with and through those persons, perhaps giving them an indemnity. It will be much more satisfactory to have the real opponent before the court as a party. Thus the judge will on some occasions be wise to use the power under paragraph (e) for this purpose. He should satisfy himself before making such an order that the society has funds sufficient to meet any order for the costs of the petitioners and court fees which may be made against it, as well of course as its own expenses.

Again, this power of designation may be useful in a few cases to enable the D.A.C. or C.C.C. to come before the court as a party in its own right. Usually any objection to the petition by either of these bodies will continue to be subsumed under the intervention of the archdeacon either to oppose the petition or to put the petitioners to proof. But in a few cases, for example, where the archdeacon does not agree with the attitude of the D.A.C. or the C.C.C. it will be more realistic to have that body itself as a party opponent subject always to it being clear that, if it is allowed the privilege of being a party, it can meet any resultant orders for costs or court fees as well as its own expenses.

There are many other bodies, mostly concerned with conservation and aesthetics, which sometimes seek to appear in cases in the consistory court. Thus in 1982 the Royal Fine Arts Commission applied to be allowed to oppose a petition and as the law then stood had to be rejected as a party.[87] Such a body could, in a few cases, usefully be designated under paragraph (e), subject to the points about costs and fees already mentioned.

---

[87] *Re St. Andrew's Church, Backwell* (1982); unreported, see n. 77 above.

As we have seen, the reason for the rule that a party must show that he has an interest is to prevent interference by persons who are not really concerned with the church in question. Therefore the intervention of outside bodies, though it can be very useful, should be kept fully under the control of the court: they can appear only under the new rule: it should be construed strictly and the powers of the judge under paragraph (*e*) should be exercised sparingly.

3. Procedure in the Consistory Court

Introductory

The proceedings in the consistory court in respect of faculties ensure the enforcement of the control of the ordinary over churches,[1] their contents, their churchyards and their curtilages.

Procedure in the consistory court is governed by the F.J.R. 1967. Those Rules were amended by the F.J.(A.)R. 1975 and the F.J.(A.)R. 1987. The Rules of 1975 were themselves wholly revoked by those of 1987. The structure of the Rules of 1987 is to write new or substituted rules into the Rules of 1967. Throughout this book therefore the Rules of 1967 are treated as being in the form in which they emerged from the amendments made in 1987. It is in this form that they are printed in Appendix A.

The proceedings are initiated by lodging a petition in the registry of the court. In the great majority of cases the proceedings are comparatively formal and serve mainly to ensure that the consultations which form the bulk of the work take place before the petition is lodged. For, as we have seen, the work to be authorised by the court, having first been mooted in the parish, should have been discussed with the archdeacon, and with the architect and other technical advisers of the parish, then presented to the D.A.C. and finally recommended by that committee for approval. There will sometimes be several exchanges between all these persons and these processes should lead to a proposal which can be presented to the court as being well thought out and uncontroversial. Time spent at these early stages is always well spent and the work deserves much care and attention; for the building endures and the work done

---

[1] Including buildings licensed for public worship to which the jurisdiction of the court has been applied by F.J.M. 1964, s.6: see at pp. 173 *et seq.*

to it endures and nothing but the best practicable is a fit offering. A most important part of the work of the chancellor lies not in deciding controversial cases but in ensuring that there are, in his diocese, such arrangements for consultation as will ensure that all, or nearly all, the cases are uncontroversial and yet that no work whatever is done without proper authority and due consideration. When all the consulting parties are in agreement, the petition should normally be presented.

If the work has already been done without authority, and therefore illegally, the petitioners should seek a confirmatory faculty. If disagreement begins to be apparent during the consultations, as can easily happen, the petition should be presented earlier, so that any further discussions that are needed can proceed under the control of the court. However, in most cases that should not be necessary. The other sort of case in which a petition should be presented early is where there is some such real urgency as arises if a building is found to have become, or to be about to become, dangerous. Then, the sooner the petition is presented the better, without waiting to consult the advisory committee. In such cases, the chancellor can ensure that what needs to be done is done expeditiously and that he gets such advice as he needs. The procedure is extremely flexible and the author has in such cases often made an interlocutory order on the telephone when the registrar has been approached summarily by those responsible in the parish: in such cases the proposed petitioners are required to undertake to present a petition at once and meantime the case proceeds as if they had done so.

Apart from cases of urgency and cases of incipient disagreement among those who are parties to the consultations, the petition should normally come to the chancellor in a state where he has only to sign the papers. Where that is so, the consultation system is working well.[2]

---

[2] There are a few instances where a hearing is required by law, *e.g.* in connection with the demolition or part demolition of a church (under F.J.M. 1964, s.2) or in some cases of sales of treasures (see F.J.R. 1967, r. 6(7)). In most cases of the sale of treasures a hearing in open court is desirable, see *Re St. Gregory's, Tredington* [1972] Fam. 236. There are also many cases about property where a hearing in chambers is desirable so as to ensure, without undue correspondence, that the documents which are to be authorised are in order. But the statement in the text is true of all ordinary cases.

The Appendix to the F.J.R. 1967 provides specimens of forms which can usefully be followed in preparing the necessary documents. The registrar can supply a print of the petition form and, if the case becomes an opposed one, skeletons of forms for the pleadings. The other forms are for documents to be issued by the registrar, and he will deal with them himself. Petitioners and other parties should always consult him as to preparing petitions and other documents.

The legislation provides that fees shall be paid on various occasions during the proceedings, including a lodgment fee to be paid with the petition. But in the author's dioceses and in a good many others no fees are called for from the petitioners in respect of any ordinary petition coming from a parish. The lodgment fee has been seen as a deterrent and as an excuse for not applying for a faculty; in dioceses where it has fallen into disuse there is no such excuse for work being done without proper authority and the number of petitions has increased greatly. Fees in less ordinary cases are dealt with more fully below (see Chapter 7).

The petition

Preparing the petition

Any petition must be lodged by a party having a sufficient interest in the subject-matter of the suit.[3] In the normal case where the proposals arise from discussions in the parish, the incumbent or curate-in-charge is normally one petitioner. He is often joined by the churchwardens, who are the bishop's officers in the parish, and their joinder is thus some guarantee that the proposals are proper in themselves.[4] In many cases the P.C.C. is also a petitioner, since it is normally paying for the work. If the subject-matter is being given or paid for by someone else, the council will still be liable to maintain, insure and repair it when installed; thus it is equally an appropriate party in these cases. In cases where authority is sought for an outside party to use church property, the essential petitioners are the incumbent

---

[3] See at pp. 43 *et seq.*
[4] Under Canon F13 it is the duty of the "minister and churchwardens" to obtain a faculty in a list of circumstances which covers most cases where a faculty is required.

(if there is one), the parochial or guild church council and the proposed licensee: see *Re St. Mary, Aldermary*.[5]

The petition form[6] deserves to be filled in with great care. Care at this stage will often save delays later.

At the head of the petition the petitioners should state their names, addresses and capacities. Over the page is a schedule in which they should detail the work that they want to do. The registry will normally use the schedule when it comes to preparing the citation. Nothing can be sanctioned which is not covered by the citation[7]: filling in the schedule therefore requires a balance between using words wide enough to cover all the work that is intended and going into enough detail to enable those who see the citation to know accurately what is proposed. Where there is an architect's or other such specialist specification, it should be referred to explicitly.

There follow five numbered paragraphs, the first of which is formal. Paragraph 2 states that the works or purposes for which authority is sought are correctly shown "on the designs, plans and other documents accompanying this petition." If these documents have been considered by the D.A.C., it is desirable that they should be identified by the committee's stamp. Paragraph 3 states, if such is the case, that the committee has been consulted, and the result. Again, it is important to show the identity of the plans considered by the committee. Paragraph 4 states the estimated cost and how it is to be provided. In dioceses where lodgment fees are payable, the amount mentioned in this paragraph largely determines the amount of the lodgment fees. This information should be accurately provided, especially in cases where large sums are about to be spent. The chancellor should beware of authorising work without a reasonable prospect that it will be paid for at the required times. For example, it would be unfortunate if a church roof were stripped off preliminary to renewal and the money then ran out. If a grant from the Department of the Environment is expected, this fact should be mentioned. The acceptance of such a grant is on certain terms, which are however not intended to be legally

---

[5] [1985] Fam. 101 at 105.
[6] It is Form No. 6 scheduled to the Rules of 1967. This form was not altered by the F.J.(A.)R. 1987; but the Rule Committee is engaged, at the time of writing, with revising the petition form.
[7] See at pp. 59 *et seq*.

enforceable by the Department: the practice in some, and perhaps most, dioceses is that the court shall see that the letter from the parish accepting the grant is so worded as to ensure that it does not create an enforceable contract.

Paragraph 5 deals with the relevant resolutions of the P.C.C. The voting must be stated correctly. If the proposal is supported only by a majority, and not unanimously or *nemine contradicente*, that information alerts the court to the fact that the proposal is not locally uncontroversial. Thus actual opposition may develop, leading to a hearing in open court or further negotiations in which the archdeacon can often help.

The form also sets out some numbered questions. The questions are not a mere formality. They are directed to satisfying the court that the petitioners have had the proper technical advice and have seen to the insurance implications, if any; the court needs to know whether the rights of any third parties (including the lay rector) are concerned, whether services will be interrupted and whether any church property will incidentally be disposed of. The length of time which the work will take is also to be specified: rule 7(2) of the F.J.R. 1967 requires the form of faculty to provide for it. In addition to the points mentioned above, the petition must, in any case of demolition or partial demolition of a church, specify which of the grounds mentioned in section 2 of the F.J.M. 1964 are relied on, giving full particulars specified in rule 4(2) of the F.J.R. 1967. Again, as will be explained later (see pp. 121 *et seq.*), a petition for leave to sell a church treasure should specify the grounds for the proposal, and a petition for leave to introduce a memorial into a church should specify the grounds on which it will be submitted that the deceased person concerned ought thus to be commemorated. Further, in all cases where work is to be done in or on a churchyard or church curtilage, the status of the site should be mentioned, showing whether it is consecrated burial ground in use, consecrated but disused burial ground, unconsecrated churchyard or church curtilage. Where work has already been done without authority, and therefore illegally, the petitioners who seek a confirmatory faculty should explain fully the circumstances and provide any apology that may be appropriate.

If the form is carefully filled in there should be no difficulty or delay in dealing with most cases; but if there is any unusual feature about the case, the petitioners should explain it by letter. This is particularly important where any dealing with property is presented for approval.

The statutory petition form is not suitable for some cases, especially grave space reservations, churchyard monuments or exhumations. Many dioceses have therefore drafted their own forms for such purposes. Rule 4 of the F.J.R. 1967 gives effect to the statutory forms, subject to rule 15 which allows flexibility in cases where any form is not wholly suitable.

Lodging the petition

Under rule 4(5) the petition and accompanying documents are to be presented by lodging them at the diocesan registry. In cases where demolition or partial demolition of a church is proposed, the subrule requires the petitioners to lodge an additional copy of the petition and of each document.[8]

Early proceedings on petition

The registrar is required by rule 5(1) to lay the petition, with its supporting documents, before the chancellor, who will give it preliminary consideration and will normally decree the issue of a general citation. But before doing so he should consider whether, on the face of the petition, the relief sought by the petition can lawfully be granted. For example, if the petitioners seek authority to introduce an ornament which has clearly been held in previous decisions to be illegal, the chancellor should so intimate, offering the petitioners an opportunity of trying to satisfy him, *ex parte*, at a preliminary hearing or by correspondence, that there are reasonable grounds for supposing that the proposals can lawfully be sanctioned. Cases about possibly illegal ornaments are, happily, now very rare; but a similar point can easily arise under the D.B.G.A. 1884, s.3, which prohibits the erection on a disused burial ground of any building except an extension of the church. If at the outset it appears to the chancellor that, though the proposals may be lawful, it is reasonably possible to argue that they are not, he can properly

---

[8] Cases of this sort are subject to a special procedure under s.2 of F.J.M. 1964. See at pp. 87 *et seq.*

allow the citation to be published while inviting the archdeacon to enter appearance in order to put the petitioners to proof of their case.[9] This situation could well arise when it is proposed that a church which is only rarely used for worship should be put to other uses which might conflict with the effects of consecration.[10] In the metropolitan area, the court itself should give notice to the enforcement authority of any case where the act of 1884 seems likely to be infringed: see on this point the discussion in *Re St. Luke's, Chelsea*.[11]

When the chancellor first sees the papers, he may consider it desirable, in an urgent case, to make an interlocutory order giving leave to proceed at once. Such an order is made upon the written undertaking of the petitioners that, in the event of anyone entering appearance in opposition following publication of the citation, the work will cease pending the further order of the court. Such orders, though not infrequent, are therefore only made when there are good reasons to assume that there will be no opposition. Such an order can be made by the court, under its inherent powers as a superior court of record.[12] But upon an application, under section 12 of the F.J.M. 1964, for an archdeacon's certificate, no such order is possible, the powers of the archdeacon being statutory and the section containing no provision for an interlocutory order. This is one of the reasons why the procedure by way of archdeacon's certificate has in many dioceses fallen into disuse.

Citation, notices and order nisi for faculty

The next stage in the great majority of cases is for the chancellor to endorse the petition, usually by using a conventional phrase such as "Fiat," importing an order for a general citation coupled with an order that, if no appearance is entered within the time limited by the citation, a faculty shall pass the seal as prayed. The endorsement should also mention the time

---

[9] As in *Re St. Luke's, Chelsea* [1976] Fam. 295.
[10] See *Re St. John's, Chelsea* [1962] 1 W.L.R. 706 on the effects of consecration.
[11] [1976] Fam. 295 at 312, 313.
[12] On the subject of temporary licences, see *Re St. Andrew's, Dearnley* [1981] Fam. 50 at 54G. In many dioceses temporary permission for purposes of experiment are granted by the archdeacon, under powers delegated to him by the chancellor.

within which the work shall be finished. This in practice is done by adding, say, "12 months" after "Fiat." The endorsement is then initialled and dated, and in cases where no opposition is entered that is usually the last that the chancellor sees or hears of the case, the remaining procedural steps being taken in the registry. Alternatively, if there are uncertainties about the proposals, as for example if the D.A.C. has expressed doubts, the first order is simply for a citation, and the chancellor directs the registry to make such other investigations as seem likely to be called for. The effect of a citation is to establish, at the outset, whether the petition is, or is not, formally opposed. An opposed case must always be heard in open court, unless all parties agree, under F.J.R. 1967, r. 6A, that it shall be dealt with by written representations. If that is to happen the subsequent directions must be shaped either with such a hearing in view or to provide for the case being dealt with under rule 6A. If the chancellor thinks it necessary to have a hearing in an unopposed case, on the other hand, he has a choice whether to hear it in court or in chambers.

Publication of citation

The issue and publication of a citation are essential stages in the procedure. For a faculty granted without there having been a citation, or after one that was not sufficiently or correctly published, is a nullity.[13]

These matters are regulated by rule 5 of the F.J.R. 1967. Form No. 7A in the schedule to the F.J.R. 1967 is to be followed in all normal cases.

This form is addressed by the Chancellor to the incumbent and churchwardens of the parish. It recites that a petition has been lodged and what the petition seeks to have authorised, normally following the schedule to the petition. It then cites "all persons having, or claiming to have, a lawful interest in the subject matter of the petition" to deliver or send to the diocesan registrar "a written notice of objection" on the form set out lower down the citation "if they or any of them wish to object to

---

[13] *Re St. Michael The Archangel, Brantham* and *St. Peter United with St. Mary at Quay, Ipswich* [1962] 1 W.L.R. 1067. But there is a statutory exception covering certain sorts of exhumation case: see at pp. 165 *et seq.*

the grant of a Faculty for the works or purposes stated above...." Appearance is to be entered by sending to the diocesan registrar. Such notice has to be given before a date stated in the citation which is to be seven days after the citation is first affixed in the parish: F.J.R. 1967, r. 5A(1). The citation ends by giving notice that if no one enters appearance the order for a faculty may be made without more ado.

Publication of citation

The citation is sent by the registry, with the necessary copies, to the incumbent or one of the churchwardens, with directions for it to be affixed in various places as required by F.J.R. 1967, r. 5(1) and (2). A copy has to be affixed in each place for a continuous period of not less than 10 days including two Sundays. This form is endorsed with a certificate to be signed by the incumbent or churchwarden certifying that such affixation has taken place: see Form 7A.

The provisions as to the places where the citation is to be affixed are new and were enacted by the F.J.R. 1987 following recommendations in the report of the Faculty Jurisdiction Commission. The intention is to ensure, in a way which the previous rules occasionally did not, that all parishioners have an opportunity to know of the petition. In cases where the citation refers to plans or other documents which cannot conveniently be affixed, the citation itself should state where and when the documents can be inspected. This must be a place to which there is ready access.

Rule 5(1)(*a*) deals with petitions relating to a parish church. Here the citation must be affixed "on a notice board or in some other prominent position inside the church" and on a notice board outside the church.

Rule 5(1)(*b*) deals with petitions relating to a church which is not a parish church. Here the citation must go on a notice board or in some other prominent position inside the church in question and inside the parish church or churches, and also inside such other church or place of worship in the parish as the registrar may determine. It must also be put on a notice board *outside* the parish church, the church concerned and any other church or place of worship in the parish which the registrar may direct.

In any case where the building has no outside notice board, the outside of its principal door must be used.

These provisions place a considerable burden on the registrar, who will not necessarily know the places which are involved. If he is in any doubt he should consult the incumbent or churchwarden by telephone.

Besides the complex provisions of rule 5(1), it is further provided, by rule 5(2), that the judge may order the citation to be displayed elsewhere in the parish (whether inside or outside a building). The idea behind this provision is to enable the judge to require the notice to be put up on an ordinary public notice board, on the village green or inside the local town hall. This power should be used where the proposals are known to be controversial, so as to prevent it being said that the notice given in or near the church was inadequate to reach the wider public.

Under the rules in force before 1988 Bullimore Ch. had to consider the effect of a citation which had not been published on the church door but on a board 70 yards distant from it: *Re St. Cuthbert's, Doveridge*.[14] He held that the publication was irregular but not void: the directions in the rules, as they then stood, were not mandatory but permissive and their object was to give the public notice; the evidence showed that that had been achieved. This decision is useful on the point of principle about such notice. But it must be looked at with some caution in future, since the rules were changed by the F.J.R. 1987.

There is one exception only to the need for a general citation: it relates to exhumation and it is created by F.J.R. 1967, r. 5(6)(*a*) and (*b*). If the judge is satisfied that any near relations of the deceased person still living, and any other person who, in the opinion of the judge, it is reasonable to regard as being concerned with the matter, are the petitioners or that they consent to the proposed faculty being granted, rule 5(6)(*a*) enables him to dispense with the issue of a citation and decree the issue and the faculty forthwith. Under rule 5(6)(*b*) in any other exhumation case he may dispense with the general citation but direct the issue of special citations to all the persons mentioned (r. 5(6)(*a*)).

[14] [1983] 1 W.L.R. 845.

Special citations and notices

Special citations are somewhat rare; but rule 5(3) of the F.J.R. 1967 provides that "if the judge directs or the law otherwise requires any person to be specially cited," the registrar is to serve on that person a copy of the citation. The provisions as to service are in rule 12.

A notice analogous to a special citation may be given where there appears to be a question as to whether the proposals in the petition will infringe the D.B.G.A. 1884. In such a case the judge may well feel it necessary to direct the registry to notify the relevant authority for enforcing the Act.[15]

In the case of certain petitions for the demolition or partial demolition of a church, a notice stating the substance of the petition is to be published in the *London Gazette* and certain newspapers: (r. 5(7)). The judge has power, under the same provision, to order other notices of the petition, in newspapers. Further, under section 2(1)(ii) and 2(3) of the F.J.M. 1964 the registrar is required to give notice of the petition to the C.C.C. and the D.A.C. It is, no doubt, for this purpose that rule 4(5) requires an additional copy of the petition and supporting documents to be lodged with the petition in demolition cases.

Where the petition is for a faculty for the "disposal" of an "article" which in the opinion of the judge is or may be of "historic or artistic interest" he may direct the registrar to serve notice of the petition on the C.C.C. If he does so, he is required also to direct the petitioner to serve on the Council a copy of the petition and all the supporting documents: rule 5(8). "Article" is defined as including a part of a building, any thing annexed to land and any part of an article; thus it includes not only all sorts of chattels but objects which until severance are part of the realty. The purpose of this provision is to ensure that in the, often controversial, cases of the disposal of church valuables the court can obtain further independent advice beyond that of the D.A.C.

At this stage it is also desirable to consider what other notices, if any, ought to be given under rule 5(4) and whether there is

---

[15] For a discussion of this subject see *Re St. Luke's, Chelsea* [1976] Fam. 295 at 312H to 313F.

any need for a special citation under rule 5(3). In cases where the petitioner seeks authority to take monuments away from a churchyard, it is expedient to see at this stage that the proposals have been adequately advertised in the local newspapers and to direct further advertisements if they have not.

Upon the expiry of the period of citation, as defined by rule 2(1), the original or a copy thereof is to be returned to the registrar: rule 5(5). It is required to bear a certificate of execution duly completed in accordance with Form No. 7A in the Appendix to the Rules. This form was new in the F.J.R. 1987. It is much more complex than the old form, since it contains not only the text of the citation but also that of a notice of objection as well as the form for the certificate of execution. This certificate has to be signed by the incumbent or a churchwarden and must set out in detail the various places where the citation was affixed, so as to ensure compliance with the requirements of F.J.R. r. 5(1). The certificate must also set out the dates during which it was affixed in the various places where it is required to be.

Appearance in opposition, pleadings and interlocutory orders

Appearance and particulars of objection

The steps to be taken where any interested person objects to the granting of a petition are governed by F.J.R. 1967, r. 5A.

Rule 5A(1) provides that he shall begin by entering appearance in opposition. This must be done within the "period of citation" as defined in rule 2(1) or seven days thereafter. The "period of citation" is the period during which a citation under rule 5(1) is required to remain in position. The objector must send a written notice of objection to the registry and to the petitioners. It is required by rule 5A(1) to contain the information called for by Form No. 7A in the Appendix to the Rules. This form is itself set out in the same document as the citation. Its effect is to require the objector to state generally that he objects and the capacity in which he does so.

A written notice of objection can only be given by an "interested person." This phrase is defined by rule 5A(2); it includes not only all persons who would be qualified to be petitioners but a number of other specified persons or bodies. This subject is fully discussed at the end of Chapter 2. Once an interested person has given his notice of objection, he is referred to as a "party opponent."

The registrar is then required, by rule 5A(3), to direct the party opponent to lodge particulars of objection at the registry. This document must set out in detail his grounds of objection, following Form No. 7B in the Appendix to the Rules. He must serve it on the petitioners within 21 days after the registrar's directions. Particulars of objection are sometimes referred to as the "act on petition."

The times mentioned above may be extended by the judge or registrar on an *ex parte* application (r. 13). The application may be granted on terms (r. 13(4)).[16] The power to enlarge the time ought to be exercised fairly freely before the date when the faculty is granted, so as not to shut out opponents in a case which is controversial; on the other hand, once the faculty has passed the seal, there being no entry of appearance and no reason to expect the case to be controversial, the matter should not be re-opened, save in the most exceptional circumstances, and especially if the petitioners have begun to spend money in reliance upon the faculty. It has indeed been held that a faculty once granted is irrevocable, save on the ground that it was obtained by fraud.[17]

Appearance by archdeacon

But cases quite often arise in which, when a case is formally unopposed, the chancellor considers that justice would best be served by ensuring that it is argued by the archdeacon under section 9 of the F.J.M. 1964. He should then invite the archdeacon to enter appearance so as either to put the petitioners to proof of their case, or by way of outright opposition; and he should extend, by a reasonable period, the time for the archdeacon to appear and to plead.[18] Sometimes the archdeacon may wish actively to oppose the petition: he will then plead more specifically than if he appears merely to put the proof. Such a case may well arise if the D.A.C. is strongly against the petitioners' proposal.

---

[16] Such a situation arose in *Re St. Mary's, Luton* [1967] P. 151 at 166D–E.
[17] *London County Council* v. *Dundas* [1904] P. 1.
[18] This was done in *Re St. Luke's, Chelsea* [1976] Fam. 295 at 305, 306.

Pleadings subsequent to particulars of objection: summons for directions

After the act on petition has been lodged, the petitioners have a further 14 days to lodge an "answer," sometimes called a "reply" (r. 5A(5)), unless the time is extended under rule 13.

Since the proceedings, unlike an action in the High Court, are started by a petition which usually states the proposals summarily, with a minimum of reasons and supporting facts, it is often the reply in which the case for the petitioners is fully deployed for the first time. It follows that pleadings subsequent to the reply may quite often be necessary. The registrar should take control of the pleadings under rule 5A(8) to ensure that the case is fully and expeditiously pleaded. Under that subrule, which was introduced by the F.J.R. 1987, the judge or the registrar is required to give directions, whenever any issues remain outstanding at the close of pleadings. The intention is that in all controversial cases he shall hold a summons for directions or a pre-trial review. The purpose of the latter would be to ensure that all the facts which are not in dispute are conceded and that all necessary documents are agreed, so that no time is wasted at the hearing.[19] Rule 5A(8) refers to the summons for directions as being held by the judge or by the registrar if authorised by the judge. It is expected that the registrar will normally deal with the summonses; but the judge can act personally if he wishes to take that course.

On the summons for directions other points should also be dealt with. Rule 5A(6) provides a procedure for any party to make an objection to the pleading of an adverse party as being "irrelevant, embarrassing, or bad in law," and rule 5A(7) provides for the objection to be dealt with in the event that the party concerned does not meet the objection by lodging an amended pleading. It may also sometimes be necessary to order security for costs, under E.J.M. 1963, s.60(1), or to issue a subpoena under section 81 of that Measure.

Directions should also be given, under rule 5A(8), limiting the number of expert witnesses to be called at the hearing and requiring their proofs of evidence to be exchanged in advance.

---

[19] This course was taken, to the benefit of all parties, in the unreported case of *Re St. Andrew's Church, Backwell* [1982] in the Bath and Wells consistory court.

The subrule is mandatory in contested cases and gives the judge or the registrar much wider powers than he had before 1988. Among other things which should be considered at this stage is whether the parties are prepared to agree to the case being disposed of, under rule 6A, by written representations.

All pleadings, notices of objection and the like have to be in writing and signed by the party concerned, his counsel or solicitor, and lodged at the registry. On each occasion a copy should to be served on the adverse party or his solicitor before lodgment in the registry and the copy lodged should be endorsed with the date of service and the name of the person effecting it. The method of service is set out in rule 12(1). The most usual form of service is by recorded delivery service through the Post Office.

Preparations for hearing

When the pleadings are closed the papers go again to the judge and, if the case is to be heard, he will then fix a time for hearing (r. 6(1)); the registrar must notify the time and place of hearing to the archdeacon and to the D.A.C. r. 6(2) if it has advised in the case. The rules do not provide a form of notice of the hearing; but it is desirable that the registry should supply such a notice to the parties and should provide the petitioners with copies to be put on the door of the church or churches where the citation was posted.

If the chancellor proposes to call judge's witnesses, the registrar is required by rule 6(8) and (9) to give all parties not less than seven clear days notice in writing that this evidence is going to be given, stating the name and address of the witness and the "nature of the evidence required of him."

Hearing

Where no one lodges a notice of objection under rule 5A(1), or where the party opponent is in default of pleading, the judge may grant the faculty without any hearing (subject to F.J.M. 1964, s.2 in demolition cases). Where he does so, the next step is for the registrar to draft the faculty and for it to pass the seal. But in a case which is opposed there must be a hearing (unless the case is to be dealt with under r. 6A or the petitioners withdraw) since all parties in a contested case are entitled to their day in court. Some unopposed cases also need to be heard, in particular unopposed cases about the demolition or partial demolition of a church. In such a case the C.C.C. and some other persons are entitled to require a hearing in open court.[20] While the hearing of an opposed case (or one about a demolition) must be in open court, the chancellor has a discretion in an unopposed case whether any hearing that he requires shall be in open court or in chambers. The former is suitable when there is a real *lis*, for example between the petitioner and the D.A.C., the case being technically unopposed only because the D.A.C. is not a competent party to enter opposition, or because a serious point of law needs to be decided. Hearings in chambers are more suitable for cases where the petition is for authority to allow a third party to use church property, and where the question for the judge is whether the terms are right and whether the parties have the proposed documents in the right shape. This practice is very common in the diocese of London.

For a hearing in chambers the chancellor usually sits in the diocesan registry, and for a hearing in open court he often sits in the church with which the case is concerned. But E.J.M. 1963, s.80 enables him to sit anywhere that is convenient for all concerned.

Photographers

The court, and its approaches, and those concerned in the case are protected against photographers by the Criminal Justice Act 1925, s.41[21] and the help of the police should, if necessary, be invoked to enforce the provisions of the criminal law. If the case is heard in church, the court is also entitled to the services of the churchwardens, as bishop's officers, to protect it against brawlers. In the last resort the wardens have a right of arrest.[22] Further, "any act or omission in connection with proceedings before any such court or commission which if occurring in connection with proceedings in the High Court would have been a contempt of the High Court shall be a contempt of such

---

[20] See F.J.M. 1964, s.2(1)(iv) and F.J.R. 1967, r. 6(6) and (7).
[21] See *St. Andrew's, Heddington* [1978] Fam. 121.
[22] See Ecclesiastical Courts Jurisdiction Act 1860, ss.2 and 3; Canon El, para. 4 and *Asher* v. *Calcraft* (1887) 18 Q.B.D. 607.

court or commission"; but the consistory court has no power to deal summarily with such a contempt which must be done by the High Court, upon motion.[23] In the unusual event of a contempt so serious as to justify proceedings in the High Court for contempt, the consistory court should adjourn until order is restored and then resume; the proceedings to punish the contemnor can follow later.

Subpoenas

The consistory court has "the same powers as the High Court in relation to the attendance and examination of witnesses and the production and inspection of documents."[24] It is thus entitled to issue a subpoena or make an order for production of documents at the hearing. But these matters should normally have been dealt with on the summons for directions.

Procedure at hearing

The hearing mainly proceeds in the same way as a hearing in any other court. It is most convenient to follow the practice of the Chancery Division of the High Court. This procedure was described by Fry J. in *Kino* v. *Rudkin*.[25] It is important to note that there is always a right of reply in Chancery, unlike some other courts. This practice is a desirable one for the consistory court to follow.

Under F.J.R., r. 6(3) the evidence at a hearing must be given orally; but the judge has power, either upon application or of his own motion, to direct that all or some of the evidence may be given before an examiner or by affidavit. He may also, in some circumstances, order that a written statement may be given as evidence by someone who is not a party to the proceedings, without the attendance of the maker of the statement. The conditions for the latter procedure are set out in rule 6(4). They are, shortly, that 21 days notice must be given before the hearing and copies of the statement must then be lodged at the registry or delivered to the parties. Under rule 6(5) the judge is

---

[23] E.J.M. 1963, s.81(2) and (3).
[24] *Ibid.*, s.81(1).
[25] (1877) 6 Ch.D. 160 at 163, 164.

entitled on receiving a copy of such a statement, to order the maker of the statement to attend for cross-examination by the parties. Likewise any party may apply to the judge for such an order. If, then, the maker of the statement does not appear, the statement is inadmissible "save in exceptional circumstances with the leave of the judge."

(1) Judge's witnesses Proceedings in the consistory court are further complicated by the facilities, fairly frequently employed, for the chancellor to call judge's witnesses and by the ability of the C.C.C. in some cases to demand to be heard.[26] These facilities are peculiar to the consistory court and place a serious burden on the judge. In the temporal courts, it is possible, within very narrow limits, for a judge presiding over a criminal trial to call a witness of his own.[27] In a civil cause or matter he may not call any witnesses without the consent of both parties and he must content himself with deciding the case upon the evidence that the parties choose to put before him, though he may at any time recall a witness who has once given evidence.[28] Even with witnesses called by the parties, his questions should be strictly confined to such as are necessary to enable him to understand the evidence that is being given and he should in no circumstances give the appearance of a cross-examiner.[29]. Under rule 6(8), the judge may of his own motion "direct the summoning of a member of the D.A.C. or any other person to give evidence at the hearing of a petition for a faculty, if he considers that the person summoned may be able to give relevant evidence and is willing to give it."[30] Under rule 6(9) he must give seven clear days' notice of his intention to call a judge's witness;[31] any such witness is liable to cross-examination by all

---

[26] As to judge's witnesses, see F.J.R. 1967, r. 6(8) and (9). As to the C.C.C. see r. 6(6) and (7).
[27] See *R. v. Harris* [1927] 2 K.B. 587; *R. v. Tregear* [1967] 2 Q.B. 574 and *R. v. Cleghorn* [1967] 2 Q.B. 584.
[28] *Fallon v. Calvert* [1960] 2 Q.B. 201.
[29] *Jones v. National Coal Board* [1957] 2 Q.B. 55. See especially the judgment of the Court of Appeal at 64, 65. Denning L.J. quoted with approval from the pronouncement of Bacon L.C. that "Patience and gravity of hearing is an essential part of justice; and an over-speaking judge is no well tuned cymbal."
[30] The effect of the last six words appears to be intended to deprive the judge of the power, which he would otherwise have had under the E.J.M. 1963, s.81(1), of issuing a subpoena to a judge's witness.
[31] Or a witness giving evidence under r. 6(6) or s.2(1)(iv) of the Measure of 1964 in a case of demolition.

the parties (r. 6(10)). The judge himself has to conduct the examination in chief, usually without a proof of evidence, and to re-examine. These arrangements are necessary to cope with the frequent situation where there is no technical opposition, but where there is an issue between the petitioners on the one hand and the D.A.C. or C.C.C., or both, on the other. It is to be hoped that the consistory courts will use their powers under rule 5A(2)(*e*) to designate these bodies or one of them as "interested persons" in any really controversial case in which there is no formal opposition. Alternatively, such cases can be argued by the archdeacon as a party opponent or intervening .

(2) Statutory witnesses In addition to the judge's witnesses, there is statutory provision in rule 6(11) making into evidence the substance of any report by the C.C.C. in cases referred to it under rule 5(8), which deals with sales of valuables, and in practice the written advice given by the D.A.C. to the judge and made formally in the proceedings is admitted as evidence: this practice is thought to be justified by section 13(2)(*a*) of the F.J.M. 1964. Such written advice should always be circulated to the parties, otherwise the case may be decided on materials not available to them, and rule 6(11) requires that to be done with the report to the C.C.C.

(3) Evidence Apart from these statutory exceptions, the ordinary law of evidence applies, both as to admissibility and otherwise. Rule 6(3)(*a*) gives the judge power to direct that all or any part of the evidence shall be given by affidavit or before an examiner. If it is given by affidavit, any party is presumably entitled to give notice to cross-examine. Where the rules are silent, the court can still make its own rules, as it did before the E.J.M. 1963 and F.J.M. 1964, and it is the practice of the author to lay down that in the absence of other provision the practice of the Chancery Division shall be followed in the courts of which he is the judge. This direction, it is submitted, is inferentially justified by the provision in Note (*b*) to Table I of the Legal Officers Fees Order 1987 (and like provisions in earlier Orders) that in opposed cases any fees of the registry not provided for are to be paid on the same scale as are allowed for court fees in the Supreme Court of Judicature; this provision appears to imply that there may be proceedings or steps not covered by the ecclesiastical legislation in general or by the Fees

Orders in particular but comparable to those in the Supreme Court.

(4) **Viewing the *locus in quo*** A further problem arises about the judge taking a view of the *locus in quo*. Of course if he is sitting in the church, that settles itself. But otherwise the occasion is one of some delicacy. Normally the judge should tell the parties that he is going to have a view and give them the opportunity to attend. Great restraint is necessary if such a view is held, and parties can do themselves much injury by being loquacious on these occasions. A view can be helpful to the judge in that he sees three-dimensionally places that he would otherwise know only from photographs or from oral descriptions. If the parties consent, it is really best that the judge together with the registrar should pay the visit unattended. The Court of Appeal discussed views in *Salsbury* v. *Woodland*,[32] to which those concerned should refer.

(5) **Memorials** In controversial cases in the consistory court there is a tendency for interested parties to collect signatures to what is described by its promoters as a "petition," or more properly a memorial. This is a document with some lines of writing expressing views favourable to one side or the other. Documents of this sort are sometimes left for signature in public houses or village shops. They are wholly inadmissible unless those presenting them prove, by sworn evidence which is available for cross-examination "the representations which were made to the signatories before their signatures were obtained..."[33] The usual form of "petition" does not even establish that any given signature is that of a parishioner, let alone what has been said to the signatories or what they thought they were signing. It is worthless as evidence even if it were technically admissible. The proper way of obtaining information as to the opinion in the parish is for the churchwardens as bishop's officers to make discreet enquiries and to report them on oath to the court.[34] Even so, the court must receive this evidence with some caution, because it is hearsay. The less that

---

[32] [1970] 1 Q.B. 324.
[33] *Rector and Churchwardens of Capel St. Mary, Suffolk* v. *Packard* [1927] P. 289 at 300, per Sir Lewis Dibdin, Dean of Arches, followed in *Re Christ Church, Chislehurst* [1973] 1 W.L.R. 1317 at 1321.
[34] This was done in *Re St. Luke's, Chelsea* [1976] Fam. 295 at 317, 318.

the court makes use of any evidence which is neither contained in a document nor sworn to and cross-examined upon, the better.

When the hearing is concluded the judge either gives judgment or reserves it. Reserved judgments are often delivered in writing and are not read out; but if that is done arrangements should be incorporated in the judgment for a further hearing on costs if any party so desires.

Disposal of proceedings by written representations

At the time of the summons for directions upon an opposed petition, at the latest, the parties and the registrar should consider whether the case would be suitable to be disposed of by written representations without a hearing.

The procedure for this purpose is comprised in F.J.R. r. 6A, which was introduced in 1987. It is appropriate for cases where no facts are in dispute and the other differences between the parties are not wide. It is doubtful whether it should be used for really large cases, and it cannot be used in those cases of demolition where there must be a hearing under F.J.M. s. 2(1).

Rule 6A is conceived as an adaptation of rule 33A of the Lands Tribunal Rules 1975 which has proved useful for relatively small and straightforward cases.

The procedure cannot be used unless the parties agree to do so: the agreement must be in writing. The judge must then consider the matter and, if he thinks it expedient, may order the case to be disposed of under rule 6A.

When the judge has made that order, under rule 6A(1), the registrar must give directions under rule 6A(2). He will require the petitioners to lodge at the registry, and serve on each of the parties opponent, within 21 days of the direction, "a written statement in support of their case, including the documentary or other evidence upon which they wish to rely." He is, similarly, to provide for each party opponent, within 21 days after the petitioners' statement, to deliver a written statement in reply. Finally, he is to give the petitioners 14 days for "a written statement in response."

The judge has power, under subrule (3) to declare any party to be in default of compliance with the directions and thereafter to dispose of the case without further reference to that party. He also has discretion, under subrule (4), to revoke such an order "on such terms as to costs or otherwise as may be just."

Under subrule (5) the judge may revoke the primary order for the case to be dealt with by written representations, "and direct that the proceedings shall be determined at an oral hearing" giving all necessary consequential directions.

Under subrule (7) the judge, or the registrar if so authorised by the judge, has a general power to give directions for the expeditious despatch of proceedings under this rule.

Further, subrule (6) provides that when the exchange of pleadings and documents is completed, and subject to any order under subrule (7) the judge is to determine the proceedings upon those materials and "his decision thereon shall be as valid and binding on all parties as if it had been made after an oral hearing."

If parties will make full use of this new procedure it will result in many cases being disposed of expeditiously and without the disturbance in a parish which is caused by an oral hearing.

Onus of proof

A petitioner is not entitled as of right to a faculty: the matter lies in the judicial discretion of the chancellor to be exercised upon the evidence presented to him. In *Peek* v. *Trower*,[35] Lord Penzance, Dean of the Arches, said that the burden of proof properly devolves on those who propose changes. One element, but only one, is the wishes of the parishioners. As Dr. Tristram Ch., said in *Folkestone Parish (Parishioners)* v. *Woodward*[36] the court should "give such weight to the opinion of the vestry as, in its judgment, it ought to give it, according to the circumstances of the case under consideration." This pronouncement might seem to leave the issue open; but in each of two recent cases[37] the Court of Ecclesiastical Causes Reserved overruled the decision of the court below on the ground, among others, that the judge had given insufficient weight to the opinions of the parishioners, who had supported the petition without dispute among themselves. Where there is serious

---

[35] (1881) 7 P.D. 21 at 27.
[36] (1880) Trist. 177 at 178.
[37] *Re St. Michael and All Angels, Great Torrington* [1985] Fam. 81 and *Re St. Stephen's Walbrook* [1987] Fam. 146.

dispute locally, the weight to be given to the opinion of the majority must presumably be somewhat less. Again, where there is substantial disagreement among the expert witnesses, the court must seek to evaluate it as a separate matter, treating the local opinion as only one of the factors in the eventual decision. But in *Re St. Stephen's, Walbrook*,[38] Sir Ralph Gibson in the Court of Ecclesiastical Causes Reserved appears to have held that, on the footing that the technical architectural evidence was evenly balanced, the unanimous wishes of the parishioners should prevail. It does not seem to be very easy to reconcile this view with two passages from the judgments of Lord Penzance, each quoted *in extenso* in the judgment of Sir Ralph Gibson. In one of those passages Lord Penzance said, somewhat scathingly, that "The notion that the matter in question should be decided by the wishes of the majority of the parishioners proceeds, in my opinion, upon an entirely mistaken view of the law,"[39] and that, if the majority opinion of the parishioners is to be decisive, "what, it may be asked, becomes of this discretion" [*i.e.* of the Court]?[40] In the other passage, Lord Penzance said that to allow the principle that the majority opinion is decisive "would open the door wide to all capricious changes."[41] Further, in *Re St. Mary's, Banbury*[42] both these passages from the older cases were cited and adopted by Sir John Owen, Dean of the Arches. There thus appears to be agreement between the two appellate courts on the weight of the views of Lord Penzance. The conflict of opinion between those views and the view of Sir Ralph Gibson will presumably have to be resolved on the principles of *Young* v. *Bristol Aeroplane Co.*[43]

Effect of building being listed

On another important point there is also a conflict of recent judicial opinion between the two appellate courts, but in this case without the weight of the views of Lord Penzance, since the matter has arisen since his day. In *Re St. Mary's, Banbury*[44] the

---

[38] [1987] Fam. 146.
[39] *Nickalls* v. *Briscoe* [1892] P. 269 at 283.
[40] *Ibid.*, at 283.
[41] *Peek* v. *Trower* (1881) 7 P.D. 21 at 27.
[42] [1987] Fam. 136.
[43] [1944] K.B. 718 at 729.
[44] [1987] Fam. 136.

Dean of the Arches upheld a decision of Boydell Ch. against allowing a major change in a listed building. In the lower court, the chancellor had said[45]: "On balance the petitioners have satisfied me, in principle, that they should be permitted to construct lavatories in the porches; but I am not prepared to grant the faculty on the basis of the plans and other material adduced at the hearing. This is a grade A listed building; and any proposal to alter the structure of such a building must be approached with the same care and be subject to the same detailed consideration as would be necessary if churches were to lose their ecclesiastical immunity and if, therefore, this were an application for listed building consent pursuant to the provisions of the Town and Country Planning Act 1971,"[46] and he directed a further and more detailed petition on the subject. There was no appeal against this part of the decision of Boydell Ch. But he had also held on grounds of law that he must refuse another part of the petition, concerning the removal of some pews, and had indicated that if on this point he had had power to grant a petition[47] he would probably not have exercised his discretion to grant it. In this part of his judgment he did not refer to the building as being a listed building. The point was, however, discussed in the Court of Arches. The learned Dean commended the judgment of the chancellor in broad and generous terms and he developed the point about listed buildings. The Dean said that it was of great importance that "St. Mary's is a building of special architectural and historic interest and the removal of the pews, which were an integral part of the design of the church and have been there since the church was built, would gravely damage those interests."[48] These words in effect apply to the pews the same reasoning as the chancellor had applied to the lavatories. The learned Dean however added that a faculty which would affect the special nature of the architectural or historic interest should only be allowed in cases of clearly proved necessity.[49] Later, the Dean made a number of general observations, clearly intended to

---

[45] *Re St. Mary's, Banbury* [1985] 2 All E.R. 611 at 618: this passage, most unfortunately, has been omitted from the Law Report [1986] Fam. 24.
[46] See p. 618.
[47] [1986] Fam. 24 at 27.
[48] [1987] Fam. 136.
[49] *Ibid*.

assist chancellors in deciding future cases, where he said, among other things:

> "When a church is listed as a building of special architectural or historic interest a faculty which would affect its character as such should only be granted in wholly exceptional circumstances, these circumstances clearly showing a necessity for such a change."[50]

These phrases, referring to "necessity" were criticised by the Court of Ecclessiastical Causes Reserved in *Re St. Stephen's Walbrook*.[51] Sir Ralph Gibson said that the extent of the obligation of the ecclesiastical courts to protect churches of special architectural or historic interest against irreversible and inappropriate changes "is not, in my view, rightly defined by the concept of 'proved necessity,' " since no such definition appears in Town and Country Planning Act 1971, s.56(3), which directs the secular authorities on the considerations to be borne in mind in granting listed building consent. Further, Sir Anthony Lloyd said that he could find nothing in the relevant legislation to justify an approach as strict as that laid down by the Dean of the Arches. He added that "the fact that an ecclesiastical building is listed is a relevant consideration in deciding whether or not to grant a faculty...".[52] Likewise, Sir Ralph Gibson said:

> "The right approach, in my view, is to exercise the discretion as I think Parliament intended that it should be exercised, namely in accordance with established principles; and that includes, of course, having full regard to all the circumstances including the interest of the community as a whole in the special architectural or historic attributes of the building and the desirability of preserving the building and any features of special architectural or historic interest which it possesses. The discretion, however, is to be exercised in the context that the building is used for the

---

[50] [1987] Fam. 136.
[51] [1987] Fam. 146. The Court of Ecclesiastical Causes Reserved appears to have considered that it would not have been bound by the remarks of the Court of Arches on this subject even if it had not deemed them to be *obiter*. But its immunity from the ordinary rules about precedent is defined in s. 45(3) of the E.J.M. 1963 as being "in relation to matter of doctrine ritual or ceremonial," not generally.
[52] *Ibid*.

purposes of the Church, that is to say in the service of God as the Church, doing its best, perceives how that service is to be rendered."[53]

His Lordship went on to say that he doubted whether the learned Dean intended to lay down any other principle, a suggestion which is somewhat difficult to reconcile with the very clear and cogent words of the Dean.

For the present purpose there the matter must rest. Meantime, the chancellor dealing with a controversial case of a listed building must walk warily, faced with the conflicting views of the two courts to one of which the appeal from him must lie. If the cause before him is one of the very few which raise issues of ritual, doctrine or ceremonial, the appellate court is the Court of Ecclesiastical Causes Reserved. In all other cases the appeal lies to the Court of Arches.

The order

Form of order

The remaining stage of the proceedings after a hearing is for the registrar to draw up the order or the faculty as the case may be, submitting it to the chancellor in draft, unless it is perfectly straightforward. Subject to any necessary amendments, the chancellor orders it to pass the seal. It is then perfected and sent to the parties. Sometimes the judge orders counsel to submit minutes of order as in the Chancery Division. Under rule 7(1) the faculty is normally to follow Form 10 in the Appendix to the Rules. This form is well designed for simple cases; but in complex ones it is better to draw up a form of order *de novo*. Provision is made in rule 7(3) and in Form No. 11 for the petitioners to certify when the work is finished. The order or the written judgment should not incorporate a certificate that the cause is, or is not, one involving doctrine, ritual or ceremonial.[54]

Mandatory order

A faculty "as its name indicates, confers liberty on a person to

---
[53] [1987] Fam. 136.
[54] *Re St. Michael and All Angels, Great Torrington* [1985] Fam. 81.

do something; it does not command him to do anything."[55] Hence, it was held by the Court of Arches in 1960, when the Faculty Jurisdiction Measure 1938 was still in force, that for a consistory court to purport to make a mandatory order in a cause of faculty was an excess of jurisdiction and a nullity.[56] Where parties are likely to be recalcitrant, the classical way for the court to deal with the matter is to grant, in a single order, a series of liberties, first to the person who ought to do the work, then if he fails to do it within one month, to the incumbent, and if he too should fail to do it within one month, to the archdeacon, who presumably will do it.[57] In such an order there would also be a provision made under section 5(1) of the F.J.M. 1964 ordering the real culprit to pay all the costs of all the works and all the costs and fees in all the proceedings. Where that is likely to be done, the person concerned must be joined by a special citation pursuant to section 5(2). This procedure worked, and works, well enough in most cases. However, the power to make a mandatory order seems to have been impliedly given to the court, by F.J.M. 1964, s.5(1). That sub-section replaced, with significant additional words, section 3(1) of the F.J.M. 1938. The present sub-section is as follows:

> "If in any proceeding for a faculty, whether opposed or not, it appears to the court that any person being a party to the proceeding was responsible wholly or in part for the introduction into or removal from a church, *churchyard or other consecrated ground* of any articles without the necessary faculty, or for the execution of any work in a church, *churchyard or other consecrated ground* without the necessary faculty, the court may order the whole or any part of the costs and expenses of the proceeding or consequent thereon, *including the cost of any works ordered by the court* (so far as such costs, cost of works and expenses have been occasioned by such introduction, removal or unlawful execution as the case may be) to be paid by such person."
> [Author's italics]

The italicised words were introduced into the section by the

---

[55] *Re St. Mary, Tyne Dock (No. 2)* [1958] P. 156 at 166.
[56] *Re St. John-in-Bedwardine, Worcester* [1962] P. 20 at 25. But see below as to the position since 1964.
[57] *Re Woldingham Churchyard* [1957] 1 W.L.R. 811.

1964 Measure, the rest being precisely the same both in 1938 and 1964. The first two additions extend the sub-section to churchyards and other consecrated ground; the third gives the court power to compel a person to pay the costs of "any works ordered by the court." This provision would be meaningless if the court had no power to make a mandatory order. Thus the court appears now to have such a power, whatever may have been the case before 1964.

This power should be used sparingly and if such an order is made it must be so expressed that the party subjected to the order knows exactly what he has to do, so that he can give his contractors proper instructions.[58] The author does not recall ever having made such an order; he suggests that it ought to be a weapon of last resort, the procedure outlined in the *Woldingham* case being normally efficacious. The legislature has expressly recognised, by section 10(*b*) of the Measure of 1964, that the *Woldingham* procedure is available.

"Until further order"

As was pointed out in *Re St. Mary, Tyne Dock (No. 2)*,[59] a faculty once made is irrevocable, and once granted it cannot be recalled except for fraud, unless, of course, it is expressly granted "until further order" or, as in the *Woldingham* case, it is granted only for a period. The phrase "until further order" should therefore always be used if the court thinks it necessary to keep control over what is being done, especially in cases about tombstones, which may easily need to be cleared away at some future date, or in cases about aumbries (see at pp. 130 *et seq.*). Provision should always be included for the archdeacon to have liberty to apply in any case in which subsequent action is likely to be necessary, as for instance where an undertaking to the court has been given and may need to be enforced. Again, where parties have been allowed to erect a building on a disused burial ground on the basis that it is part of the church, it may be necessary later to ensure that it continues to be part of the

---

[58] See *Redland Bricks* v. *Morris* [1970] A.C. 652, especially *per* Lord Upjohn at 666, 667.
[59] [1958] P. 156, *per* Wigglesworth, Deputy Chancellor, at 166. See also *London County Council* v. *Dundas* [1904] P. 1.

church and does not become something else. Therefore in such a case it is desirable for the archdeacon to have liberty to apply.

Supervision by archdeacon

Another useful provision in an order, under section 10(*a*) of the Measure of 1964, is that all or some of the work authorised shall be carried out under the supervision of the archdeacon or of any other person nominated for that purpose by the court. Any other party to the proceedings can be ordered, under section 10(*c*), to pay for the costs of the archdeacon in this matter.

Conditions

It appears to be accepted that a faculty can be granted subject to conditions, in addition to the condition which appears in all faculties requiring that the work shall be done within a time limit. But conditions of other sorts should be worded very precisely just as much as if there were a mandatory order, since it is a contempt of court to infringe the conditions. It is generally better, instead of the court imposing a condition *in invitum*, to require the petitioner to give an undertaking in writing and to incorporate that undertaking in the order. Then the words which are to be enforced against him are his own words; breach of an undertaking to the court is always contempt of court.

Confirmatory faculty

In some cases the work in question has already been done before the petition is presented. Where that is so, the successful petitioner should be given a confirmatory faculty authorising the work illegally done to remain. But, as Garth Moore Ch. has pointed out,[60] a confirmatory faculty cannot be retrospective and the work continues to have been done illegally, notwithstanding that its continuance is legitimated from the date of the confirmatory faculty. Further, since the work was illegal, the persons who actually give the order have no right to expect the

---

[60] *Re St. Mary's, Balham* [1978] 1 All E.R. 993: see also *Re St. Agnes', Toxteth Park* [1985] 1 W.L.R. 641; and *Re St. Mary's, Barton-upon-Humber* [1987] **Fam. 41.**

P.C.C. to pay the debt if they are sued by the supplier: see *Re St. Agnes', Toxteth Park*.[61]

Costs and fees

In all cases, and not merely in those of illegal works discussed above, the most effective sanction available to those who are exercising the faculty jurisdiction is the power to make an order for costs, *i.e.* to decide how the court fees and the costs and expenses of the parties themselves in respect of the litigation are to be borne. This power is now expressly vested in the court under E.J.M. 1963, s.60,[62] which also provides, by section 61, for the recovery in the county court of any costs which may be so awarded.

Appeals

In causes of faculty not involving matter of doctrine, ritual or ceremonial the appeal lies to the Arches Court in the Province of Canterbury or to the Chancery Court of York in that Province,[63] at the instance of any party to the proceedings.[64] In causes of faculty involving matter of doctrine, ritual or ceremonial it lies, at the instance of any party to the proceedings, to the Court of Ecclesiastical Causes Reserved.[65] For the purpose of determining "in a cause of faculty" to which of these courts the appeal lies "it shall be the duty of the chancellor to certify upon the application of the party desiring to appeal whether or not a question of doctrine, ritual or ceremonial is involved and such certificate shall be conclusive."[66] The point to be certified appears, on the wording of section 10(3), to be whether any point of doctrine, ritual or ceremonial is involved in the *cause*, not whether it is going to be involved in the proposed appeal. Thus a certificate can, and normally should, be given before any notice of appeal is framed.

Appeals to the Court of Arches are quite common; in the smaller northern province appeals to the Chancery Court of

---

[61] [1985] 1 W.L.R. 641 at 643 F–G.
[62] As to how this power should be exercised and enforced see Chap. 7.
[63] E.J.M. 1963, s.7(1)(*b*).
[64] *Ibid.*, s.7(2)(*a*).
[65] *Ibid.*, s.10(1) and (2).
[66] *Ibid.*, s.10(3).

York. are necessarily less frequent. But appeals to the Court of Ecclesiastical Causes Reserved are rare.[67] There are also provisions in sections 8 and 11 of the E.J.M. 1963 for further appeals to the Privy Council from the Court of Arches and the Chancery Court of York, and to the Crown, by a special procedure, from the Court of Ecclesiastical Causes Reserved. The facilities prescribed by these sections have not so far been used.[68]

The time limits for appeal are dealt with in the Ecclesiastical Jurisdiction (Faculty Appeals) Rules 1965. They are 28 days after the judgment of the consistory court was given, or 14 days after the date of the chancellor's certificate, whichever period last expires. These provisions proved troublesome to apply in practice in *Re St. Luke's, Chelsea (No. 2)*[69] where they are fully discussed in the judgment of Goodman, Deputy Chancellor. A party considering an appeal should begin by consulting the report of that judgment. This should be done within a day or two of the judgment of the consistory court being delivered, since the time limits are very short.

It is not the purpose of this book to discuss appeals to the Court of Ecclesiastical Causes Reserved, the Court of Arches or the Chancery Court of York in any detail. But it may be convenient to note that the appeal lies as of right and that no leave is necessary. The powers of the appellate court and the principles for their exercise have in recent times been discussed fully by the Court of Arches in *Re St. Edburga's, Abberton*,[70]; *Re St. Gregory's, Tredington*[71]; *Re St. Helen's, Brant Broughton*[72] and *Re St. Mary's, Banbury*[73]; and by the Court of Ecclesiastical Causes Reserved in *Re St. Michael and All Angels, Great Torrington*[74]; and *Re Stephen's Walbrook*[75].

---

[67] The court has so far sat only twice: see *Re St. Michael and All Angels, Great Torrington* [1985] Fam. 81; and *Re St. Stephen's Walbrook* [1987] Fam. 146.
[68] The most recent reported case in the Privy Council under the faculty jurisdiction appears to be *Rector and Churchwardens of St. Nicholas Acons* v. *London County Council* [1928] A.C. 469.
[69] [1976] Fam. 318.
[70] [1962] P.10.
[71] [1972] Fam. 236.
[72] [1974] Fam. 16.
[73] [1987] Fam. 136.
[74] [1985] Fam. 81.
[75] [1987] Fam. 146.

4. Fabric and Contents of the Church

The fabric of the church

Repairs

Since the Inspection of Churches Measure 1955, there is a statutory requirement that every church shall have an architect, approved by the D.A.C. for the purposes of that Measure, and that he shall inspect the church and report at least once every five years.[1] His fees for the inspection are to be paid out of a fund set up by the Diocesan Synod,[2] and a copy of every report so made is to go to the relevant archdeacon.[3] The Measure provides for the archdeacon to arrange an inspection, at the cost of the fund, of any church which has not been inspected for at least five years.[4]

The Measure does not provide expressly what is to happen next; but the intention is made clear in the preamble, which recites that under the Canons Ecclesiastical then in force it is the duty of the churchwardens to "take care to provide that churches be well and sufficiently repaired, kept and maintained..." and that "all powers, duties and liabilities of the churchwardens relating to the care, maintenance, preservation and insurance of the fabric of the church have been transferred to and are vested in the parochial church council."[5] This transfer of responsibilities was originally effected by the Parochial Church Councils (Powers) Measure 1921 and it continues under the Parochial Church Councils (Powers) Measure 1956, s.4(1)(ii).

---

[1] Inspection of Churches Measure 1955, s.1(1) and s.1(2)(c).
[2] *Ibid.*, s.1(2)(b).
[3] *Ibid.*, s.1(2)(d).
[4] *Ibid.*, ss.2 and 3.
[5] The present Canons E1 and F13 do not throw on the churchwardens any duty as to repairs except to ensure that repairs are not done without a faculty or an archdeacon's certificate.

Canon F13 does not expressly refer to the responsibility of the council, but it requires that churches and chapels "shall be decently kept and from time to time, as occasion may require, shall be well and sufficiently repaired": this must be a reference to the duty of the council under section 4(1)(ii) of the Measure of 1956. In case the P.C.C. in any parish is remiss in performing its duties, the archdeacon is required and empowered, by Canon C22, to "give direction for the amendment of all defects in the walls, fabric, ornaments and furniture" of any of his churches or chapels. If these directions are not obeyed, he can obtain a faculty to do the work himself, under section 10 of the F.J.M. 1964. The weakness of this procedure is, however, lack of an effective sanction. Though section 5 of the F.J.M. 1964 enables an order to be made that the culprit shall pay all the expenses when the wrong act consists in something positive, it does not appear to cover work that has to be done because the responsible authority, the P.C.C., has failed to do anything at all or has otherwise been remiss in performing its duties, even if its inaction involves disobeying a lawful direction of the archdeacon under Canon C22. In practice, however, this sort of situation does not arise. If it did, steps would have to be taken to get the neglected church declared redundant.

Canon C22 requires the archdeacon to hold an annual visitation and also "to survey in person or by deputy all churches chancels and churchyards" within his archdeaconry. This clause does not say how often he is to make this survey, so that each archdeacon has his own practice. Sometimes the part of the duty which can be done by deputy is delegated to the rural dean; and indeed it may be necessary to depute it in a large archdeaconry where there are two or three hundred parishes. But the more of his duties that an archdeacon performs in person the better. He is the central figure in the whole business of looking after churches; both the parish officers below him and the chancellor above him rely on his knowledge and judgment, as does also the D.A.C. Moreover visits of this sort are a pastoral opportunity.

In the case of an old building, there are always works of some sort that need to be done, and it is the duty of the churchwardens, as officers of the ordinary,[6] to alert the archdeacon, as

---

[6] Canon E1, para. 4.

representative of the ordinary, to the fact that work needs to be done. A certain archdeacon used to tell churchwardens when he charged them, that they should go and stand by the church during heavy rain to see whether the gutters were blocked or broken. Conscientious attention to this sort of detail can save all concerned much trouble and expense.

Unblocking gutters is, of course, *de minimis*, so far as the consistory court is concerned, and therefore needs no faculty. But whenever contractors, or still more unpaid volunteers, are going to work on the fabric of the church the church architect ought to be instructed to supervise. Work on churches, and especially old churches, is for a specialist and it is dangerous to rely on unsupervised local or voluntary help, however well-intentioned.[7] The main function of the court in cases of routine repair is to see that there is in all cases a proper specification and that a qualified architect, usually the architect appointed under the Inspection of Churches Measure 1955, is in professional charge.

It is only a generation since the Measure of 1955 was enacted and there are still, unfortunately, too may cases of long accumulated neglect, which lead finally to emergency work and crippling bills. Something of this sort has usually occurred in cases where the officers of a parish come to the consistory court asking for leave to sell one of the church treasures to pay a large bill for repairs. The court cannot withhold sympathy from petitioners if they show that they inherited a situation of impending disaster from neglectful predecessors. The successors are themselves genuinely intending to make a fresh start and get the affairs of their church into proper order and therefore should be helped. But the primary remedy for a badly neglected church is to make it redundant, since its parishioners have shown by their neglect that they have not cared to look after it. This is one of the reasons why no relief by way of selling church treasures ought to be granted unless the chancellor has heard the case himself in open court and so has seen the petitioners and has satisfied himself that redundancy can properly be avoided because a new generation of parishioners is intending to take more trouble than those whose neglect has

---

[7] Supervision by the church architect is essential when work is being done by public or charitable bodies using voluntary or trainee workmen.

produced the crisis.[8] What must not be allowed in these cases is that a treasure shall be sold, the crisis surmounted and the old carelessness start afresh. If there are no treasures to sell, the right solution will normally be redundancy, so that the work of the church can be concentrated in buildings supported by a congregation that has taken the trouble to look after them.

In this connection, grants are sometimes now available from English Heritage under arrangements with which every archdeacon is familiar. The court's concern is to ensure that parish officers, in accepting such a grant, do not give pledges for the future conduct of themselves and their successors which will hamper the proper care of the building and the proper pastoral work of the parish for the future. In a circular letter of May 21, 1979, the Secretary-General of the General Synod explained that the set of conditions normally required by English Heritage is not intended to create legally enforceable obligations; but it is important in every case that the letter accepting the grant shall be expressed to be subject to the terms of the Secretary-General's circular. In every diocese the registrar should have a form of words and should insist on its being used in every such case; and the chancellor, in considering whether to grant a faculty for the works, should make sure that that has been done.

Many cases of repairs to the fabric of a church arise out of a quinquennial inspection under the Measure of 1955, and there should normally in these cases be a full specification. If so, it can be recommended in principle by the D.A.C. but the chancellor should still make sure tht the money required will be forthcoming when the bills have to be paid. It would be unfortunate, for instance, if the roof of a church were taken off so as to enable work to be done to rotten joists, and then there was no money to put it on again. This is, no doubt, an extreme case; but upon a faculty petition for a large amount of accumulated repairs the chancellor should investigate the arrangements for paying for the work and he should, in some cases, make an order that the work, while approved in principle, is not to be started save with the leave of the court or of the registrar. The power thus reserved can be used to ensure that the work is undertaken in stages, and that no stage is begun until the money to pay for it is in hand or is fairly certain to be so when needed. Apart from

---

[8] *Re St. Gregory's, Tredington* [1972] Fam. 236 especially at 242.

anything else, if the chancellor gives unconditional authority for work costing a large amount of money, he may find himself in difficulties if the parish authorities come, six or 12 months later, and say that they wish to sell the chalice to pay for the work that he himself has recently authorised.

These things being said, ordinary cases of repair to a fabric, even at a very large cost, are not particularly difficult for the petitioners to present or the chancellor to deal with. For the case is usually supported by the report of a competent architect, with a full specification which the D.A.C. has recommended. The fact that the papers must eventually be seen by the chancellor, and the work must be sanctioned by him, ensures that the earlier stages of preparation are properly and meticulously considered with adequate professional advice. Hence, there is no case for some easier procedure, since the sanction would be lost, and the system would still fail. This would give the state a better case for stepping in and taking over churches which are thought to be part of the national heritage and which the state would say are being neglected by their proper custodians.[9]

Demolition of a church or part of a church

Before the F.J.M. 1964 a petition for the demolition of a church was dealt with in the same way as any other petition.[10] It is now subject to restrictions imposed by section 2 of the F.J.M. 1964 and to special procedural provisions in the F.J.R. 1967, rr. 4(2), 5(7) and 6(6).

Briefly, the section forbids the court to grant a faculty for "the demolition or partial demolition of a church" except in the cases provided for in the section.

The word "church" is not defined in the Measure of 1964, but it is defined in the Interpretation Measure 1925, s.3 as "any church or chapel which has been consecrated for the purposes of public worship according to the rites

---

[9] Although the duty of keeping a church in repair lies on the P.C.C., the lay rector, if there is one, is liable at law to pay for the repair of a chancel. Quite a number of parishes have the Church Commissioners or one of the colleges at Oxford or Cambridge as lay rector; all these bodies are very generous and helpful in that capacity.

[10] *e.g.*, in *Re St. George's, Birmingham* [1960] 1 W.L.R. 1069.

and ceremonies of the Church of England."[11] It is doubtful whether this definition covers a building erected on land previously consecrated as a burial ground and used merely for funeral services without any consecration of the building as such. There is no indication in section 2 of the Measure of 1964 that demolitions of any part of a church are too small to be within the scope of the section. Thus a redundant turret, chimney, pinnacle or other excrescence, even if on the point of collapse, is apparently within the section.

By section 2(2) of the F.J.M. 1964, a faculty for demolition of the whole or any part of a church may be granted "if the court is satisfied that another church will be erected on the site or curtilage of the church in question or part thereof to take the place of the church," provided that the procedure described in sub-section (1) is observed. Such cases are not very frequent but an order under sub-section (2) was made by Newey Ch. in *Re Christ Church, Croydon*.[12]

Further, section 2(3)(i) states that the court may grant a faculty for the demolition of *part* of a church if it is satisfied that "the part of the church left standing will be used for the public worship of the Church of England for a substantial period after such demolition," provided that the procedure described in sub-section (1) is observed. This provision has been held to cover a case where the only part of a church to be "left standing" was a crypt and the walls of the church up to three feet above the surface of the ground.[13] It has also been applied to the demolition of a chancel, the rest of the church being left standing.[14]

The procedure described in section 2(1) is as follows:

(i) The petitioner must within four weeks after the petition is lodged at the registry[15] publish "a notice stating the substance of the petition for the faculty,"[16] in the *London Gazette*. He must also publish a like notice in such other newspapers as the court may

---

[11] *Re St. John, Chelsea* [1962] 1 W.L.R. 706 at 708 as to the form and effect of consecration.
[12] [1983] 1 W.L.R. 830.
[13] *Re St. Luke's, Cheetham* [1977] Fam. 144.
[14] *Re St. John the Evangelist, Ford End* [1984] 1 W.L.R. 1194.
[15] F.J.R. 1967, r. 5(7)(a).
[16] F.J.M. 1964, s.2(1)(i).

direct within such period as is specified in the direction. If no period is specified in the direction, publication must be within 14 days after the giving of the direction.[17]
  (ii) An officer of the court (*i.e.* the registrar) must give notice of the petition to the C.C.C.[18] and to the D.A.C.
  (iii) The judge must consider "such advice as the Advisory Committee has tendered to the Court."[19] There is no time limit, but if, within a reasonable time, the committee has tendered no advice, then the court, by doing nothing, will have considered "such advice as the Advisory Committee has tendered," *i.e.* no advice at all.
  (iv) The C.C.C. is given the right to insist on the chancellor hearing in open court "a member of the Council or some person duly authorised by the Council."[20] In order to exercise this right, the council must give a notice (as provided in Form No. 8 in the Rules): this notice must be "lodged at the diocesan registry not more than six weeks after the Council receive notice in writing of the petition under section 2(1)(ii) of the Measure."[21]
  (v) Any other person may give the notice in Form No. 9 applying to give evidence in open court, and this application must be granted "unless in the opinion of the judge his application or the evidence which he gives is frivolous or vexatious."[22] Such an application has to be made within four weeks after the last publication of notice of the petition in the *London Gazette* or a newspaper.[23]

There is no provision in the Measure or Rules entitling the court to order the C.C.C., or any other person who applies to give

---

[17] F.J.R. 1967, r.5(7)(*b*).
[18] F.J.M. 1964, s.2(1)(ii).
[19] *Ibid.*, s.2(1)(iii).
[20] *Ibid.*, s.2(1)(iv)(*a*).
[21] F.J.R. 1967, r. 6(6)(*a*).
[22] F.J.M. 1964, s.2(1)(iv)(*b*): for a case where a representative of the local planning authority gave evidence under this provision see *Re St. John the Evangelist, Ford End* [1984] 1 W.L.R. 1194.
[23] F.J.R. 1967, r. 6(6)(*b*).

evidence, to pay the costs of the hearing which it or he has forced on the petitioners, even if the case is otherwise unopposed and the D.A.C. recommends the petition for approval. No doubt the C.C.C. will behave responsibly; but there is no protection for petitioners against any other person who applies to give evidence save the power of the judge to exclude that person as frivolous or vexatious: see section 2(1)(iv)(b). This power will not be easy to exercise except after the hearing has begun, and considerable costs have already been incurred. These provisions are accordingly capable of abuse.

But the court has power under section 2(3)(ii) to grant a faculty for the demolition of *part* of a church if it is satisfied that such demolition is "necessary for the purpose of the repair, alteration or reconstruction of the part to be demolished or of the whole of the church." Before this can be done the registrar must give written notice of the petition to the C.C.C., and the judge must consider "any advice which the Council may tender to the court."

There are also provisions in section 2(4)[24] that give the court power to grant a faculty "for the demolition or partial demolition of any church..." where certain emergencies have arisen, namely:

   (i) If a court of competent jurisdiction has made an order under the Building Act 1984, s.77. This is an order requiring work to be done to dangerous or dilapidated buildings made by a magistrates' court on the application of the local authority.

  (ii) If the appropriate local authority has served a notice "requiring the taking down, repair or securing of that church"; this is a notice under section 62(2) of the London Building Acts (Amendment) Act 1939, "or under the provisions of any other local Act empowering the council of a county, city, borough or district to give such a notice on the grounds that a building or structure is dangerous."

 (iii) If the appropriate local authority has given a notice under the Building Act 1984, s.78, that they propose to

---

[24] As amended by the Building Act 1984, s.132 and Sched. 6.

take immediate action to deal with the church as a dangerous building.

(iv) If the appropriate local authority has given notice under the Building Act 1984, s.79, requiring the execution of works of repair or restoration to the church.

In *Re All Saints', Plymouth*[25] the court had to consider the effect of a very ill-drawn notice given by a local authority and purporting to be given under the Public Health Acts 1936 and 1961 without identifying the section or sections invoked. The notice alleged that the local authority considered "certain loose slates" on the church to be in such a condition as to be dangerous. The chancellor expressed "the gravest doubts" whether the notice was a valid notice at all; but he held that it was sufficient for him to decide that it was not a notice within either section 2(4)(iii) or section 2(4)(iv) of the F.J.M. 1964,[26] and that accordingly he had no jurisdiction to grant a faculty for the demolition of the church. He also said that since it was clear that the legislature intended to restrict very severely the power of the court to grant faculties for the demolition of churches, "the court should be scrupulous to ensure that it in fact has jurisdiction."[27] He further stated that if he had had jurisdiction he still would not have granted the faculty. All that the local authority had complained of was loose slates, but "where jurisdiction arises under section 2(4) total demolition ought not to be permitted unless the physical condition of the building is such that total demolition is the only sensible course in all the circumstances."[28]

In the cases which can be dealt with under section 2(4) of the F.J.M. 1964, there is no special procedure. Disused churches, especially in towns, awaiting redundancy, become the subject of vandalism and thus become dangerous. In such cases, once there is action by a competent local authority, and where total demolition is the only sensible course in all the circumstances, matters can proceed very swiftly in the consistory court. The

---

[25] [1981] Fam. 1. The relevant sections of the Public Health Act 1961 are set out on the first page of the report.
[26] *Re All Saints', Plymouth* [1981] Fam. 1 at 5.
[27] *Ibid.*, at 3F–G.
[28] *Ibid.*, at 5H.

petition can be lodged without preliminaries and a case of real urgency can be dealt with by an interlocutory order allowing the work to be begun. Such an order can be made *ex parte*, by telephone if necessary. Procedures of this sort have been used on a number of occasions in the London diocese. But while the procedure in the consistory court is far quicker than any possible procedure under the Pastoral Measure 1983, the intention of the legislature fairly clearly is that the slower process should normally be followed in getting rid of the church altogether, and the receipt of a notice ostensibly under section 2(4) should not be made an excuse for cutting matters short unless there is a real emergency.[29]

Where the court does make an order for demolition, it should give consequential directions as to the removal of human remains and the furnishings of the building.[30]

It appears that the *partial* demolition of a listed church which is in ecclesiastical use does not require listed building consent.[31] But if a church is listed, a faculty for *total* demolition should be made conditional on any necessary listed building consent being obtained.

Extension of churches

In the twentieth century, and more especially since about 1950, there has been a tendency to organise the life of a congregation so as to provide a number of activities beyond the worship which is the primary purpose of a church. These activities are usually best pursued in immediate physical proximity to the places where the worship takes place. Sometimes they can be housed within the walls of the existing church by cutting off and adapting areas of the church which are not needed for worship.[32] But it is often necessary to extend the church by means of structures which are used and designed for purposes ancillary to worship rather than for liturgical services. Thus, a building was erected as long ago as 1927 on the disused

---

[29] See the remarks of Calcutt Ch. in the *Plymouth* case, especially at 6, 7.
[30] See *Re St. George's, Birmingham* [1960] 1 W.L.R. 1069 at 1070 and *Re St. Luke's, Cheetham* [1978] Fam. 144 at 147, 148.
[31] *Att.-Gen.* v. *Howard United Reformed Church Trustees* [1976] A.C. 363 and *Re St. Luke's, Cheetham* [1978] Fam. 144. See also Appendix C.
[32] See at pp. 99 *et seq.*

burial ground of the cathedral church of St. Nicholas at Newcastle-on-Tyne (then still under the faculty jurisdiction), which comprised a hall and various vestries and offices connected to the church itself by a corridor. A similar proposition was put forward in the middle of the 1960s in respect of *Re St. Mary's, Luton*.[33] This case went to the Court of Arches and resulted in the proposed building being erected. Since then there have been a good many cases of the same sort; however, few of them have been litigated.

These cases present peculiar difficulties of preparation and can only be brought to fruition by long and hard work. The problem for the architect is to design a structure which can be added harmoniously to an existing building. If that building is modern or undistinguished or both, his task is not particularly difficult. But it is otherwise if the existing building is of great artistic merit, whether it is medieval or of later date. The plans therefore should always be discussed fully with the D.A.C. from the earliest stage. Further, it is necessary to work closely with the local planning authority, since planning permission is necessary. The D.A.C. should indeed go out of its way to foster an understanding relationship between itself and the planning authorities in the diocese; in the experience of the author this can normally be achieved. Similarly, it may well be desirable in a good many of these cases to consult the C.C.C. on the relevant aesthetics and any of the statutory amenity societies which are concerned with a church of the relevant period. Thus in *Re St. Ann's Church, Kew*,[34] Garth Moore Ch. found support for his views in favour of allowing the extension by accepting those of the Georgian Society, Victorian Society and the Society for the Protection of Ancient Buildings. On the other hand in *Re St. Thomas, Lymington*[35] Phillips Ch. allowed the proposals notwithstanding the contrary views of the Lymington Society, and in *Re St. Andrew's Church, Backwell*[36] the chancellor declined to give effect to the views of the Royal Fine Arts Commission.

---

[33] See [1967] P. 151; and [1968] P. 47 in the Court of Arches.
[34] [1977] Fam. 12 at 14.
[35] [1980] Fam. 89 at 94.
[36] (1982); unreported. The registrar of the diocese of Bath and Wells can no doubt supply copies of this important judgment, which the law reports unaccountably do not include.

Since April 1, 1988, under the amended form of the F.J.R., most of the amenity bodies are entitled to become parties opponent or can be made so entitled by the chancellor: see F.J.R. 1967, r. 5A(2) and Chapter 3 above. If any of these bodies wish to oppose the petition it should therefore be required to enter appearance in opposition.

It is not in every case that a hearing is necessary. If, for example, the D.A.C. commends a proposal and there is no parochial opposition, the chancellor will hesitate before deciding upon a hearing if its only purpose would be to enable some outside body to send a representative to give evidence, especially if that body could enter appearance in opposition and has not done so. On the other hand, if there is local opposition, or if for aesthetic reasons the chancellor feels it necessary to invite the archdeacon to intervene to put the petitioners to proof, witnesses from the amenity societies can be called by the party opponent: the expense will be part of the general costs of the proceedings, with which the court will deal at the end of the case. In a really controversial case, however, the parties opponent are likely to have their own expert witnesses, so that a witness sent by the amenity body will not necessarily add to the elucidation of the aesthetic problem. But such a witness can be helpful if he is professionally qualified, and if he states his own professional opinion and does not merely voice, at second hand, the opinion of the amenity body. Thus in the *Backwell* case,[37] the chancellor regarded the Secretary of the Royal Fine Art Commission, a qualified architect, as a useful expert witness in his own right, though he did not in the end prefer his evidence to that of the experts for the petitioners.

In 1980 the Royal Fine Art Commission and the Historic Buildings Council made an attempt to stop all building on churchyards by sending out a circular to all local planning authorities. A local planning authority could be excused if it supposed that this circular, written on paper bearing the royal arms, was in some degree binding upon it. This was not so. For in the *Backwell* case[38] the Royal Warrants constituting the Royal Fine Art Commission were put in evidence and examined by the court. It was held that to issue such a circular was not within the

---

[37] (1982); unreported.
[38] *Ibid*.

terms of reference of the Commission. Moreover, the Department of the Environment's Circular No. 22/80 makes it clear that planning authorities should decide cases on their own professional advice and not otherwise, which the local authority had very properly done in the *Backwell* case. On the other hand, in the case of *St. Mary Baldock* the local planning authority refused planning permission, apparently on the basis of this circular, but the Minister later allowed the appeal of the parochial authorities and granted them permission to erect the desired building in their churchyard.[39]

In a case where the petitioners seek to extend the church, the court must consider the status of the ground on which the extension is to be erected. It may be either a consecrated burial ground or an unconsecrated churchyard or curtilage. The consecrated burial ground may be either in use or disused. The legal considerations affecting each of these possibilities are different.

If the proposed new building is on unconsecrated churchyard, or church curtilage, there is no specific legal difficulty. For land of this sort is under the jurisdiction of the court mainly in order to protect the church itself. Thus the matters for decision in such a case are aesthetic and practical rather than legal. If the new building is to be connected structurally to the church, a faculty is in any event needed for the connection, and in so far as the new building might, for example, darken the church or be used for unsuitable entertainments, its erection on curtilage of the church will need consideration. A case of this sort can arise not merely when the land in question has always been unconsecrated churchyard, but also if land which has been a disused burial ground is de-consecrated and freed from the D.B.G.A. 1884 by a scheme made under section 30 of the Pastoral Measure 1983 for the express purpose of facilitating the erection of the new building.[40] There is no legal need for the new building on curtilage to be connected structurally to the church; but it is in most cases convenient that it should be so

---

[39] Information about the case can no doubt be obtained from the diocesan registry of St. Albans.
[40] This situation arose some years ago in the case of *Watford Parish Church* and again at *St. Mary's, Baldock*. These unreported cases were both in the diocese of St. Albans and the registrar or diocesan secretary can no doubt furnish information about them.

connected in order that persons may be able to get from one building to the other under cover.

If the site of the proposed new building is a consecrated burial ground which is not disused, the legal question is whether the new building will be consistent with the perpetual sacred uses imposed by the sentence of consecration. The leading modern case on this subject is *Re St. John's, Chelsea*,[41] where the restrictions imposed by consecration were examined exhaustively by the consistory court of the diocese of London.[42] A building which is designed to be an extension of the church appears to be permissible, as is also an "ecclesiastical building" for example a church school.[43] Such a building is not required as a matter of law to be connected structurally with the church unless the site is a *disused* burial ground. A building for secular purposes would normally not be permissible. Where the building is to be an extension of the church, the court should usually impose conditions or undertakings to ensure that it is not used for purposes that are unsuitable for part of a church.[44] The most important provisions are:

(1) that the building, like a church, shall be under the exclusive control of the incumbent, so that if there is any suggestion of impropriety he can be dealt with by disciplinary processes; and

(2) that any required undertaking shall be given by the P.C.C. which, unlike the transient incumbent and churchwardens, is a perpetual corporation aggregate.

The archdeacon for some time being should always be given, in the faculty, liberty to apply to enforce the conditions and undertakings.

When the building is on part of the churchyard which has been used for burials, attention must also be paid to the very sensitive issues raised by the need, which occasionally arises, to move some of the human remains and, more often, to remove tombstones. The former should be avoided if at all possible,

---

[41] [1962] 1 W.L.R. 706.
[42] This decision has been approved in the appellate court of the Northern Province in *Re St. Mary the Virgin, Woodkirk* [1969] 1 W.L.R. 1867. It appears not to have been considered in the southern province by the Court of Arches.
[43] *Corke* v. *Rainger* [1912] P. 69.
[44] This was done, *e.g.*, in *Re St. Andrew's Church, Backwell*, see n. 36 above.

since the remains of the deceased in consecrated ground are under the court's protection; but it can if really necessary be allowed.[45] There was, however, impressive technical evidence in the *Backwell* case that the method of driving very slender piles, current in 1982, made it unnecessary to exhume any human remains at all or to transfer them elsewhere. Any remains which have to be disturbed should be reburied reverently by the incumbent in another part of the churchyard, or in consecrated ground elsewhere, under arrangements sanctioned by the court.[46] Any tombstones that need to be removed can be removed under faculty, but the owners have the rights reserved to them by section 3 of the F.J.M. 1964, which must be observed scrupulously. If under this section the owner of a tombstone does not elect to take it away from the churchyard, it should be erected elsewhere in the same churchyard as directed by the court. These aspects of such cases cause a good deal of emotion to some relatives of the deceased and much tact and care should always be exercised in providing for them. This should be done at a very early stage of each case.

It has apparently been suggested in some quarters that it is generally objectionable to build anything at all on a churchyard, and that if more space is really needed it could be obtained better by constructing a subterranean building under the churchyard. It is true that at least two recent cases have occurred in the diocese of London where faculties have been granted to enable new rooms to be constructed under a church. In one of them there were no burials and all that was needed was to excavate the soil which lay between the piers which supported the church. In the other, there was already a vault with coffins in it and authority was given for the removal of the coffins to consecrated ground elsewhere. But if the proposition is to make an underground room by excavations outside the body of the church, in land that has been buried in extensively, perhaps at more than one depth, very great practical difficulties are likely to arise and successful opposition to the proposals can well be expected. It is very doubtful whether indiscriminate mechanical excavation should ever be permitted.

---

[45] *Re St. Ann's Church, Kew* [1977] Fam. 12 at 19 and *Re St. Andrew's Church, Backwell*, see n. 36 above.
[46] See *Re St. Thomas, Lymington* [1980] Fam. 89 at 95.

The third class of case is where the site of the proposed building is a *disused* burial ground within the meaning of section 3 of the D.B.G.A. 1884, as amended by the Open Spaces Act 1887, s.4. This situation was considered in *Re St. Mary's, Luton* in the St. Albans consistory court and the Court of Arches.[47] The effect of these decisions is that if, and only if, the proposed building is truly an extension of the church, it is permissible by virtue of the proviso in section 3 of the Act of 1884, which in that case alone allows the erection of a building on a disused burial ground. In practice this has meant that the new building must always be contiguous to the church and structurally connected with it.[48] Further, the conditions and undertakings as to user, which are in any event requisite, are all the more necessary in their fullest stringency. There have been many other decisions on the effect of the Act of 1884; there is no need to set them out here, since the law was exhaustively discussed in *Re St. Mary's, Luton* (and also in the case of *Re St. Luke's, Chelsea*,[49] though the "building" there proposed was a massive obelisk and not a church room.) In cases of disused burial grounds it is, of course, just as important to attend to any questions which may arise in regard to the removal of human remains and tombstones as it is in the case of consecrated land which is not a disused burial ground.

All cases of new building on churchyards are difficult for the court to decide and it is essential that the evidence for the petitioners and their submissions shall be prepared and presented with great care so that the chancellor may be satisfied that the new building really is necessary, that it is lawful, that it is aesthetically satisfactory in itself, and that it will not be used for unsuitable purposes. Further, considering the new building as an adjunct to the church, he must be of the opinion that to place it there will not to an unacceptable extent impair the aesthetic value of the existing church. For church authorities have "a special responsibility for the protection of these historic buildings and churchyards which they may be said to hold in trust as part of the national or local heritage."[50]

---

[47] [1967] P. 151 and [1968] P. 47; see also *Re St. Luke's, Chelsea* [1976] Fam. 295.
[48] See, *e.g.*, *Re St. Ann's Church, Kew* [1977] Fam. 12 at 16.
[49] [1976] Fam. 295.
[50] *Per* Phillips Ch. in *Re St. Thomas, Lymington* [1980] Fam. 89 at 94.

Internal conversion of church

In some cases the space which is needed for purposes ancillary to worship can be provided within the existing fabric of the church itself, and faculties have often been granted for this purpose. There are obvious aesthetic difficulties in such an arrangement where the existing interior of the church is a harmonious whole. On the other hand, in a good many cases the church is of no outstanding aesthetic merit, and an aisle, or even one end of the church, can be cut off without serious harm, leaving a smaller area for worship and making space for vestries; meeting halls and so forth. There is no legal or doctrinal objection to any such arrangement. Sometimes, where a relatively small amount of new space is needed, it can be provided inside the structure of the tower, either on the level of the church floor or as an upper room, either already existing or made for the purpose by putting in an extra floor. Again, many such schemes may also include reordering of the worship area, as for example by bringing the altar nearer to the congregation or putting it in the middle of the north wall of the church.[51] One advantage of an internal conversion is that, since the areas to be used for ancillary purposes are in fact within the church itself, which continues after such conversion to be a church, those areas continue to be subject to the control of the incumbent. Even so, it may sometimes be expedient to require express conditions or undertakings to ensure that they will at all times be used for purposes wholly consistent with their being a part of the church.

Secular use of part of church

It happens quite often, especially in towns, where land is scarce and expensive, that there is a part of a church, often a crypt, which is not needed for worship or for any purpose ancillary to worship. In such cases, and under careful arrangements, it is admissible for the court to allow such an area to be used by third parties for suitable secular purposes, so as to provide revenue which will assist in maintaining the church and its services. Such an arrangement can be made in a number of

---

[51] *Re St. Peter, Roydon* [1969] 1 W.L.R. 1849.

different ways; but it can never be made by way of lease for two reasons. First, no legal estate can be created in consecrated land[52]; second, no tenancy, legal or equitable, should ever be created, nor should it give the appearance of being created, so as to enable a person to claim, even plausibly, that he is in occupation under a tenancy protected by the Landlord and Tenant Act 1954. Consequently, the person who is to be allowed to use part of the church should always be put in the position of a mere licensee. Nor should the licence be for so long a period as to produce an arguable bar to the church being in due time deconsecrated and dealt with under the Pastoral Measure 1983: the court should therefore always enquire, before allowing a licence to be granted, of the Diocesan Pastoral Committee whether it has any plans or proposals for redundancy with which the suggested licence would be in conflict.

The licence can be granted by the incumbent, as freeholder[53]; alternatively, whether there is, or is not, an incumbent, it can be granted by the court itself.[54] In either case there should, in addition to the faculty granting the licence, be a contractual document between the P.C.C. and the licensee by which the latter enters into covenants as to user and for payment of fees; conversely the P.C.C. sometimes contracts under the licence to keep the structure of the building in good repair. These documents are always elaborate and must be worked out carefully in respect of such practical matters as the right amount of the licence fees, insurance and the covenants protecting the church and its services against noise, other interruptions or against conduct which is a breach of Canon F15 "Of churches not to be profaned." A great many of these cases have arisen in the past 20 years in the diocese of London, and advice on the

---

[52] *Re St. Paul's, Covent Garden* [1974] Fam. 1, and the earlier cases discussed therein. See Pastoral Measure 1983, s. 56(2) and (3), which expressly prohibits any sale, lease or other disposition of any part of a church, but allows a faculty to be issued for "a suitable use" of part of a church.

[53] Technically, the interest in fee simple in consecrated land is in abeyance, but the incumbent has an interest analogous to a life interest, which is an interest of freehold: see *per* Lord Selborne L.C. in *Ecclesiastical Commissioners for England and Wales* v. *Rowe* (1880) 5 App.Cas. 736 at 744. See also *Re St. Paul's, Covent Garden* [1974] Fam. 1 at 4.

[54] *Re St. Paul's, Covent Garden* [1974] Fam. 1.

contents of the documents can be obtained from the registrar of that diocese.[55] Any money that is to be paid by the licensee should always be made payable to the P.C.C. and not to the incumbent, so that it does not become in law part of his income, with the numerous complexities which would result both as to income tax and the computation of his diocesan minimum stipend.

In a good many cases licences have been allowed for use by charitable bodies of crypts or other parts of churches not wanted for worship or purposes ancillary thereto. In these cases, of course, the object is more to help the charity than to produce income, so that the licence fees may be small or even minimal. But attention should always be paid to the other terms so as to protect the church against damage and its services against noise or other interruptions. It is desirable that any such charity should be incorporated, so that the covenants of the charity may be enforceable at law against a perpetual body and not merely against those persons who happen to be trustees at the time of the case.

The petitioners should be the incumbent, if there is one, the P.C.C. and the proposed licensee. They should ask the court either to grant the licence, or to authorise the incumbent to grant it, and for authority for the P.C.C. to enter into the contractual document containing the terms. The reason for making the proposed licensee a petitioner is that he may be ordered to pay the costs of proceedings and to give any undertakings to the court which it may be desirable to exact. The proposed documents should be submitted in draft with the petition and there should be clear evidence that the terms are adequate and proper and that the space in question is not for the time being needed for other church purposes. The period of the licence should always be comparatively short, so that if, in changed circumstances, it is desirable to use the space in question for church purposes, such purposes can be resumed at fairly short notice. The overriding consideration is always that the whole of the church continues to be a church and that nothing should be done which will prevent its use as a church whenever that user

---

[55] Various procedural matters were discussed by the court in *Re St. Mary, Aldermary* [1985] Fam. 101. This case concerned a churchyard, but much of the reasoning applies to a case concerning a church. The proposed licensee should always be one of the petitioners.

is expedient, and that in the meantime the use of the rest as a church will not be disturbed. In a recent case in the diocese of London,[56] the whole of a church, which was a chapel of ease very little used for worship, was put at the disposal of a religious and educational charity for a considerable period on terms ensuring that part of the floor would be available for regular worship once or twice a week and requiring that it should continue to be used in that way. The legal problems which arise in such a case derive from the fact that the building is consecrated for worship, and accordingly has a status which requires respect. Indeed, this status is reinforced by Canons F15 and F16 which forbid profanation of churches. The law on consecration was discussed very fully in *Re St. John's, Chelsea*,[57] to which careful reference should always be made in preparing or presenting a case.

The documents are inevitably complex and it is not desirable for the court to enter into prolonged correspondence about them. The most practical method of proceeding is for the citation to be issued, so as to discover whether the petition is opposed in principle. Normally, it is unopposed. In that event the matter should be set down for hearing in chambers, so that the details and the documents may be discussed expeditiously. If there is opposition, or if it appears that a serious question of law needs to be argued, the hearing must be in open court. Further, in quite a number of cases it is expedient to arrange that the archdeacon shall enter appearance in order to argue a point of law or to subject the documents to criticism, especially in the light of *Re St. John's, Chelsea*.[58] If, in the end, he and the petitioners agree the documents, the matter can be brought before the chancellor in chambers for approval of the agreed documents. It is seldom that a case is so simple that it can be dealt with finally otherwise than by a hearing; but in the experience of the author it is very rare for such a case to need to be heard otherwise than in chambers. In the case of *Re St. Peter, Vere Street* mentioned above the archdeacon had been active in the negotiations preceding the petition and very properly preferred not to be a party opponent. A solicitor was thereafter

---

[56] *Re St. Peter, Vere Street*, unreported.
[57] [1962] 1 W.L.R 706.
[58] *Ibid.*

appointed as acting archdeacon and gave the court much assistance.[59]

Fixed equipment

Organs

The organ is normally the most expensive thing in a church, either to buy, to replace or to repair. The problems of the organ are almost always troublesome, and it is not desirable that any of them should be dealt with except by the chancellor himself by faculty.

Consequently, when these problems arise, the parish officers need to discuss them from a very early stage with the archdeacon and with the member or members of the D.A.C. who are specially concerned with organs, whether those persons be ordinary members of the committee or are designated as organ advisers or organ consultants. Large amounts of money are involved and the music at most of the services of a church is important. Therefore no decisions should be taken in a hurry. Parish officers should resist any tendency by organ builders, or by vendors of organs, to press for an immediate or early decision; parishes are sometimes urged to hurry in return for a reduction in price or an implied threat that the price is about to rise. These suggestions are always irrelevant; organs should last for decades.

Chancellors who happen to know about organs or music should be aware of the insidious temptation to substitute their own opinions for those of the witnesses. Thus, in *Re St. Mary's, Balham*[60] Garth Moore Ch. said, "Even though I am not completely ignorant of such matters, I know enough to know my own limitations." As in any other case, the decision should be made upon the evidence adduced. Conversely, a chancellor who is not, of his own knowledge, equipped to form a personal opinion, should remember that it is not he, but the congregation, who will have to live with the organ in question, whether it be a new instrument or an old one undergoing repairs. It is not

---

[59] The same procedural device was used successfully in the very different case of *Re St. Mary's, Barton-upon-Humber* [1987] Fam. 41.
[60] [1978] 1 All E.R. 993 at 997e.

for the court, as such, to have a policy about organs, save to ensure that the best is done for the church and for the congregation.

For a good many years there has been an unresolved issue on which expert opinions have differed, as to the use of what are generically called electronic or electrostatic organs as against pipe organs. The former class produces sounds by means of electrical impulses and devices; the latter produces sounds made by the passage of currents of air through pipes, whether or not the currents are produced with the aid of electrical motors.

Every D.A.C. should include at least two persons closely acquainted with the musical problems and the way in which the music that is so necessary in a church can be produced. In the diocese of London there has for some years been an organs sub-committee of the D.A.C., presided over by an archdeacon and including all the committee's experts on organs. This arrangement sometimes operates slowly, but it ensures that advice on cases about organs is tendered by the collective expertise of all the organ specialists, tempered by the practical wisdom of the archdeacon. Such a sub-committee is appropriate in a large diocese; smaller ones need something simpler. The committee in a small diocese needs to guard against the danger of confiding its duties and judgment to a single specialist, however knowledgeable or understanding. All cases about organs are difficult, and the needs and resources of no parish are exactly the same as those of any other.

The only two reported cases about the merits of particular sorts of organs since 1950 are *Re St. Mary's, Lancaster*[61] and *Re St. Martin's, Ashton-upon-Mersey*.[62]

In the *Lancaster* case, as part of a larger scheme, it was proposed by the parish officers that a pipe organ, built about 1873, should be removed from the church and an electronic organ, costing about £35,000, should be substituted for it. Five experts, provided by the C.C.C. and the D.A.C., all said that in their considered opinion the old organ should be preserved, but four experienced church organists spoke very highly of the electrostatic organ. The chancellor said that the evidence of the

---

[61] [1980] 1 W.L.R. 657.
[62] [1981] 1 W.L.R. 1288.

former group of witnesses showed "that pipe organs set the standard against which all organs in places of worship are judged,"[63] and that electrostatic organs are "held out by their manufacturers as simulating the sound made by a pipe organ."[64] It followed, he said, that "there must be pipe organs played and heard at as many places as possible where the services of the church are sung. By 'as possible' I mean as is consistent with the exercise of the informed, collective conscience of the Church in the use and deployment of its forces and resources, whether spiritual, financial or material."[65] But nevertheless the chancellor concluded that there would be no objection to the substitution of the electrostatic organ for the pipe organ in the particular context of *St Mary's, Lancaster* at the time of the case. This decision shows that there are cases where electrostatic organs can properly be allowed.

But in applying the decision to other cases one must not overlook that the particular electrostatic organ in question was an extremely expensive one and that the practical organists were all enthusiastic about it. It by no means follows that every such organ is everywhere appropriate. The chancellor said that pipe organs are the norm, and those who wish to substitute an electrostatic one have an onus to discharge. It is sometimes argued that a proposed electrostatic organ is much cheaper than the corresponding pipe organ; again it is said that the latter will last for a century, while the former is likely to need to be replaced in a little over a decade and so will cost a parish much more over a long period. The evidence on points of this sort needs in each case to be sifted carefully and objectively. Evidence is also needed as to the stability of the manufacturer and therefore the worth of his guarantee of spare parts and services.

In the *Ashton-upon-Mersey* case, Lomas Ch. concentrated mainly on the financial considerations and decided against the electronic organ which the petitioners sought authority to introduce into the church.

Where questions about the repair of organs arise it is important for the petitioners and their advisers to ensure that

---

[63] [1980] 1 W.L.R. 657 at 660e.
[64] *Ibid.*, at 660f.
[65] *Ibid.*, at 660g.

the specification does no avoidable damage to the organ case. Where the organ is old, the case is a matter of considerable interest for the experts and should be protected carefully.

Bells

By Canon F8 "In every church and chapel there shall be provided[66] at least one bell to ring the people to divine service," and the Canon also enacts that "no bell in any church or chapel shall be rung contrary to the direction of the minister." Like all goods of the church, the bells and bell ropes are vested in the churchwardens; but since, under the Canon, the control of the bells is vested in the incumbent, it appears that it is he who should be sued in tort if the bell-ringing amounts to a common law nuisance to a neighbouring owner or occupier.

The value of bells and their materials is very considerable and nothing should be done to or about bells except under expert advice. A specialist on bells is an essential participant in every D.A.C., whether as a full member or as a consultant. There appears to be no reported case in recent times about the installation or repair of bells. In practice such cases are common, and the fact that none is reported suggests that proper advice has been sought and accepted in most of the cases.

It was recognised by Sir Robert Phillimore in *The Ecclesiastical Law of the Church of England*,[67] that "A faculty may be granted to sell ornaments or utensils found to be unnecessary, as in the case of old bells when a new peal is set up, and the like."[68] Bells from a redundant church sometimes have to be disposed of and while the authority of a faculty is no longer necessary for them to be removed from the redundant church, they cannot be set up in another church except with such authority.[69]

While the Canon deals only with bells "to ring the people to divine service," bells are used in churches for other purposes as well, in particular for ringing at the consecration of the Eucharist. Such objects have repeatedly been held illegal, most

---

[66] I.e. at the cost of the P.C.C.: Canon F14.
[67] (1873 1st. ed.), Vol. II at p. 1792.
[68] Cited with approval in *Re St. Gregory's, Tredington* [1972] Fam. 236 at 240.
[69] For an example of such a case see *Re West Camel Church* [1979] Fam. 79; but note, in regard to the redundant church, that Pastoral Measure 1968, s.49 had not then been amended to make a faculty unnecessary.

recently by Hylton Foster Ch. in *Re St. Mary, Tyne Dock*,[70] where the older cases are enumerated. All of them seem to stem from *Elphinstone v. Purchas*,[71] where no reasons were given and the reported argument throws no light on what those reasons may have been. However, the explanation appears to be that bells are not included in the ornaments mentioned in the prayer book of 1549.[72] It is not altogether clear that these decisions continue to stand at the present time, when so much has changed since 1870 in the normally accepted pattern of observances at the Eucharist. If upon the issue of a citation for a sanctuary bell a qualified party enters appearance in opposition this point will need careful judicial attention. Meantime, such ornaments seem to be used in some churches without causing litigation.

In the *Tyne Dock* case the incumbent sought to evade the effect of an order for the removal of the sanctuary bell by making a hole in the ceiling and passing a rope through it so that a bell in the belfry could be rung at the appropriate moment instead. These arrangements were characterised by Dr. Wigglesworth, the Deputy Chancellor, in *Re St. Mary, Tyne Dock (No. 2)*[73] as "unworthy subterfuges." The vicar had given up using the bell in question before the hearing and apologised for his conduct. There was therefore no order about it. Though in the particular circumstances the "subterfuge" was no doubt improper, there is no general decision in either of the *Tyne Dock* cases that the ringing of one of the ordinary bells in the belfry is an illegal procedure at the Eucharist. The old cases all deal with small bells inside the church. In *Re St. John The Evangelist, Clevedon*,[74] Chadwyck-Healey Ch. held that to toll a bell in these circumstances was illegal. He did so with evident reluctance, citing three distinguished authorities from the thirteenth century to the contrary and saying "I am quite aware that the ringing of a bell at the time of the celebration of the Holy Communion is a matter of comfort to many people who cannot, either by reason of sickness or other causes, be present in church." The bell calls their attention if they are within earshot, which many are, especially in the country, so that they can for a moment join

---

[70] [1954] P. 369 at 379.
[71] (1870) L.R. 3A and E 66 at 98, 99.
[72] See *Rector and Churchwardens of Capel St. Mary v. Packard* [1927] P. 289 at 305.
[73] [1958] P. 156 at 169.
[74] [1909] P. 6 at 14.

their prayers with those of the congregation. It is difficult to see how this tolling is any more objectionable than the tolling of a bell when the curate says his daily office (expressly enjoined in the preface to the book of common prayer). Whatever the propriety of ringing a bell inside the church, it is surely a different matter to call the attention of people outside it to what is happening inside the church at the time. Chadwyck-Healey Ch. said that he could trace no distinction between the two sorts of case: however the matter was not professionally argued before him and if it had been he might easily have come to a different conclusion. Recently, and also in the same diocese, a bell for this purpose was allowed to be installed: but here too the point was not argued.[75]

Pews

Pews are normally thought of as pieces of furniture in a church, usually of wood and often fixed to the floor. The moving, or removing, of pews is a common item in schemes of reordering. Quite often, when a citation is issued in respect of a petition for a faculty to execute such a scheme, it turns out that some parishioners object on grounds either sentimental or practical. A great many pews are comparatively modern and are of no particular aesthetic value, either in material or design. On the other hand, there are many pews of great distinction which ought to be preserved, especially for their carving or because they are of intrinsically beautiful wood or of handsome shape. All these considerations require to be evaluated carefully by the D.A.C. and the evidence weighed by the chancellor. In many cases there is no particular legal difficulty or problem. In a minority of cases, however, such problems do arise. For there is a considerable body of common law and statutory law about pews and the legal rights of individuals to them. It would be out of place in a book on the faculty jurisdiction to give a full account of this branch of the law of property; if such a case arises those concerned should refer to other textbooks.[76]

---

[75] *Re West Camel Church* [1979] Fam. 79 at 82, 83.
[76] There are accounts of this branch of the law in the following works: *Halsbury's Laws of England*, (4th ed.) Vol. 14, paras. 1086 *et seq.*; *Phillimore's The Ecclesiastical Law of the Church of England*, (1st ed., 1873) Vol. II at pp. 1797 *et seq.*; *Blackstone's Commentaries* (19th ed., 1836), Vol. II at p. 429; *Theobald's Law of Land*, (2nd ed., 1929) at pp. 233, 234; *Carson's Real Property Statutes*, (3rd ed., 1927) at pp. 114 *et seq.*: this is perhaps the fullest collection of cases.

The effect of the authorities can be stated shortly. In every church, seats have to be provided for the use of the parishioners and those who attend divine service (Canon F7.) By the same Canon the churchwardens, as officers of the ordinary, are normally required to allocate the seats. But a right to occupy a seat at service times, which is in the nature of an easement, may be acquired by faculty or by prescription from which a faculty may be presumed.[77]

A similar right may be acquired under a private Act of Parliament. In such a case it was held in 1870 that the proprietor of a pew did not acquire a freehold interest in the soil of the church so as to entitle him to vote at parliamentary elections.[78] Similar pew rights can be acquired under the Church Building Acts, where the pew rents paid by those with such rights often provided the incumbent's stipend.

For the first time in many years the effect of the grant of a right to a pew for worship arose in *Re St. Mary's, Banbury*.[79] In this case there was a petition for a faculty to authorise the internal reordering of a church rebuilt under a private Act of Parliament of 1790. The Act had provided for raising the cost of rebuilding the church; a main source of money was to be the sale of pews and seats. Certain parishioners lodged objections to the petition, grounded on the allegation that they were the present owners of rights to seats created under the Act. Boydell Ch. concluded that the right established by the parties opponent in their respective pews "is a right to use (the pew) during divine service and other religious observances at times when the church is open for worship."[80] On the other hand, he said that "there is no right of access to the pew or to use it for other purposes."[81] Further, he held that the parties opponent could not "be compelled to accept chairs in substitution of their rights to their numbered pews"[82]; and that "the right to use the pew...cannot be removed by faculty."[83] The petition for

---

[77] *Phillips* v. *Halliday* [1891] A.C. 228.
[78] *Brumfitt* v. *Roberts* (1870) L.R. 5 C.P. 24. According to Bovill C.J., at 232, a "pew" signifies "a seat enclosed in a church."
[79] [1986] Fam. 24 (in the consistory court) and [1987] Fam. 136 (in the Court of Arches).
[80] [1986] Fam. 24 at 33.
[81] *Ibid.*
[82] *Ibid.*
[83] *Ibid.*

reordering the church, to which the removal of the pews was essential, could therefore not be granted. On appeal to the Court of Arches the petitioners argued that the statutory right was not "in an individual geographically fixed pew or seat, but in a seat or seats of some kind in an area from which the originally allotted pew and its geographical location may have been excluded."[84] On the construction of the Act, the learned Dean held that the Act empowered the trustees of the original scheme to create pew or seat rights to individual and identifiable pews or seats and that the rights so to be conferred were perpetual. He said that he was satisfied that the pews could not permanently be removed without the consent of the owners; accordingly the petition for their removal must fail and the appeal was dismissed.

This litigation, therefore, calls attention to a hazard which must be run by those who petition for any reordering which involves interference with pews in which third parties have or claim prescriptive or statutory rights. If a claim of this kind appears likely to be made, the petitioners should at once seek advice from someone knowledgeable in this specialised branch of the law.

The holy table

It would have seemed strange, even 30 years ago, to treat the holy table as "fixed equipment." For there was a body of learning, conveniently summarised by Dr. Tristram Ch. in *The Rector and Churchwardens of St. Luke's, Chelsea* v. *Wheeler*,[85] to the effect that the holy table must not be of stone and must be moveable. The two leading cases in the nineteenth century were *Faulkner* v. *Litchfield and Stearn*,[86] a decision of Sir Herbert Jenner Fust, Dean of the Arches, and *Liddell* v. *Westerton*,[87] where the Privy Council approved that judgment of Sir Herbert Jenner Fust. (These very long cases are mines of learning and information which the curious may study.)

Since then, the Holy Table Measure 1964, s.1 provided that "The Holy Table used at the celebration of the Lord's Supper or

[84] [1987] Fam. 136.
[85] [1904] P. 257.
[86] (1845) 1 Rob.Eccl. 184.
[87] (1857) 2 L.T.O.S. 54.

Holy Communion in any Church or Chapel may be either moveable or immoveable and may be made of wood, stone or any other material suitable for the purpose for which the Table is to be used."

This Measure was repealed by the Church of England (Worship and Doctrine) Measure 1974, s.6(3) and Sched. 2. The matter is now governed by Canon F2 which provides, by paragraph 1, that "In every church and chapel a convenient and decent table of wood, stone or other suitable material shall be provided for the celebration of the Holy Communion..."

The Canon does not expressly refer to the question whether the table may be moveable or immoveable; but it seems clear that the Canon, following as it does the Measure of 1964, does not restore the restriction on immoveability required by *Faulkner v. Litchfield* and *Liddell v. Westerton*.

In *Re St. Stephen's, Walbrook*[88] the petitioners sought a faculty to introduce into the church, as the main altar, a cylindrical piece of marble three feet five inches in height, eight feet in diameter and some 10 tons in weight. It was argued by the party opponent in the consistory court that, whatever else this artefact might be, it was not a table, and that, whatever else the Measure of 1964 had done and the Canon had continued, the holy table must still be a table. This argument prevailed before the chancellor who held that the artefact was not a table, and in reaching that conclusion he followed the observations about tables contained in *Faulkner v. Litchfield* and *Liddell v. Westerton*, the former being a decision of the Court of Arches and the latter one of the Privy Council and so both binding on him.

The case went, on appeal, to the Court of Ecclesiastical Causes Reserved; this court is, by section 45(3) of the E.J.M. 1963 "not...bound by any decision of the Judicial Committee of the Privy Council in relation to matter of doctrine ritual or ceremonial." The court held that the artefact under consideration was a "table," so that this ground of decision of the court below was reversed. Their Lordships also dealt with the history of the subject and Sir Anthony Lloyd stated that "One could be forgiven for thinking that the whole object of the Holy Table Measure 1964 was to reverse the decision in *Faulkner v. Litchfield*

---

[88] [1987] Fam. 146.

and Stearn"[89] and he expressed doubts whether the court below was bound by that decision, despite it having been approved in *Liddell* v. *Westerton*.

So far as the law is concerned, the result of this litigation appears therefore to be that the holy table may be any artefact which can properly be called a table, and of any material and whether moveable or immoveable, the only two controlling considerations being, under the wording of Canon F2, that the material must be "suitable" and the table "convenient and decent." On the other hand in the *St. Stephen's* case Sir Ralph Gibson appears in his judgment to have accepted the view expressed by the Dean of the Arches in *Re St. Mary's, Banbury*[90] that churches are to be protected from "irreversible" changes, though he did not accept that the change effected in the *St. Stephen's* case was irreversible despite the size and weight of the artefact and the great cost of introducing or removing it.[91] The question of "irreversibility" arises in the case of many reorderings of the furnishings of churches and is further discussed below, at pp. 118 *et seq*.

Assuming that what is proposed is lawful, the further question remains whether, as a matter of discretion, the introduction of any particular object ought to be allowed. This is usually an aesthetic matter, but sometimes the court excludes an object which is likely to lead to unease in the parish. A great part of all the judgments in the *St. Stephen's* case was addressed to the aesthetic issue; but since it depended on the particular evidence given in that case this matter calls for no further comment in the present context.

Moveables

Generally

The moveable objects in a church are of two categories, *i.e.* (i) those which are used in the performance of the services and rites of the church, and (ii) others. The former are technically known as "ornaments": the latter are sometimes, equally

---

[89] [1987] Fam. 146.
[90] [1987] Fam. 136.
[91] As to which see the judgment of the chancellor in *Re St. Stephen's, Walbrook* [1987] Fam. 146.

misleadingly, called "decorations."[92] The distinction, used in the troubled days of the nineteenth century, is considered to be important in that an "ornament" superficially innocuous, might be said to have become tainted by use, or expected use, for superstitious reverence and thus either to be illegal or at least to be something which the court should not allow to be brought into the church. Those days are, happily, at an end. Unless and until the old quarrels break out again,[93] it is more useful to approach the matter differently. As Spafford Ch. has drily observed "The Church of England has many major matters of concern. I doubt if the use of electric 'candles' in a church is one of them."[94]

The new Canons require certain things to be provided in every church; they are detailed in Canons F1 to F12 inclusive. Canon F14 requires them to be provided at the charge of the P.C.C. The items are a font (F1), a holy table (F2), communion plate (F3), communion linen (F4), surplices (F5), reading desks and a pulpit (F6), seats for the congregation (F7), at least one bell "to ring the people to divine service" (F8), a bible and a book of common prayer for the minister (F9), an alms box (F10), register books (F11), and a register book of services (F12). In several of these Canons provision is made for disputes to be settled by the ordinary (*e.g.* as to where the font should be if not near the principal entrance to the church).

These Canons are designed to help in stilling old controversies. In particular, Canon F2 provides that the holy table is to be "convenient and decent" and that it shall be "of wood, stone or other suitable material," thus seeking to put an end to the old disputes about stone altars. Further, in two recent cases the court has intimated that the position of the altar is not a matter of doctrinal significance.[95] It has also been held that the

---

[92] See the discussion in *Phillimore's Ecclesiastical Law of the Church of England* (1st ed., 1873) Vol. I at pp. 920 *et seq*. The definition in the text comes from *Westerton* v. *Liddell* (1857) Moo.Spec.Rep. 133 at 156 and was recently cited with approval in the judgment of the Court of Ecclesiastical Causes Reserved in *Re St. Michael and All Angels, Great Torrington* [1985] Fam. 81 at 89.
[93] The leading 19th century cases in this field are *Westerton* v. *Liddell* (1857) Moo.Spec.Rep. 133 at 157, summarised by Lord Cairns in *Martin* v. *Mackonochie* (1868) L.R. 2 P.C. 365 at 390, *Clifton* v. *Ridsdale* (1876) 1 P.D. 315, affirmed (1877) 2 P.C. 276.
[94] *Re St. Andrew's, Dearnley* [1981] Fam. 50 at 51.
[95] *Re St. Peter, Roydon* [1969] 1 W.L.R. 1842, at 1856 and *Re St. Luke's, Cheetham* [1977] Fam. 144 at 147.

presence or absence of a crucifix is not necessarily indicative of a high church, a middle church or even a low church.[96] On the other hand Canon F2 has been the subject of considerable recent litigation on the question of whether the holy table still has to be a table. It was held that a cylindrical piece of marble, eight feet in diameter and weighing 10 tons was a table.[97]

But the Canons leave intact the *aesthetic* control over the appearance of all the objects in question, exercised by the ordinary through the faculty jurisdiction, though in practice the jurisdiction is not normally enforced in respect of linen and the various sorts of book. But the Canons exclude, so far as possible, all issues as to the *legality* of those objects. This is again for the peace of the church.

In *Re St. Michael and All Angels, Great Torrington*,[98] there was considerable discussion in the judgment of the Court of Ecclesiastical Causes Reserved of the proposition that there is a distinction between the introduction into a church of an item ordered by the canons and an item "not ordered though lawful."[99] It was said that the former class "in general" do not need to be authorised by faculty. This proposition, however, cannot be intended to remove the court's control over the aesthetic quality of the item in question: thus no one seems to have suggested in *Re St. Stephen's, Walbrook*,[1] that it was wrong to apply for a faculty in respect of the altar table in question, which was aesthetically controversial. In regard to the latter class it was said that while a faculty is strictly required "minor matters, may often be introduced without a faculty."[2] This proposition seems to be little more than an affirmation that matters *de minimis*, if uncontroversial aesthetically or otherwise, are not usually the subject matter of a faculty.

In regard to all the other moveable objects in a church, the "decorations" in the old sense of that word, the test is

---

[96] *Re St. Mary the Virgin, Selling* [1980] 1 W.L.R. 1545. As to crucifixes generally see *Re St. Mary, Tyne Dock* [1954] P. 369 at 380.
[97] See *Re St. Stephen's, Walbrook* [1987] Fam. 146.
[98] [1985] Fam. 81 at 89–90.
[99] *Ibid.*, at 89.
[1] [1987] Fam. 146.
[2] [1985] Fam. 81 at 89.

primarily aesthetic; but the chancellor, in exercising the faculty jurisdiction, has to consider two other factors. First, some objects appear in the past to have been held to be illegal in themselves: such objects cannot be permitted, but they are few. Secondly, objects otherwise unobjectionable can become undesirable to be allowed if there is evidence that they are likely to be used for purposes of superstitious reverence. The latter class can usually be dealt with by requiring an undertaking against superstitious user, and expressing the faculty to be operative only until further order, with liberty to apply so that the archdeacon or other interested parties may easily approach the court for the rescission of the faculty if the undertaking is broken. The church is, indeed, much indebted to the late Hylton-Foster Ch. and to Garth Moore Ch. who dealt with some of these ancient controversies in two cases; *Re St. Mary, Tyne Dock*[3] and *Re St. Peter, St. Helier, Morden*,[4] which between them did more than any other reported cases to bring a reasonable attitude into this subject-matter. The particular objects discussed in these cases are mentioned further below.[5] Except for four items declared illegal in *Re St. Mary, Tyne Dock*[6] and *Re St. Mary, Tyne Dock (No. 2)*[7] and stations of the cross held illegal by Ellison Ch. in *Re St. Mary the Virgin, West Moors*[8] there is no reported case in or after 1950 in which any object has been either held to be illegal *per se* or has been held tainted by illegality due to expected superstitious reverence.

The objects held illegal in the *Tyne Dock* cases were a tabernacle, a sanctuary gong, a sanctuary bell and some portable candle holders. Those which were there held to be unobjectionable were an aumbry, a thurible, a confessional table and chair, an additional altar, certain stations of the cross, a holy water stoup and a cruet for oil. The chancellor declined to authorise

---

[3] [1954] P. 369. This dispute had a sequel, dealt with by Dr. Wigglesworth as Deputy Chancellor [1958] P. 156.
[4] [1951] P. 303; this case was followed by Elphinstone Ch. in *Re St. Augustine's, Brinksway* [1963] P. 364; but Ellison Ch. declined to follow it in *Re St. Mary the Virgin, West Moors* [1963] P. 390.
[5] Of a piece with the Canons discussed above and these decisions is Canon B8 which deals with the vesture of ministers during the time of divine service and recognises the diversity of such vestures as having no particular doctrinal significance.
[6] [1954] P. 369.
[7] [1958] P. 156.
[8] [1963] P. 390.

the retention of a particular large statue of the Blessed Virgin, on the ground that its retention would tend to keep alive dissensions in the parish.

There seems to be no doubt that a tabernacle for the purpose of housing the reserved sacrament is illegal; but since an aumbry or hanging pyx are not,[9] there is no practical difficulty.

In respect of stations of the cross there are two problems. Of the 14 commonly used, four (St. Veronica and the three falls of Our Lord) are not expressly warranted by scripture, though Garth Moore Ch. in the *St. Peter, St. Helier, Morden*[10] case has given some grounds for thinking that the falls might be factual; a question is therefore said to arise whether the non-scriptural stations can be allowed at all. This seems rather ridiculous when pictures of mythological scenes are common, for example of St. George and the dragon. It has further been suggested that the stations as a whole are illegal as tending towards superstitious reverence.[11] It is the practice of the author, hitherto unchallenged, to follow Garth Moore Ch. and authorise all 14 stations as an aid to worship.

All the rest of the moveable objects in a church are to be judged primarily by usefulness and good artistic taste. But the court has a duty to "safeguard sound doctrine": thus in *Re St. Edward the Confessor, Mottingham*[12] Garth Moore Ch. was asked to allow an "aesthetically satisfactory plaque depicting in bas-relief the washing of the Babe of Bethlehem"[13] in immediate juxtaposition to the font. He declined to allow it to be so placed lest it should suggest that the baptism of Our Lord took place in infancy or that an ordinary washing can be equated to a solemn initiatory baptism.

But the court should beware of allowing churches to become dumping grounds for chattels unwanted because the church which formerly housed them has become redundant, or because they belonged to a parishioner, however worthy, whose residuary legatees do not want them. The same applies to moveables bequeathed by a testator to the church. Gift horses to

---

[9] In addition to the *Tyne Dock* cases, see *Re Lapford (Devon) Parish Church* [1955] P. 205 and *Re St. Nicholas, Plumstead* [1961] 1 W.L.R. 916: see also at pp. 130 *et seq.*
[10] [1951] P. 303.
[11] See the cases in n. 4 above.
[12] [1983] 1 W.L.R. 364.
[13] *Ibid.*

a church should always be looked in the mouth, and no gift, however well intentioned, should be introduced without a faculty. All, if allowed in a church, become a liability of the P.C.C. for their maintenance and insurance. Every case of a gift must of course be subjected by the D.A.C. to exactly the same critical aesthetic consideration as the committee would give to something which the P.C.C. itself wished to buy. The tests are, will it embellish the church, or at least will it be useful without being so ugly as to disfigure the church?

There are innumerable things that are needed in, and will embellish, a church, from an expensive chalice, through beautiful tapestries and altar frontals, to the candlesticks[14] and the humbler but still necessary chairs, pews or carpets. Each such object deserves the most careful consideration as to its shape, size and colour, and in all these respects intending petitioners should pay great attention to the informed views of the D.A.C. Some particular sorts of more important chattels are particularly discussed below.

Petitions for leave to accept gifts and to introduce the object in question into a church should normally be made by the churchwardens who will become their owners; by the incumbent, into whose church they will be put; and by the P.C.C., which will be financially responsible for them.

Moveables brought into a church and dedicated to the service of God become the property of the churchwardens, who cannot part with them except under the authority of a faculty, even if their introduction was not similarly authorised.[15] Though title to goods belonging to a church can be adjudicated upon by the secular courts, it is also justiciable in the consistory court. Indeed the latter is the more convenient tribunal. For, whatever the title, the goods once in a church cannot be removed without a faculty.[16]

The diocesan board of finance now has charge of the moveables in a redundant church once the declaration of

---

[14] There is no legal objection to having six candlesticks on an altar, but the old English tradition was to have two: *Re St. Saviour's Church, Walthamstow* [1951] P. 147.
[15] *Re Escot Church* [1979] Fam. 125.
[16] *Ibid.,* per Calcutt Ch. at 127D–E. On the jurisdiction to decide questions of title see also the judgment of Newey Ch. in *Re St. Mary of Charity, Faversham* [1986] Fam. 143, where a great many of the older cases were considered.

redundancy has been made and may without a faculty remove them for safe-keeping. This provision does not authorise them to be put into another church without a faculty. The same applies to the various items, altar, communion plate and so on, which the bishop may move after a redundancy scheme has been made.

Re-ordering

Petitions are very frequently lodged for authority to rearrange moveable objects in a church, with or without some additions to, or subtractions from, existing moveables or things only slightly affixed, like pews.[17] Such a petition is said to be for "re-ordering." Re-ordering can be very drastic as, for instance, by placing the altar on the north wall as authorised by Forbes Ch. in *Re St. Peter Roydon*[18] or by Newey Ch. as in *Re All Saints', Whistable*.[19]

Such petitions are justified by changing or developing ideas as to the physical framework of worship, in particular the now current idea that the altar should be near the congregation. Such petitions are often opposed on the ground that the opponents prefer to see the church as they remember it in their childhood. Some of these arguments are highly unprofitable and often show little but the opponents' ignorance of church history. For the church has evolved through the ages and so have the tastes of the congregations. History did not start or stop in the reign of Edward VII, and many people would be interested, and perhaps surprised, if they could see their familiar church as it was in the time of Elizabeth I or George III. On the other hand, some clergy, supported by a band of enthusiasts, are a little too much inclined to press ahead with reforms of this sort without sufficient effort to educate, or to consult with, the general body of the congregation.

There is very little law on this subject because the issue is one of discretion. But it has been helpful that in the Canons and in the decided cases about ornaments, noted in the previous

---

[17] Where there are claimed to be legal rights to individual pews, such claim may be a bar to reordering. See p. 108 and *Re St. Mary's, Banbury* [1987] Fam. 136.
[18] [1969] 1 W.L.R. 1849 at 1856.
[19] [1984] 1 W.L.R. 1164.

section, the efforts of the legislature and the courts have been directed to putting an end to archaic controversies by indicating that doctrinal significance does not attach to particular objects or the positions of particular objects in a church.

One point that is common to all these cases is that, since tastes have changed and will certainly change again, a reordering should not be irreversible. In *Re St. Stephen's, Walbrook*[20] the Archdeacon of London told the court that while there had been numerous cases of reordering in the London diocese, all had been reversible. The consistory court held that the introduction of a stone altar weighing 10 tons would violate this principle. The Court of Ecclesiastical Causes Reserved, while not questioning the principle, held that the proposals before them would be reversible. The Dean of the Arches in *Re St. Mary's, Banbury*[21] dealt with this point, saying that when a reordering is desired by the incumbent and P.C.C. it should normally be allowed "if this can be done without necessitating a permanent *and* irreversible change to the building."[22] Further, he added that: "Where such a change would be necessitated it will be necessary to balance the claims of the congregation against the claims of conservation."[23]

While some parts of the Dean's judgment were criticised by the Court of Ecclesiastical Causes Reserved in *Re St. Stephen's, Walbrook*, they did not comment on this passage, which can be taken as a practical guide to cases of this sort. It means, in broad terms, that to pull down structural features of the building or to remove them is likely to be objectionable, but to shift, introduce or remove moveable objects is not in itself objectionable on this ground. To introduce new structural features or bring in new and very heavy objects may well violate the principle of reversibility; but each case depends on its own facts.

Few issues can be more divisive and harmful in a parish than a case of re-ordering which becomes controversial and has to be heard in open court. Occasionally this extreme course is necessary, but great efforts should be made to avoid it. Cases of this sort seldom appear in the reports; although *Re St. Peter,*

---

[20] [1987] Fam. 146.
[21] [1987] Fam. 136.
[22] *Ibid.*
[23] *Ibid.*

Roydon[23a] is an exception; since they are always decided on particular facts; but the following observations may be of some help.

When the responsible officers of a parish first conceive the idea of re-ordering, they should consult the archdeacon and discuss the idea with him, preferably on the spot. They should keep the P.C.C. informed of what they are doing at every stage. With the help of the archdeacon they should approach the D.A.C. and invite it to send a delegation to inspect and discuss. In cases where it is physically practicable, they should invite the archdeacon to use the power, which is in many dioceses delegated to him, of allowing the proposed re-arrangements to be made for an experimental period of a few months. If, while the discussions are pending, there is an annual parochial church meeting, the matter should be reported to it fully and minuted. An opportunity should be given for the report to be debated. If the discussions are at a different time of year, a special parochial church meeting should often be called. In either case it is often wise to invite the archdeacon to preside, since that enables the incumbent to say what he wants to say without being open to the accusation that he has used the chair to say too much. Time, in many cases months, spent on consultations is well spent, and parish officers should aim, eventually, to present a petition which is backed by a unanimous P.C.C. and commended by the D.A.C. If so, and if the general body of the congregation feels that it has been fully informed and its views noted, there is a good prospect of the petition being unopposed. If so, the chancellor will seldom think a hearing necessary before he grants the petition. If a determined minority declares itself, the case will usually have to be heard. On such a hearing the chancellor is likely to look for evidence that the congregation has been fully and fairly consulted and its views considered. If that has indeed been done, the prospect is that he will allow the views of the incumbent and P.C.C., commended by the D.A.C., to prevail, at least if the proposals are reversible. But he is not likely to be, and should not be, too easily satisfied that proper consideration has been given to the views of all who are concerned.

One element in all these cases, which tends to be forgotten, is the cost. Petitioners should ensure that, if a hearing is needed, their witnesses can give full and convincing evidence that the

[23a] [1969] 1 W.L.R. 1849.

necessary money for the scheme can be found. While the P.C.C. is financially responsible for all the work to a church, and its views are entitled to great respect, it must not ride roughshod over a reasonable minority. It is particularly unhelpful, in a controversial case, to find that the critical decision of the P.C.C. was in fact that of its standing committee. The fullest and most open discussion in the parish is needed.

If there has been an experimental period sanctioned by the archdeacon, and if at the end of it the P.C.C. asks the court to make the arrangement permanent, that is usually an easy matter. By that stage, any reasonable opposition will have declared itself.

Disposal by sale or otherwise

Churches are in many cases equipped with more things of great value than they need, and in some cases the officers of a parish are anxious to part with some of those items by gift to a church which has recently been erected or to a church (especially in some diocese outside England) which is less well provided with property than most churches in England. An unselfish proposal of this sort deserves help and encouragement.[24] But the court must exercise a degree of caution before authorising a gift of this sort. It must be sure that enough plate will remain for the continuing needs of the donor church. It should also be slow to allow plate which has a long historical connection with the donor church to be given away, if there is some other object which could be given without destroying the historical link. Further, if the object to be given away was originally given in memory of some particular person, the court should make sure that that person will continue to be commemorated adequately in the place with which he was connected. These considerations, however, are not likely to produce much practical trouble, since parish officers are not often inclined to give away their best treasures. More commonly, indeed, they are disposed to turn their surplus treasures to immediate financial advantage and applications of this sort

---

[24] That faculties authorising gifts to religious and charitable purposes can properly be granted was expressly recognised by the Court of Arches in *Re St. Gregory's, Tredington* [1972] Fam. 236 at 243, 244 and 246.

require to be scrutinised with special care. They are not lightly to be encouraged. The Court of Arches dealt with the principles governing cases of this sort in *Re St. Gregory's, Tredington*.[25]

Any parties contemplating a sale of church treasures should be referred to the full text of this definitive judgment.[26] The main points which emerge are as follows[27]: first, churchwardens have the legal property in the goods of the church and can sell them with the consent of the vestry (now the P.C.C.) under the authority of a faculty: any sale without such consent and authority is void. Secondly, some special reason for a sale must be proved: that the goods in question are "redundant" is one possible ground, but not an essential ground nor is it the only possible ground: this is not a jurisdiction to authorise changes of investment. In assessing the "special reason" advanced by the petitioners, the court must take into account any "special character" of the ministry of the church in question.[28] Thirdly, the granting of a faculty is a matter for the discretion of the chancellor. In order to exercise it he is entitled to have the case fully argued and the witnesses adequately cross-examined. Therefore, if the case is otherwise unopposed the archdeacon should always enter appearance to put the petitioners to proof. Faculties of this sort should seldom, if ever, be granted without a hearing in open court. In the *Tredington* case the Court of Arches acted upon findings that the plate in question was redundant, in the sense that the church had plenty without it, and that there was a financial emergency, though saying that these were not the only grounds for allowing a sale. But they are much the commonest.

The evidence must, of course, be prepared elaborately. The petitioners must prove what plate the church has and the

---

[25] [1972] Fam. 236. In this case the court overruled the decision of Kempe Ch. in *The Vicar and Churchwardens of St. Mary, Northolt* v. *Parishioners of St. Mary's, Northolt* [1920] P. 97 (see at page 241H) and generally adopted *St. Mary's, Gilston* [1967] P. 125, *Re St. Mary's, Westwell* [1968] 1 W.L.R. 513 and the remarks of Sir Robert Phillimore in *Ecclesiastical Law* (1st ed., 1873) Vol. II, at pp. 1792 and 1797.

[26] Sir Harold Kent, Q.C., Dean of Arches stated in *Re St. Helen's, Brant Broughton* [1974] Fam. 16 at 18F that he was in agreement with the judgment of the Deputy Dean in the *Tredington* case on these matters.

[27] [1972] Fam. 236 at 239–246.

[28] This proposition derives from the observations of Sir Harold Kent, Q.C., Dean of the Arches, in *Re St. Martin's-in-the-Fields* (1972); unreported. The Dean, while accepting the principles of the *Tredington* judgment, reversed the decision of the consistory court in the case before him, applying this gloss to those principles. See *Re St. Mary le Bow* [1984] 1 W.L.R. 1363 at 1365–1368.

sufficiency of what will be left after a sale, and they must prove the financial emergency. To do so they will need to show why the proceeds of sale are wanted (*e.g.* that great and unexpected repairs are urgent or that some important project like building a church extension is unable to proceed for lack of money), explaining the finances of the P.C.C. fully and also the efforts which they have already made to find the money. And of course they must prove how much a sale is likely to raise. The D.A.C. and the C.C.C., and in some cases the national amenity societies, can help by providing the archdeacon with expert witnesses to evaluate the artistic and historical qualities of the object which is proposed for sale, and the need for any works which the proceeds of sale are designed to finance. It is to these points that the D.A.C. should from the beginning address itself. It is not called upon to say whether it is for or against a sale. That is a matter for the discretion of the court and the function of the advisory bodies is to supply relevant facts and expressions of artistic, architectural and historic opinion to help the court in what it has to do. The judgment in the *Tredington* case has been considered and applied in a number of subsequent cases both to allow and refuse disposals.[29]

If a sale is allowed, provision should be made as to the destination of the proceeds of sale and of any surplus which there may be after meeting the financial emergency. The money should be settled so that income is either paid to the P.C.C., or accumulated for a period.[30] The capital should not be touched without a further application to the court. But there have been cases in the diocese of London where goods of very great value have been sold and have brought a disproportionate windfall to the church. In these cases some of the proceeds have been diverted to other religious and charitable purposes elsewhere in the diocese. Proper provision should also be made for the

---

[29] *Re St. Mary's, Broadwater* [1976] Fam. 222; *Re St. Mary's, Warwick* [1981] Fam. 176; *Re St. Mary le Bow* [1984] 1 W.L.R. 1363; and *Re St. Agnes, Toxteth Park* [1985] 1 W.L.R. 641 (in each of which the disposal was allowed): and *Re St. Helen's, Brant Broughton* [1974] Fam. 16; *Re St. Andrew's, Thornhaugh* [1976] Fam. 230; *Re St. Mary's, Barton-upon-Humber* [1987] Fam. 41; *Re St. Mary of Charity, Faversham* [1986] Fam. 143 (in each of which the disposal was refused).

[30] See *Re St. Mary's, Gilston* [1967] P. 125. The accumulated fund after defraying the expenses which had given rise to the emergency was, by the end of 1987, many times more than the original proceeds of sale, a considerable protection for a small parish. The same was true at Tredington.

continued commemoration of the original person in whose memory, or by whom, the object was given. Detailed directions were given on these points by the Court of Arches in the *Tredington* case, which was then remitted to the court below to carry through the execution of the order.

Following the *Tredington* judgment a number of sales of treasures have been allowed on a sufficient cause having been shown.[31] But in 1983 the London Consistory Court was informed in *Re St. Mary le Bow*[32] by a former partner in Christies that, so far from the floodgates having been opened, the *Tredington* decision has produced a distinct shortage of church silver on the market. The *Tredington* decision was not designed to make it easy for parishes to employ what past parishioners have given so as to enable the current generation to evade its responsibilities and not to effect all necessary current repairs. Nor will anything short of the requirements in the *Tredington* judgment be sufficient, as appeared in *Re St. Helen's, Brant Broughton* where the Court of Arches upheld the decision of Goodman Ch. who declined to grant a faculty for the sale of a picture which was extremely expensive to protect and insure.[33]

Apart from cases where the officers of a parish wish to sell one of their treasures in order to raise money, or to give it or its proceeds away to a deserving cause which is both religious and charitable, there are often cases in which, consequent upon the re-ordering of the contents of a church, redundant goods, such as old pews and occasionally cracked bells, become disposable. These sales require the same consents as are necessary for the sale of a treasure and the authority of a faculty as well; otherwise the purchaser gets no title.[34] Sales of this sort tend to be made too readily to the first dealer in old wood or the like who offers. The things in question are often more valuable than the local

---

[31] In *Re St. Andrew's, Heddington* [1978] Fam. 121, a sale was allowed for reasons which appear to be within the rules laid down by the Court of Arches, in the *Tredington* case, although the learned chancellor did not expressly refer to them.

[32] [1984] 1 W.L.R. 1363.

[33] [1974] Fam. 16. On the other hand in an unreported case in the diocese of London a piece of wood used as a shelf in the vestry turned out to have a picture by an early Flemish Master on its underside. This picture was not in any real sense part of the equipment of the church having been given by a friend to the previous vicar and then employed by him as a shelf. The court allowed it to be sold.

[34] See *Re St. Mary's Barton-upon-Humber* [1987] Fam. 41.

people realise, and the views of the D.A.C. and its advice as to the sale should always be obtained.

Where a petition seeks authority to sell a church treasure the reasons for proposing the sale should be stated explicitly in the petition or in a document annexed thereto. The F.J.R. 1967 moreover make special provision for such cases in that, if the chancellor is of the opinion that the "article" in question is of historic or artistic interest, he may direct the registrar to serve notice on the C.C.C.; the petitioners must then send to the Council a full set of the papers. The Council is required to report to the judge within six weeks, and is allowed to give notice asking the court to hear evidence on its behalf. Such an application would normally be granted and the person nominated would appear as a judge's witness. The substance of a report by the Council is to be disclosed to all parties.[35]

Parochial libraries

In some parishes there are collections of books belonging to the churchwardens as part of the goods appertaining to the church. Any such library falls within the faculty jurisdiction in the ordinary way.

There is, however, a special sort of library existing in some parishes, but governed by the Parochial Libraries Act 1708. This Act begins by a recital that the clergy "in many places in the south parts of Great Britain called England and Wales" are so ill-provided for that they cannot afford to buy books "for the better prosecution of their studies." The recital continues by stating that recently charitable persons had "erected libraries within several parishes and districts in England and Wales but some provision is wanting to preserve the same and such others as shall be provided in the same manner from embezzlement." Section 1 deals with "such a library" and requires rules to be made by the founders. Sections 2 to 9 inclusive provide elaborate safeguards to discourage a clergyman from making away with any of the books in such a library and empowering the ordinary to enquire into the state and condition of such libraries at his vistitation. Finally, section 10 makes the books in such a library inalienable without the consent of the ordinary,

[35] F.J.R. 1967, rr. 5(8), 6(7), 6(11).

and then only where there is a duplicate of the book. It also empowers any Justice of the Peace to issue a search warrant if such book is "taken or otherwise lost out of the said library."

To relax the strictness of section 10 it was enacted by the E.J.M. 1963, s.6(1)(b)(ii) that the consistory court shall have jurisdiction in a cause of faculty for authorising the sale of books comprised in a library within the diocese, being a library to which the Parochial Libraries Act 1708 applies. Further, section 4(1) of the F.J.M. 1964 provides that a book in such a library may be sold under the authority of a faculty and "the proceeds of sale shall be applied for such of the ecclesiastical purposes of the parish as in such faculty may be directed." It further requires that the judge shall obtain and consider the advice of the D.A.C. before granting a faculty of this kind.

In section 4(1) a "parochial library" is qualified by the words "appropriated to the use of the minister of any parish or place within the operation of that Act [Parochial Libraries Act 1708.]" and by section 4(2) any question whether a library "is within the said Act and is so appropriated" is to be determined conclusively by the Charity Commissioners. The phrase "appropriated to the use of the minister of any parish or place" derives from section 4 of the Act of 1708.

Clearly the Parochial Libraries Act 1708 is of very limited application, being confined by its preamble to books presented for the use of the minister. Collections of books for the benefit of parishioners in general are within the normal rules for chattels appertaining to a church. Similarly the provisions cited above from the Measures of 1963 and 1964 can seldom be applicable.

There has, however, been one reported case under these sections[36] where Gage Ch. authorised a sale of a parochial library (admitted by all concerned to be a parochial library) to a university which had been housing it for the previous 20 years. The faculty was made subject to conditions (i) that the university should not sell the library for at least 100 years and (ii) that the library should be available "for

---

[36] *Re St. Mary's, Warwick* [1981] Fam. 170.

consultation by anyone with a genuine interest, including particularly officers and parishioners of St. Mary's, Warwick, and representatives of diocesan bodies."[37] The proceeds of sale[38] were made available to pay for the "repair of fabric, glass and ancient ornaments,"[39] of the church.

It does not appear why the books in question were admitted to be a "parochial library"; but it is clear from the judgment that the result would have been the same if the library had been treated as an ordinary church treasure to be dealt with under the principles laid down by the Court of Arches in *Re St. Gregory's, Tredington*[40], which indeed Gage Ch. expressly applied.[41]

Loan to museum or to cathedral treasury

It often happens that a parish has some really valuable objects which in practice have to be housed in a bank for security and are therefore seldom or never seen. In such cases, under due precautions as to insurance and security, the churchwardens should be encouraged to apply for a faculty authorising them to lend the things in question to a museum, or to the cathedral treasury if there is one.

The goods in question are held by the churchwardens on behalf of the parish and the same local consultation, should be held as in any other case where a faculty is necessary. In view of the decision in *Re St. Gregory's, Tredington*,[42] treasures are an ultimate security to the parish for dealing with financial emergencies. The P.C.C. should therefore have the opportunity to insist that anyone who borrows their treasures shall insure them for their full current value throughout the period of the loan. There is no difficulty about this point if the borrower is a museum, but it was proposed in the case of one cathedral treasury that the insurance should be for the true current value or £1,000 whichever would be *less*. It is difficult to see how any

---

[37] [1981] Fam. 170 at 175.
[38] £30,000.
[39] [1981] Fam. 170 at 175.
[40] [1972] Fam. 236.
[41] In an unreported case in 1982, the Bath and Wells consistory court authorised arrangements under which a library appertaining to Bath Abbey and long housed in the basement of a municipal building at Bath was removed to the skilful custody of the Cathedral Library at Wells.
[42] [1972] Fam. 236.

P.C.C. could be advised to accept such an arrangement. And the court would obviously have to consider the matter closely before granting a faculty on such terms.

Where the loan is to a great national or municipal museum, the court can rely for proper security on the public bodies who own these places. But where the loan was to a small country museum the author insisted on the museum trustees installing a specially fortified showcase with a wire connecting it direct to the police station. At St. Paul's Cathedral most elaborate security arrangements have been provided under experienced advice from museums. The dean and chapter undertook to insure the things lent to their full value. It was thus possible to prepare a set of forms of agreement between the dean and chapter and each set of churchwardens and a standard petition form. In all cases, after due citation, the faculties applied for passed the seal. These arrangements, once worked out, afford the necessary protection to each parish in lending its treasures to the cathedral and the scheme is very successful.

Heating, lighting and sound reinforcement

Adequate heating arrangements in a church are desirable for the reasonable comfort of the congregation and for the protection of the contents of the building against damp; but the equipment should never be allowed to injure the appearance of the building, as was the effect of many old-fashioned installations with festoons of ugly pipes or black stoves. Nor is all modern apparatus attractive to see. Particular attention should be given to the arrangements outside the church for housing large oil tanks.

The C.C.C. and most D.A.C.s have accumulated a great deal of information about heating in current use. While heating apparatus can scarcely improve the appearance of a church, good lighting should do so and bad lighting can do great harm. Wherever problems about lighting arise, there should be very full consultation before any petition is lodged. Some churches benefit by a bright light to show up the beauties of a vault; others may be better treated by retaining much upper darkness, with its numinous suggestions, and concentrating the lights on the prayer and hymn books of the congregation. Adequate light is essential for a lectern, a pulpit or the priest's stall. Care should be taken not to have unsightly wiring and switchgear.

Sound reinforcement is often extremely valuable in a large church or one which happens to have bad acoustics; but the loudspeakers are not necessarily beautiful, and can easily do damage to the look of the church.

On all these subjects it is important that there should be full consultation, before any petition is lodged. In addition to the archdeacon, who should be consulted at the outset, the church architect should always be concerned as well as the relevant kinds of contractors and other experts. Cases of these sorts practically never need, or should, be the subject-matter of a hearing in court. The function of the consistory court is to make sure that every project is thoroughly discussed and competently advised upon. In every case the D.A.C. should be concerned from an early stage and the intending petitioners should provide it with full specifications and diagrams. Photographs will often help, and it is frequently desirable that a delegation from the committee should visit the church before giving its formal advice. The statutory form of petition for a faculty includes a question whether the approval of the church's insurers has been obtained: this applies to all lighting and heating cases and the court will check that in these cases an adequate answer is given, with supporting documents.

Since 1950 there has been no reported decision about heating or sound reinforcement. In regard to lighting there is, as we saw, a decision of the Court of Arches that six candles on an altar or retable are not unlawful, though the tradition in England is in favour of there being two.[43] It has also been held that a sanctuary lamp on an altar is a legal ornament,[44] and that electric "candles" on an altar are undesirable.[45] These decisions are no doubt interesting, but they do not touch the great problems of lighting a church so as to help the worshippers and

---

[43] *Re St. Saviour's Church, Walthamstow* [1951] P. 147. See also *Re St. George's, Southall* [1952] 1 All E.R. 323 and *Re St. Mary, Tyne Dock* [1954] P. 369.
[44] *Re All Saints, Leamington Priors* [1963] 1 W.L.R. 806.
[45] *Re St. Andrew's, Dearnley* [1981] Fam. 50. This decision contains a useful summary of the customs and practice of the Church of England about the use of lights. The objection to electric "candles" was that they purported to be something which they are not, *i.e.* candles.

add to the beauty of the building. These are practical and aesthetic issues and not legal ones.

Reservation of the sacrament

Sixty years ago there was much controversy about the reservation of the sacrament. By reservation is meant that, at the end of the celebration of the Holy Communion, bread and wine which have been consecrated are taken away from the altar and put in a place of safety to be used, as occasion arises, for the communion of persons who were not present at the celebration. This practice started long before the Reformation and was expressly recognised, for the purposes of the communion of the sick, in the first prayer book of Edward VI.[46] However, the prayer book of 1662 contained a rubric which required that such of the elements as had not already been given to communicants should be consumed at the end of the service and not carried out of the church.[47] The reasons for this rubric have been in controversy, though there is at least some reason to suppose that it may have been directed against "profanation [of the sacrament] by the taking away of the consecrated elements and consuming them as though they were common food at an ordinary meal."[48] However that may be, the prayer book of 1662 had the authority of Parliament in the Act of Uniformity and the rubric has been held to have made reservation of the sacrament illegal.[49] Whether it was theologically objectionable is quite another matter, though some authorities found that it was contrary to the 25th and 28th of the 39 articles. However, in the prayer book of 1927, which was approved by all Houses of the Church Assembly, and again in that of 1928 which was similarly approved, but both of which failed to obtain the approval of the

---

[46] See *Re St. Mary, Tyne Dock (No. 2)* [1958] P. 156; the text of the rubric of 1549 is set out at 159.
[47] See *Re Lapford (Devon) Parish Church* [1955] P. 205. The text of the rubric is set out at 210.
[48] See *per* Garth Moore Ch. in *Re St. Michael and All Angels, Bishopwearmouth* [1958] 1 W.L.R. 1183 at 1187.
[49] *Re Lapford (Devon) Parish Church* [1955] P. 205 at 210. Reservation was earlier held to be illegal in a number of cases including at least one decision of the Court of Arches, see *Bishop of Oxford* v. *Henly* [1907] P. 88. But these decisions were before the events in connection with the prayer books of 1927 and 1928 discussed below.

House of Commons, there were express provisions for the reservation of the sacrament for the communion of the sick. On the failure of these prayer books to be passed by Parliament, the bishops were in a dilemma. Reservation in uncontrolled circumstances was common, despite its illegality, but its theological propriety had been established by both prayer books having been adopted by all Houses of the Assembly.

In 1929, therefore, the bishops issued a statement[50] which prayed in aid their *jus liturgicum* to regulate the practice on the lines laid down by the prayer books which the Assembly had approved, notwithstanding the technical illegality of this practice. This statement has become the basis of modern practice and the church is much indebted to the courage of the bishops in issuing it "for the purpose of keeping peace within the church in 1928 (*sic*), which at that time was threatened by disintegration,"[51] which the action of the bishops has prevented.

The practice is, in effect, that a bishop treats himself as entitled in his diocese to authorise reservation of the sacrament in a place of safety, for purposes which he defines. Usually, but not necessarily always, these are for the communion of the sick, and also for some groups of parishioners whose work prevents them from being present at the services in church.[52] The conditions prescribe the place of safety in which the consecrated elements are to be kept and the circumstances in which they may be used.

Since the arrangements for the place of safety invariably include work which can only be done under faculty, the ecclesiastical courts had to decide what they should do, faced, as they were, with the illegality of the whole practice. Their action was first discussed in a judgment of Vaisey Ch. in the Wakefield

---

[50] Quoted in full by the Dean of the Arches in *Re Lapford (Devon) Parish Church* [1955] P. 205 at 213.

[51] See *per* Garth Moore Ch. in *Re St. Peter & St. Paul, Leckhampton* [1968] P. 495 at 500A. But the details of the Bishops' statement are not necessarily binding in the changed circumstances of 60 years later, and effect should be given to the express directions of the reigning bishop, as Garth Moore Ch. there pointed out.

[52] It was only the communion of the sick which was contemplated in the rubric of 1549 or in those of the abortive prayer books of 1927 and 1928. In the *Lapford* case [1955] P. 205 at 211 the bishop had allowed it for a somewhat wider class; the Dean of the Arches regarded the matter as in the bishop's discretion, but he said "Any such extension should be carefully watched..."

consistory court in 1941,[53] emphasising that their action is ancillary to that of a bishop and is concerned with the reverent security of the consecrated elements which, as Vaisey Ch. observed, might otherwise have been "housed in some unworthy place such as a cupboard in the vestry" (or, perhaps, in the parsonage house).

This view of the matter was upheld by Sir Philip Baker-Wilbraham, Dean of the Arches, in *Re Lapford Church* notwithstanding certain earlier decisions to the contrary.[54]

The normal practice in the dioceses where the author is chancellor, which he believes is almost universally followed by his brethren, is for the reservation to be in a locked aumbry or safe,[55] usually on the north wall near the main altar, or the altar of the side chapel, the aumbry often being covered by a curtain and nearly always accompanied by a light[56] to indicate the presence of the sacrament. There must always be an express authorisation in writing by the diocesan bishop, or in London the area bishop; and the exact position and arrangements must be approved in writing by the archdeacon. The faculty is always expressed to operate only until further order, so as to enable the court to keep control in case of any abuse.[57]

Though an aumbry is the usual receptacle, there is authority that a hanging pyx, or cage, is equally legitimate though in such cases it is necessary to look rather more carefully to security than is necessary in the case of an aumbry.[58] On the other hand a tabernacle, that is a cupboard, in the middle of the altar, is still held to be illegal.[59] The difference between a pyx and a tabernacle is not at all obvious; but historically a pyx was

---

[53] *Re St. Mary Magdalene, Altofts* (1941); unreported. This decision was approved by the Dean of the Arches in the *Lapford* case at 214; but it is published only as a note at the end of *Re St. Mary, Tyne Dock (No. 2)* [1958] P. 156 at 172.

[54] [1955] P. 205 at 214.

[55] See *Re St. Mary, Tyne Dock* [1954] P. 369, *per* Hylton-Foster Ch. at 377; *Re St. Mary, Tyne Dock (No. 2)* [1958] P. 156, *per* Wigglesworth Deputy Chancellor at 169 and *Re St. Michael and All Angels, Bishopwearmouth* [1958] 1 W.L.R. 1183, *per* Garth Moore Ch. at 1185 *et seq*. Thereafter the matter has not been sufficiently in controversy to have been worth reporting.

[56] As to the light, see *per* Vaisey Ch. in *Re St. Mary Magdalene, Altofts* [1958] P. 156 at 173 and *per* Garth Moore Ch. in *Re St. Michael and All Angels, Bishopwearmouth* [1958] 1 W.L.R. 1183 at 1191.

[57] See *Re St. Mary, Tyne Dock (No. 2)* [1958] P. 156 at 166.

[58] See *Re St. Nicholas, Plumstead* [1961] 1 W.L.R. 916 at 920.

[59] See *Re St. Mary, Tyne Dock* [1954] P. 373 at 375 and see the earlier cases there cited.

common in England before the Reformation while tabernacles were never in general use in England.[60] The arrangements, above described, have worked without any difficulty at all in all the dioceses with which the author is acquainted and there has in fact been no reported case anywhere on this form of practice since 1967.[61]

Moreover as Garth Moore Ch. pointed out in *Re St. Peter and St. Paul, Leckhampton*,[62] it is at least doubtful whether reservation is now illegal in all cases. For the rubrics[63] in the alternative service book, authorised by virtue of the Prayer Book (Alternative and Other Services) Measure 1965, are not in the same terms as the rubric of 1662 in that they only say that "the consecrated bread and wine when it is not required for the purposes of communion" shall be consumed, a phrase which Garth Moore Ch. held referred to communion in general and did not indicate communion at that or at any particular service. This reasoning, strictly, does not apply to elements consecrated at a service conducted under the prayer book of 1662. But at least it does apply to all services conducted under the alternative service book, and it serves to establish that it is not longer axiomatic that reservation is universally illegal as was previously in theory the case. Thus the controversies, which caused so much trouble in the church earlier in the present century, have happily been laid to rest, though it remains true that the procedure described above must be scrupulously followed in every case.

Burial in church of cremated remains

Cremated remains may be buried in a church under the authority of a faculty,[64] and this privilege is occasionally accorded to a benefactor of the church or a person very closely connected with it, for example an incumbent. But the privilege

---

[60] *Re St. Nicholas, Plumstead* [1961] 1 W.L.R. 916 at 918–920.
[61] *Re St. Peter & St. Paul, Leckhampton* [1968] P. 495, a case where the aumbry was not in the normal position. For a case about a "sacrament house" see *Re St. Matthew's, Wimbledon* [1985] 3 All E.R. 670.
[62] [1968] P. 495 at 499.
[63] Rubric 49 in rite A or rubric 42 in rite B. In the *Leckhampton* case Garth Moore Ch. was referring to rubric 40 in the "second series" book: it was in the same terms.
[64] *Re Kerr* [1894] P. 284.

must be closely guarded; otherwise there would be nowhere to draw the line and much embarrassment would ensue. The privilege should be regarded as extremely rare. A faculty for this purpose was refused in *Re St. Peter's, Folkestone*,[65] notwithstanding that the court allowed a tablet to be erected in the church in memory of the person whose ashes were concerned.

Occasionally faculties are granted for a "columbarium," so called because it is an architectural device which consists of pigeonholes[66], in which caskets containing ashes can be placed. The author has been concerned with columbaria in the dioceses of London, St. Albans and Bath and Wells. Specimens of the documents can be sought in the registries of those dioceses. It is important that the regulations for operating a columbarium, which the faculty authorises, should be drawn up with minute care. The problem is to define whose ashes can be put in the columbarium and in what sort of containers and who is to make the decision. A difficulty is that once the ashes of any member of a family are thus deposited, there can easily be applications in respect of all the relatives of that person; the space will soon become full. On the whole, though the author has allowed the creation of a number of columbaria, he is doubtful whether the practice should be encouraged. A call for a columbarium arises in respect of churches without churchyards; but almost all churches have land round them in which a cremation plot can be set aside and where there is much more room than there ever could be inside the church. Since it is only ashes and not bodies which require interment, there is no need for the plot to be consecrated as a burial ground. That being so, there is no general right of burial in one of these areas; the matter is one of grace and can be regulated by the faculty, so that the facilities may continue for as long as possible.

Armorial bearings

In connection with the Coronation of 1953 a number of parishes wished to erect the royal arms in their churches and a controversy ensued between Garth Moore Ch. and Macmorran Ch. on the one side and the Home Office on the other. The latter

---

[65] [1982] 1 W.L.R. 1283.
[66] From the Latin, *Columba*; a pigeon.

asserted that its leave was necessary for the erection of the Royal Arms. Each of these learned chancellors held that if the Royal Arms were being erected to symbolise the royal supremacy (in the same way as the same arms are put up in secular courts of law) no leave, otherwise than by faculty, was required. The two judgments deserve to be studied in full.[67] It also appears from these judgments that the arms of the diocese or the province can be put up under faculty without any other leave, but that the arms of other persons or bodies, for example the local authority, should be put up only with the leave of the person whose arms are concerned.

Heraldry is an exact science, and it is far too easy for uninstructed persons to get it wrong. Thus in any case involving coats of arms, expert advice should be sought. Since this is not a subject which arises very often, a good many D.A.C.'s include no such expert and advice should in those cases be sought elsewhere.

Memorial tablets

To be commemorated by a memorial tablet in a church "is never a matter of right, but is always one of privilege, and it is a privilege which should be sparingly conceded."[68] This view was repeated recently by Phillips Ch.,[69] and again by Owen Q.C., Dean of the Arches, in *Re St. Margaret's, Eartham*.[70] No memorial in a church can be erected save under the authority of a faculty and the present Dean of the Arches has pointed out that failure to realise the need for a faculty is likely to lead to hardship, heartache and financial waste.[71] Moreover, the dean said that "Incumbents have a responsibility to prevent breaches of this rule."[72] Accordingly every tentative approach by members of the family of a deceased person, enquiring whether they may put up a memorial to him, should be received by the incumbent

---

[67] *Re St. Paul's Church, Battersea* [1954] 1 W.L.R. 920 and *Re West Tarring Church* [1954] 1 W.L.R. 923.
[68] *Per* Sir Philip Baker Wilbraham, Dean of the Arches, in *Dupuis* v. *Parishioners of Ogbourne St. George* [1941] P. 119 at 121.
[69] *Re St. Nicholas, Brockenhurst* [1978] Fam. 157. For another case where a memorial was allowed, see *Re St. Peter's, Folkestone* [1982] 1 W.L.R. 1283.
[70] [1981] 1 W.L.R. 1129.
[71] *Ibid.*, at 1133G.
[72] *Ibid.*, at 1134B and C.

with extreme caution and subjected to a full process of consultation from long before any petition is lodged with the court.

Those who seek this privilege must present a case of "exceptionality," examples of which were given by the dean as follows:

> "The character of, or outstanding service to church, country or mankind by the person to be commemorated... a desire to record by the memorial some important or significant aspect of local or national history, and some family history or tradition of such memorials especially, but not necessarily, if any future application based on the family connection would be impossible."[72a]

The onus of proof is, throughout, on the petitioners. Moreover, the dean stated that the exceptionality upon the basis of which the petition is based must be expressly stated in the petition.

Further the monument, if erected, must be such as will embellish the church, since nothing ugly should ever be allowed to be introduced and moreover it must not contain anything that could cause offence.[73]

The tests to be passed are therefore severe. Some chancellors have thought it desirable to hold a preliminary hearing on the issue of exceptionality, so that, if a petition would fail on that point, the petitioner can be spared the considerable expense of obtaining a design. On the whole, however, it is better that both aspects of the case, exceptionality and embellishment, should proceed together through the consultative process and it may be as well for the archdeacon to find out informally from the chancellor whether he thinks at an early stage that there are the makings of a case of exceptionality. Embellishment, on the other hand, is a matter on which the views of the D.A.C. are important, since they are the advisers of the chancellor on matters of aesthetics. The committee must, of course, give close consideration to the appearance of the memorial itself and must consider it in its physical context. One element which arises frequently is to

---

[72a] [1981] 1 W.L.R. 1129 at 1134B and C.
[73] *Dupuis* v. *Parishioners of Ogbourne St. George* [1941] P. 119 at 121.

consider whether the church is in danger of becoming cluttered with memorials.[74] The process of preparing to present a petition for a memorial in a church is bound to be lengthy and indeed some chancellors have taken the view that the petition should only be presented, say, five years after the death of the person to be commemorated, so that his career may be seen in perspective and so that the matter is not dealt with in the pangs of recent bereavment. It is important to give much thought to the inscription, not only for its lettering but for its content, so as to avoid the boastful, the sentimental or the banal.

In earlier days inscriptions sometimes gave rise to controversy in that they included requests for prayers for the deceased person in such terms as to imply the doctrine of purgatory condemned by the 22nd article of religion. This was indeed the ground on which the memorial was refused in *Dupuis* v. *Parishioners of Ogbourne St-George*.[75] Since then, however, Ellison Ch. in *Re Parish of South Creake*,[76] has delivered a learned and exhaustive judgment explaining that it has been the custom of the church, since at least the days of St. Ambrose, to pray for the repose of the souls of the departed and that such prayers do not inherently import the forbidden doctrine. This judgment, it is submitted, is definitive.[77]

The memorial, if erected, does not become the property of the incumbent as freeholder of the church to which it is attached, still less does it belong to the churchwardens as goods of the church. In *Re St. Mary's, Broadwater*[78] Buckle Ch. allowed churchwardens to sell a helmet which had been one of the accoutrements of a tomb that had become detached from it and was kept in a bank. This decision could, perhaps, be supported on the ground that the churchwardens were in *de facto* possession and the heir at law of the person commemorated had expressly said that he raised no objection to the sale. Even so, it is a little difficult to see what title the churchwardens could have transferred to the purchaser, except bare possession. Another

---

[74] It was on this very point that controversy arose in the parish in *Re St. Mary the Virgin, Selling* [1980] 1 W.L.R. 1545.
[75] [1941] P. 119.
[76] [1959] 1 W.L.R. 427.
[77] See also *Re St. Mary The Virgin, Ilmington* [1962] P. 147, which concerned an inscription on a memorial in a churchyard.
[78] [1976] Fam. 222.

case about a helmet arose in the following year in *Re St. Andrew's, Thornhaugh*[79] where a rector and churchwardens were refused a faculty for the sale of the helmet. Though this case was not professionally argued, Fitzwalter Butler Ch. had the assistance of a number of very distinguished persons and the matters of title were fully investigated. His decision, it is submitted, is a more reliable guide to the general situation in cases about armorial appurtenances than is that of Buckle Ch. in the *Broadwater* case. On the other hand there are contradictory elements in the remarks of Fitzwalter Butler Ch. about the effect of section 3 of the F.J.M. 1964.[80] However, since that section applies to all monuments, it will be more conveniently discussed below in relation to memorials in churchyards.

The present section has been concerned with memorials which are only memorials and nothing else. Objects of all sorts including for instance stained glass, which are proposed to be given to a church in memory of someone, raise quite different considerations. Petitions for their introduction are to be considered on the practical and aesthetic merits of the object concerned in the ordinary way: a small and unobtrusive plaque or inscription attached to or engraved on the object, stating in whose memory the object was given, is of course readily permissible, as is also wording in a stained glass window to the same effect.

---

[79] [1976] Fam. 230.
[80] *Ibid.*, at 235.

5. Churchyards

Introductory

Churchyards are of various kinds. First, there is the churchyard, either adjacent to a church or elsewhere, which has been consecrated and set apart for the burial of the dead. Such a churchyard may be either in present use or disused. If disused, it may either have been closed by Order in Council or merely have fallen into disuse because it is full. Churchyards which are being used, or have been used, for burials, are presumed to have been duly consecrated unless there is strong reason for suggesting the contrary. Most churchyards adjacent to ancient churches are of this sort, and are as such within the jurisdiction of the consistory court. Occasionally one finds a consecrated public burial ground adjacent to an ordinary churchyard as was the case in *Re Coleford Cemetery*.[1]

Secondly, there are unconsecrated churchyards adjacent to churches; this situation is fairly common where the church was erected during the nineteenth or twentieth century. In such cases it is usually easy to discover, in the registry of the diocese in which the church was when it was consecrated, exactly what is provided by the original sentence of consecration.[2] In these modern, or relatively modern, cases the church alone was consecrated and the surrounding enclosure, usually in the ownership of the incumbent, is unconsecrated churchyard.

---

[1] [1984] 1 W.L.R. 1369. This consecrated area was vested in the (civil) parish council.

[2] Documents of this sort have in many cases, though not always, been lodged for safe custody with the local County Records Office. They are not usually transferred when the church is transferred from one diocese to another. Thus the documents discussed in *Re St. Peter's, Bushey Heath* [1971] 1 W.L.R. 357 were found with the records of the diocese of London in which that church originally was and not with those of the diocese of St. Albans in which it now is. Similarly, many documents relating to churchyards in Bedfordshire are still at Lincoln in which diocese Bedfordshire was until the 19th century, or in Ely in which diocese Bedfordshire was for a time during that century. Now it is in the St. Albans diocese.

Such churchyards are and always have been within the jurisdiction of the consistory court. A complication was introduced by section 7 of the F.J.M. 1964, which declared that the curtilage of a church is within the jurisdiction of the consistory court. "Curtilage" is a comparatively narrow word and parts of an unconsecrated churchyard may well not be within the scope of the word "curtilage"; but the greater includes the less and since unconsecrated churchyards have always been subject to the jurisdiction of the court it is difficult to see what practical difference section 7 made.[3]

The importance of these distinctions is that if a churchyard or curtilage is unconsecrated it is possible for the court to make orders enabling legal estates or interests in it to be created or transferred, and what can properly be allowed by such an order is determined primarily by the need to protect the church (*i.e.* the building). On the other hand, in a consecrated churchyard vested in the rector or incumbent the legal fee simple is in abeyance, so that no legal or equitable interest can be created out of the fee simple, and what can properly be allowed by licence is determined primarily by the need to uphold the status of the churchyard as a place for the repose, under the protection of the court, of the mortal remains of the deceased and only secondarily (though often importantly) by the need to protect the church to which such churchyard is adjacent, if there is one.

If a consecrated churchyard is closed by Order in Council it is permissible for the court to allow a limited category of works (*e.g.* road-widening) if there are good reasons of public advantage for doing so, even if that involves moving, reverently, to other consecrated ground some human remains. But if the churchyard is still open, nothing can be authorised which will prevent any part of it being used for future burials as and when it may be required.[4] The

---

[3] "Curtilage" was discussed in *Re St. John's Church, Bishop's Hatfield* [1967] P. 113 and *Re St. Peter's, Bushey Heath* [1971] 1 W.L.R. 357. Both "curtilage" and unconsecrated churchyard are discussed in *Re St. George's, Oakdale* [1976] Fam. 210, *Re Christ Church, Chislehurst* [1973] 1 W.L.R. 1317 and *Re St. Mary Magdalene, Paddington* [1980] Fam. 99. The word is used in other legislation, *e.g.* the Gun Licence Act 1870, s.7 and the Larceny Act 1916, ss.26 and 46(3).

[4] In a large country churchyard not closed for burials there may well be space not already used for burials and not required for that purpose in the immediate future. In at least two cases in the diocese of Bath and Wells a faculty has recently been granted for the temporary erection of an ecclesiastical building, in one case an extension of the church school, on such an area. The faculty provided for the removal of the building when the space is eventually needed for burials.

question what can lawfully be allowed in a consecrated burial ground was fully discussed by the London consistory court in *Re St. John's, Chelsea*,[5] which was approved by the Chancery Court of York in *Re St. Mary The Virgin, Woodkirk*.[6] *Re St. John's, Chelsea* has not so far been considered by the Arches Court of Canterbury; but it is not likely that that court will take a different view from the appellate court of the northern province, and in practice the decision in the *Chelsea* case is normally regarded as correct throughout both provinces. Apart from principle, it is expedient that the limits imposed by the sentence of consecration be observed scrupulously. The legislature has provided, in particular by the Pastoral Measure 1983 and also the Town and Country Planning Act 1971, methods by which, in defined circumstances and subject to special and usually somewhat prolonged procedures, the effect of consecration can be cancelled. However it is not for the judges to lend themselves to evading the statutory safeguards.

Yet a further complication is introduced by section 3 of the D.B.G.A. 1884, which prohibits any building whatever on a disused burial ground unless the building is an extension of the church. This legislation has been much discussed in recent times, mainly in connection with the vestries and halls which are now commonly erected contiguous to churches.[7] Apart from this one exception, the prohibition is absolute and has been held in a series of cases to prohibit all sorts of projects which might have been deemed useful.[8]

Here again, despite apparent inconvenience, and indeed the irrationality of some of the results of the enactment, it is not for the judges to lend themselves to evasions of its strict application.[9] It is to be hoped that this legislation, the origins of which are obscure, will be repealed. In the meantime it must be

---

[5] [1962] 1 W.L.R. 706.
[6] [1969] 1 W.L.R. 1867.
[7] See pp. 95 *et seq.*
[8] See further pp. 153 *et seq.*
[9] In *Paddington Corporation* v. *Attorney-General* [1906] A.C. 1, the House of Lords seems to have held that a screen erected on a disused burial ground for the purpose of preventing the acquisition of a right of light over it is not a "building" for these purposes. Similarly, it is thought that scaffolding, erected temporarily for the purpose of constructing or repairing a building, perhaps the church itself, adjacent to the disused burial ground is not in itself a building within the meaning of the Act.

enforced scrupulously by the ecclesiastical courts so far as their jurisdiction allows. There are arrangements also for enforcement by secular proceedings, and the ecclesiastical court should give notice to the secular enforcement authority of any case coming to its notice where an infringement of the Act seems likely to occur.[10]

The particular applications of the distinctions discussed generally in this section are discussed further below. It is essential, in a case involving work to, on, or under a churchyard for the court to discover, at a very early stage, exactly what is the status of the churchyard concerned. If the case starts on the wrong basis, a great deal of time and effort is bound to be wasted.

Finally, there are many cases of consecrated areas in municipal cemeteries. These areas are sometimes, though not always, away from any church and the only powers enforced by the consistory courts in respect of such cases are those which are directed to protecting the remains of the dead, which are in such consecrated ground under the protection of those courts. Accordingly, they do not in practice seek to control what tombstones can be erected in such places as they do in the case of ordinary churchyards. In fact the municipal control of the introduction of tombstones is often a good deal more stringent than that imposed in ordinary churchyards by the consistory courts. It is the municipal authority which pays for the maintenance and upkeep of the cemetery and within wide limits it is entitled to make what arrangements it pleases. Where, as happens occasionally, a consecrated municipal cemetery is immediately adjacent to a churchyard surrounding a church, the court will concern itself more fully with it, as occurred in *Re Coleford Cemetery*[11], for example, where the court refused to allow a line of posts and wires for supplying electricity to a nearby house. In such a case it may also be expedient for the parochial authorities to come to some special arrangements in regard to that area so as to protect the church and its churchyard.

---

[10] See the discussion of secular enforcement in *Re St. Luke's, Chelsea* [1976] Fam. 295 at 312, 313, following the earlier authorities there mentioned.
[11] [1984] 1 W.L.R. 136.

Burial rights

In a parish where there is a consecrated churchyard, every parishioner has a right for his remains to be buried in the churchyard,[12] without any need for the leave of the incumbent, "but permission of the ordinary is necessary before any monument can properly be erected."[13] A person whose name is on the electoral roll of a parish at the time of his death now has a like right.[14] So has a person dying in the parish, whoever he is.[15] Normally, no other class of persons may be buried in the churchyard, except with the consent of the parishioners and churchwardens, whose parochial right is thereby invaded and also of the incumbent whose soil is broken.[16] The necessary consent must now be given by the P.C.C. rather than by the vestry, as in the case of the sales of valuables.[17] If the incumbent declines to allow the burial of a person who has no right of burial, his decision cannot be called in question in the consistory court.[18]

The position in a churchyard where any given burial is to take place is a matter for the incumbent to decide, and he is entitled at his discretion to prescribe any position, including one where there has been a former burial, except such positions as are reserved by faculty.[19] Thus, over the centuries, most churchyards have been buried over more than once, but the fact that the remains of a particular person are in a particular place gives

---

[12] This ancient legal right was for the interment of corpses. Canon B38 implies that it now extends, at least as a matter of canon law, binding on the clergy, to ashes.

[13] *Per* Sir William Scott in *Maidman* v. *Malpas* (1884) 1 Hag.Com. 125 at 208 cited by Graham Ch. in *Re St. Paul, Hanging Heaton* [1968] 1 W.L.R. 1210 at 1211. The power of the ordinary in this instance is exercised by the consistory court: *per* Garth Moore Ch. in *Re Woldingham Churchyard* [1957] 1 W.L.R. 811 at 812.

[14] Church of England (Miscellaneous Provisions) Measure 1976, s.6(1).

[15] See Phillimore, *Ecclesiastical Law* (1st ed., 1873) Vol. I, at p. 843. This right can cause difficulties if there is in a parish a large public institution which does not have its own burial ground. One possible solution is to seek the closure of the churchyard and then to apply for a faculty reserving an area for the interment of the ashes of ordinary parishioners and persons on the electoral roll.

[16] Phillimore, *Ecclesiastical Law* (1st ed., 1873) Vol. I, at p. 843. See also Church of England (Miscellaneous Provisions) Measure 1975, s.6(2).

[17] Compare *Re St. Gregory's, Tredington* [1972] Fam. 236 at 240G; and see *Re St. Nicholas, Baddesley Ensor* [1983] Fam. 1 at 5.

[18] *Re St. Nicholas, Baddesley Ensor* [1983] Fam. 1.

[19] See at pp. 163 *et seq*. Such faculties may be granted either for corpses or for cremated remains, the latter usually in an area set apart for them.

no legal right to the successors of the deceased save that his remains may not be disturbed in their resting place in consecrated ground otherwise than under the licence of the ordinary.[20]

These ancient arrangements are interfered with by the modern practice of erecting monuments over a large proportion of all burials; for the monument belongs to those who erected it[21] and cannot be moved except under faculty. The freedom of the incumbent to choose where a burial is to take place is thus much restricted in practice. The presence of a great number of monuments much increases the cost to the P.C.C. of keeping the grass cut and generally maintaining the churchyard in a good condition[22]; this has led to many petitions for clearing away monuments or parts of monuments (especially kerbstones), if they are untended.[23] Further, in most dioceses the chancellor has issued instructions as to the shape of any new monuments which are to be introduced without a faculty, particularly by forbidding incumbents to permit the introduction of kerbstones and controlling the size and shape of the monuments themselves.[24]

The general management of the churchyard is a matter for the P.C.C., which is entitled to make reasonable regulations relating to such matters as mounds and flowers; but its actions cannot validate or invalidate anything that needs to be done by the ordinary. One of the most satisfactory ways of keeping a churchyard in good shape has been found lately to be to put sheep into it, reverting to the ancient practice. In the rural diocese of Bath and Wells, the chancellor issued a circular of advice on this subject in 1980; but it is not a matter requiring a faculty. Such arrangements operated successfully for several years in the churchyard of Bishop's Cannings in the diocese of Salisbury. They do not in any way interfere with the rights of burial discussed in this section.

---

[20] Phillimore, *Ecclesiastical Law* (1st ed., 1873) Vol. I, at p. 879; see also *Re Dixon* [1892] P. 386.
[21] Or to the heirs of the person commemorated, see p. 146.
[22] This liability falls on the P.C.C. under the Parochial Church Councils (Powers) Measure 1956, s.4(ii)(c).
[23] See pp. 145 *et seq*.
[24] See pp. 169 *et seq*.. See also *per* Graham Ch. in *Re St. Paul, Hanging Heaton* [1968] 1 W.L.R. 1210 at 1212.

In a churchyard closed for burials by Order in Council, cremated remains may nevertheless be buried under the authority of a faculty.[25] Faculties setting apart one area in a closed churchyard for the burial of cremated remains are common.

Re-ordering of churchyards

Faculties are often applied for by the authorities of parishes for re-ordering their churchyards. By "re-ordering" is meant the removal, altogether or to a new position, of monuments or parts of monuments, either so that the ground under the places which these objects have occupied may be used for further burials, or to make it easier to cut the grass, or both.

Such applications raise issues of considerable delicacy, legal, historic, aesthetic and emotional; they must be handled with quite exceptional care. These issues are discussed in Chapter 11 of *The Churchyards Handbook*.[26] The first step to be taken by anyone who contemplates promoting such an application is to study that chapter; the next is to consult the archdeacon, the D.A.C. and the church architect.

While most tombstones of the seventeenth or eighteenth centuries, or earlier, are individual works of art, and should therefore normally be retained (though not necessarily in the same positions) the same cannot be said of those of later date. Kerbstones are seldom of aesthetic merit and they cause quite disproportionate inconvenience to those who have to maintain the churchyard: provision is normally made for removing them altogether, unless they are part of a grave which is still tended. It is not appropriate, even if it is feasible, to reduce the churchyard simply to an open lawn; its essence is that it is a consecrated burial ground, normally close to a church. Every case differs from every other, and there can be no standard form of scheme. Spafford Ch. in the Manchester consistory court[27]

---

[25] See *Re Kerr* [1894] P. 284. This case actually concerned the burial of cremated remains in a church; but the reasoning of Tristram Ch. about the effects of closure applied equally to a churchyard.

[26] (2nd ed., 1976), by the Revd. H. Stapleton, F.S.A. and P. Burman, F.S.A., published by C.I.O. Publishing, Church House, Dean's Yard, London, SW1P 3NZ.

[27] *Re St. James', Heywood* [1982] 1 W.L.R. 1289.

stated recently some of the considerations which appeared to him to be helpful in dealing with cases of this kind. His remarks are for that reason of interest, but they are not in any way binding, even in his own diocese; for the chancellor was not dealing with any questions of law but those of discretion; in every case the discretion has to be exercised upon its own facts.

The present section is concerned with cases in which a petition has been lodged after the fullest consultations, as suggested by *The Churchyards Handbook*.

The court is concerned to see that no rights of property are violated and to ensure that all persons having relevant interests are given sufficient opportunities to assert their rights and to state their cases.

Normally, therefore, the court gives directions for advertisements to be put in the local press on several occasions before the citation is issued. It enquires whether local archaeologists and other knowledgeable persons have had an opportunity to study the monuments while they are *in situ*, to record them, and to decipher any that may seem to be illegible, bearing in mind that to the skilled eye many that seem illegible can in fact be read. Then the court must look at the plans submitted, showing the stones that are proposed for removal, and must satisfy itself that the plans are sufficiently specific. In decreeing the issue of a citation, it is often best to provide for the citation to refer to the plan and to make arrangements for the plan to be deposited in the church or elsewhere in the parish where it is easily available to be inspected, and for the citation to refer expressly to these arrangements.

Prima facie tombstones are private property and cannot be interfered with in the absence of the consent of the owners. The court must therefore pay special attention to section 3 of the F.J.M. 1964, which in some circumstances enables an order for the removal of a monument to be made without the consent of the "owner." This section was new in the Measure of 1964; that it was enacted shows that the legislature recognised a need to facilitate churchyard re-ordering.

Subsection (4) defines "owner" as meaning "the person who erected the monument in question and, after his death, the heir or heirs at law of the person or persons in whose memory the monument was erected..." This definition follows the ancient rules as to the title to monuments. But it cannot fail to give rise to difficulties at a period when the concept of an heir at law has long become unfamiliar. Until 1926, real estate devolved (in the absence of other testamentary provision) upon the heir at law of the owner, that being his nearest surviving relation under a system of primogeniture with males taking priority over females. This system of devolution ceased to have any practical application in the law of real property as a result of the provisions of the Administration of Estates Act 1925, and at the present time it would in most cases be difficult, once the person who erected the monument is dead, to say who in fact is the "owner" within subsection (4).[28] In practice the court pays attention to anyone who, in answer to the advertisements or citation, evinces an interest in the given monument and shows some fairly close relationship to the person commemorated.

The effect of subsection (2) is that the court may grant a faculty to move, demolish, alter or do work to any monument whenever erected in the church or churchyard without the consent of the owner, or if after reasonable efforts the owner cannot be found, notwithstanding that the monument was originally erected under a faculty. But under subsection (3) the faculty must not be granted in respect of a particular monument if the owner withholds his consent and satisfies the court "that he is, within a reasonable time, willing and able to remove the monument (or so much thereof as may be proved to be his property) and to execute such works as the court may require to repair any damage to the fabric of any building or to any land caused by such removal." The court is given power by faculty to authorise such removal and to make "such orders as may be just as to the execution and cost of all necessary works."

This is a drastic enactment and decisively negatives any suggestion that once a monument is erected its owners are entitled to have it stay *in situ* perpetually. Thus the legal status of the monument is quite different from that of the mortal remains of the person commemorated, which are to remain forever in the churchyard unless the court, for some very good reason, allows them to be transferred elsewhere.[29] Section 3 is

---

[28] The question of title to a monument is discussed in connection with a monument inside a church in *Re St. Andrew's, Thornhaugh* [1976] Fam. 230. There is no difference in principle between monuments inside a church or monuments in a churchyard.

[29] See Exhumation, discussed at pp. 165 *et seq.*

the clearest possible intimation by the legislature that churchyards shall be available over and over again for burials when the processes of dissolution have gone far enough. This idea has not been fashionable for the last century, though it was well understood in earlier times.

In practice what is necessary for the court to do, in respect of a petition for a faculty for "re-ordering," is to ensure that adequate notices are given and that any parties who come forward as parties opponent know their rights and are given ample opportunity to exercise them. Generally speaking, once opposition has emerged and is defined, the petitioners come to terms with those parties opponent who have reasonably good cases, and the faculty can be granted subject to the agreed conditions.

Special considerations apply to a mausoleum, that is to an edifice, above or below ground, often contiguous to the church. Such buildings present intractable problems and occasion a great deal of expense. Sometimes they are of considerable aesthetic or historical value. They are normally in ownership other than that of the incumbent. In one recent unreported case in the diocese of St. Albans, the Department of the Environment was sufficiently interested in a mausoleum to take over its maintenance altogether, under special arrangements worked out between the owners, the church authorities and the Department, which were sanctioned by the consistory court. Occasionally it may be desirable to invoke section 1 of the F.J.M. 1964, which gives the court power to make a vesting order in favour of the incumbent and to determine the rights of the owners. There is no reported case on this section and the author has never in practice been invited to apply it; but it is one of the possibilities in dealing with the problems of a mausoleum. It would not be appropriate in a general book on faculties to elaborate further on this little known section; and it suffices to say that every case of a mausoleum needs to be thought out as a separate issue.

In some cases one element in a scheme for re-ordering is to set aside for the time being an area for car parking and to put on the surface gravel or other materials. This is often a desirable arrangement and there is nothing illegal about it. In particular the surfacing material is generally accepted as not constituting a "building" within section 3 of the D.B.G.A. 1884. If the parking area is later needed for burials, it should be made available under a fresh scheme, since that is the purpose for which the land is consecrated.

Introduction of new monuments

As we have seen, no monument can be introduced into a churchyard without the permission of the ordinary, that is of the chancellor as judge of the consistory court. But "in most cases the chancellor is content to delegate to the incumbent his authority to grant permission for the erection of an ordinary tombstone and to dispense with the need of a faculty."[30] This is a fiduciary power:

> "The incumbent of a church has a duty laid upon him as trustee of the church and churchyard for posterity to see that only those things are placed in it which may be fit for posterity and which are aimed at keeping our great heritage of churches as beautiful as they are now."[31]

Of course, the family of a deceased person can put up whatever monument they like on their own private property away from the public gaze, "but since they desire to erect it in a public place to which the public come to enjoy the sanctity and peace of the churchyard, they cannot complain if it offends the general opinion as to what is or is not appropriate in such a place."[32]

Since these cases almost always arise at the instance of a bereaved family, at a time when their loss is recent, the responsibility falling on the incumbent is not an easy one, and it often takes a good deal of courage to say "no," as Gage Ch. expressly recognised in *Re St. Peter, Kineton*.[33] The present Dean of the Arches has recently said: "The easy course would be to accede with sympathy to the petition; but this would not be right."[34] However, some assistance can be given by a chancellor to the incumbents in his diocese if he issues an instrument of delegation defining the powers of the incumbent to admit those monuments which conform to the specifications set out in the

---

[30] *Per* Garth Moore Ch. in *Re Woldingham Churchyard* [1957] 1 W.L.R. 811 at 812.
[31] *Per* Gage Ch. in *Re St. Peter, Kineton* [1967] 1 W.L.R. 347 at 348.
[32] *Ibid.*
[33] *Ibid.*
[34] *Re St. Mary's, Fawkham* [1981] 1 W.L.R. 1171 at 1175G.

instrument, and no others. Then, if an applicant asks to be allowed to introduce a monument not within those specifications, the incumbent has to say that any permission which he were to give would be a nullity and that if the applicant wishes to proceed further he can apply for a faculty. The incumbent is under no obligation to exercise the powers conferred upon him: if he feels uneasy about any proposal which he would have power to allow, he is fully entitled to say that he asks the applicants to seek a faculty.

Arrangements of this sort are very common. In *Re St. Peter, Kineton*[35] decided in 1966, Gage Ch. said that for the last 25 years white marble had been prohibited and native stone recommended "all over the country." That was perhaps an exaggeration, because there were no "regulations" at all in the St. Albans diocese until 1960, and the same may well have been true in other places. But some time towards 1950 there seems to have been the beginning of a change from the very loose system of advice which appears from *Re Little Gaddesden Churchyard*[36] to have been operative in 1933, to the system of mandatory limits on the extent of the delegated power of the incumbent which is general now. Thus in *Re St. Peter, Kineton*[37] and *Re St. Paul, Hanging Heaton*,[38] Gage Ch. and Graham Ch. were both dealing with cases where leave was sought to introduce a tombstone which did not comply with existing "regulations," and each refused to grant the faculty. There has further been a change in the attitude of the Court of Arches in these cases. For in *Re Little Gaddesden Churchyard*,[39] Sir Lewis Dibdin, Dean of the Arches, allowed the introduction of a white marble monument for which both the incumbent and the consistory court had refused permission, saying that he had never heard of a case where the material of a proposed monument was in dispute, that there was no legal objection to the proposal and that the matter was merely one "of taste, the taste of today. That is a smaller matter, and in my opinion it ought not to prevail against the wishes of the petitioner."[40] On the other hand, in *Re St. Mary's,*

---

[35] [1967] 1 W.L.R. 347 at 348.
[36] [1933] P. 150.
[37] [1967] 1 W.L.R. 347.
[38] [1968] 1 W.L.R. 1210.
[39] [1933] P. 150.
[40] *Ibid.*, at 153.

Fawkham,[41] Owen Q.C., the present Dean of the Arches, had to consider an application for a headstone including two porcelain tiles containing colour photographs of the deceased, a pure matter of taste (though it was incidentally in breach of the diocesan "regulations"). He upheld the decision of the chancellor to refuse a faculty on the ground that such a memorial "would be so alien to an English country churchyard, and especially an ancient country churchyard, that it cannot be allowed."[42] Here, then, unlike what occurred in the *Little Gaddesden* case, the court decided against the petition on a matter of taste. It did so on the evidence of the D.A.C.

In the *Kineton* and *Hanging Heaton* cases, cited above, the diocesan "regulations" forbade white marble, so that here too there was a considerable change from the state of affairs at the time of the *Little Gaddesden* case. In fact most, if not all, sets of current "regulations" prohibit all marble and all polished granite. The tendency is to encourage the use of local stone, as blending naturally with the colours of the local countryside. This was so in the *Hanging Heaton* case, despite evidence that the local Yorkshire stone tends to go black as it ages. There appears in 1980 to have been a sudden attempt to introduce colour photographs; for a case of that sort arose in the Liverpool diocese[43] as well as in the *Fawkham* case in the Rochester diocese. In view of the decision of the Appellate Court in the latter case, there are not likely to be many others.

The wording of inscriptions also gives trouble, the more so that it cannot, in the nature of things, usefully be made the subject of "regulations." Thus in the *Kineton* case and again in the *Haydock* case the court rejected the proposed inscriptions on grounds which were really those of taste. It is best if incumbents endeavour to secure that inscriptions shall usually be short and factual giving the name and date; if a quotation is desired, it should if possible be confined to an excerpt from the bible or the prayer book.

An embarrassing situation can arise in these days of unstable marriages where each of two competing persons wishes to put up a monument on the grave of one deceased person. In *Re St.*

---

[41] [1981] 1 W.L.R. 1171.
[42] *Ibid*., at 1175H.
[43] *Re St. Mark's, Haydock* [1981] 1 W.L.R. 1164.

Mark's Haydock (No. 2)[44] Hamilton Ch. resolved this question in favour of the estranged widow rather than of the lady with whom the deceased had been associating at the time of his death.

The contents of the "regulations" contained in an Instrument of Delegation are matters to be discussed between the chancellor and his advisory committee.[45] Broadly, the normal form is to prohibit all but native stone, or stone very like it, and oak. It is also normal to restrict the dimensions of the monument to something comparatively small. Regulations invariably prohibit kerbstones because of the difficulty which they cause in keeping the grass cut and chippings are forbidden as an alien intrusion. There is much valuable advice on the form of "regulations" in *The Churchyards Handbook*.[46]

The person to whom the power is delegated should be the incumbent or curate-in-charge, with a provision that if the benefice is vacant the power should be exercised by the rural dean; it should never be conferred on sequestrators or churchwardens. Vacancies must be expressly provided for; experience has shown that most undesirable precedents are too often set during a vacancy in the living.

In granting or withholding permission a person to whom the power is delegated should seek to ensure consistency; otherwise a sense of unfairness will be created. In considering an application for a faculty, the court should have the same end in view. But, while the court should normally proceed by analogy with the "regulations" when the proposed monument is of a mass-produced sort, the position is very different if the monument is specially designed and would be an artistic embellishment to the church and churchyard. Such monuments ought positively to be encouraged. In some dioceses a special power is delegated to archdeacons, with the consent of the D.A.C., to permit the introduction of specially designed monuments.

---

[44] [1981] 1 W.L.R. 1167.
[45] A specimen of an Instrument of Delegation is printed in Appendix B.
[46] (2nd ed., 1976). The expense of maintaining the churchyard falls on the P.C.C.: Parochial Church Councils (Powers) Measure 1956, s.4. To have the churchyard grazed by sheep has been found in rural areas a satisfactory substitute for the motor mower. It was, after all, the old way but has been re-introduced lately in some places.

Where "regulations" are newly introduced, or are amended, it is often desirable, again on grounds of fairness, for the court to allow, during a transitional period, a certain latitude in areas where there are gaps in a row of graves which all have, for instance, white marble monuments. In such a case, no harm need be done if the gaps are likewise filled with white marble monuments introduced under faculty. But this is a matter to be watched closely and the court should make it clear that there are distinct limits on what will be allowed. That a faculty is necessary is itself a deterrent and the "regulations" should confer no latitude upon the incumbent.

Finally it is important that every faculty allowing the introduction of a monument shall be expressed to be "until further order." Although section 3 of the F.J.M. 1964 enables the court to make an order for the removal of a monument introduced under faculty, it is as well to make clear from the beginning, by the use of this language, that no monument is guaranteed a place in the churchyard for ever, and that the grant of a faculty for its introduction gives no such guarantee.

Monuments introduced without leave are in position illegally, and the court can order their removal, with penal consequences as to expenses and costs.[47]

The Disused Burial Grounds Act 1884

As we have seen, the consecration of the land as a burial ground imposes perpetual sacred uses upon it and subjects it to the jurisdiction of the consistory court of the diocese.[48] Thus, no change in it can lawfully be made without a faculty, and the sacred uses restrict the matters for which a faculty can properly be granted. But if the consecrated land is not only a burial ground but a *disused* burial ground, no faculty can lawfully be granted at all for the erection of any building upon it, including any temporary or moveable

---

[47] See Enforcement, Chapter 7; *Re Woldingham Churchyard* [1957] 1 W.L.R. 811 and *Re St. Mark's, Haydock* [1981] 1 W.L.R. 1164.
[48] *Re St. John's, Chelsea* [1962] 1 W.L.R. 706 and *Re St. Mary The Virgin, Woodkirk* [1969] 1 W.L.R. 1867.

building,[49] save "for the purpose of enlarging a church, chapel, meeting house or other places of worship."[50] Such is the effect of section 3 of the D.B.G.A. 1884.

As originally enacted, the Act of 1884 applied only to such burial grounds as had been closed for burials by Order in Council. But section 4 of the Open Spaces Act 1887 provided that, in the Act of 1884, the term "burial ground" should have the same meaning as in the Metropolitan Open Spaces Act 1881, as amended by the Act of 1887 itself: the term is therefore defined as "including any ground, whether consecrated or not, which has at any time been set apart for the purposes of interment." Section 4 of the Open Spaces Act 1887 goes on to define "disused burial ground" as meaning "any burial ground which is no longer used for interments, whether or not such ground shall have been partially or wholly closed for burials under the provisions of any statute or Order in Council."[51]

The first requirement is, therefore, that the ground must at some time have been "set apart" for the purposes of interment; there may be many other ways of doing that, but in the case of an ordinary churchyard of the Church of England, consecration is clearly such a setting apart. A second requirement is that the ground "is no longer used for interments." The secular courts have held, in the case of an unconsecrated burial ground, that if the whole of the ground has once been set apart, and if burials are later discontinued, the prohibition applies even to those parts of the ground, once set apart, which never were at any stage used for interments.[52] But where land, though acquired for the purposes of interment, was never used at all for those purposes and was left derelict, it was not "set apart," and the D.B.G.A. 1884 did not apply to it.[53]

---

[49] Temporary or moveable buildings were included by s.4 of the Open Spaces Act 1887.
[50] There are, however, statutory exceptions in London: see below.
[51] This complicated referential legislation is discussed in full in the judgment of Kay L.J. in *Re Ponsford and Newport District School Board* [1894] 1 Ch. 454 at 465 *et seq.* and is set out textually in a footnote in *Re Bosworth and Gravesend Corporation* [1905] 1 K.B. 403 at 407.
[52] See *Re Ponsford and Newport District School Board* [1894] 1 Ch. 454 and *Re Bosworth and Gravesend Corporation* [1905] 1 K.B. 403. In *Nicholl* v. *Llantwit Major Parish Council* [1924] 2 Ch. 214 at 220, 221, Tomlin J. expressed the view that some of the remarks in the judgments in the *Ponsford* and *Gravesend* cases were not "directed to anything material to the determination of those cases."
[53] *Nicholl* v. *Llantwit Major Parish Council* [1924] 2 Ch. 214.

Section 3 of the Act of 1884 creates a statutory prohibition but provides no penalty for an infringement. A person guilty of such an infringement can be indicted for a misdemeanour[54]; alternatively, it is enforceable by the Attorney-General in a relator action or *ex officio* as representing the public.[55] In London there is special legislation which conferred powers on the former London County Council to enforce the section and that body did so on a number of occasions,[56] sometimes in faculty proceedings, either as petitioner or as a party opponent, and sometimes in Chancery proceedings for an injunction.[57] Similarly, a person individually aggrieved can bring an action for an injunction.[58] The duties of the London County Council were imposed by a private Act, the Metropolitan Board of Works (Various Powers) Act 1885, and in *L.C.C. v. Dundas*[59] Tristram Ch. stated that the London County Council had communicated with the chancellor of the London diocese asking to be given notice before cases possibly infringing the Act were heard, and that he had made an order under the Ecclesiastical Courts Act 1829 that the registry should give such notice on every application of the sort. The Act of 1829 was repealed by the E.J.M. 1963, and the order of Tristram Ch. was, most regrettably, lost to view. The matter came to light again in *Re St. Luke's, Chelsea*,[60] where it turned out that, upon the re-organisation of local government in London, the successor authority was the Greater London Council, but that in inner London the powers and duties had been delegated by that council to the borough councils and to the Common Council of the City. Thus, the petitioner, the Council of the Royal Borough of Kensington and

---

[54] *Per* Lindley L.J. in *Re Ponsford and Newport District School Board* [1894] 1 Ch. 454 at 464.
[55] See *Attorney-General v. London Parochial Charities* [1896] 1 Ch. 541 and *Paddington Corporation v. Attorney-General* [1906] A.C. 1 and in the Court of Appeal at [1903] 2 Ch. 556, 561.
[56] *L.C.C. v. Dundas* [1904] P. 1; *Rector and Churchwardens of St. Margaret, Lothbury v. L.C.C.* [1909] P. 310 and *St. Nicholas Acons v. L.C.C.* [1928] P. 102, [1928] A.C. 469.
[57] *L.C.C. v. Greenwich Corporation* [1929] 1 Ch. 305.
[58] *Boyce v. Paddington Borough Council* [1903] 1 Ch. 109; but in the Court of Appeal the Attorney-General was added as a plaintiff in respect of the rights of the public [1903] 2 Ch. 556 at 561, and the case is reported in the House of Lords as *Paddington Borough Council v. Attorney-General* [1906] A.C. 1.
[59] [1904] P. 1 at 16.
[60] [1976] Fam. 295 at 312H–313F.

Chelsea, was itself the enforcement authority. This state of affairs was discovered at a late stage of the hearing. Directions were accordingly given to the registry of the London diocese in future to notify the relevant enforcement authority of any petition in which a point under the Act seems likely to arise.

There is also other metropolitan private legislation stemming from the London County Council (General Powers) Act 1935, ss. 42 and 51, by which local authorities are entitled to provide a number of recreational facilities in respect of any open space in their area, and buildings in connection therewith, notwithstanding the provisions of any other statute. The then state of this legislation was discussed at length in *Re St. Luke's, Chelsea*.[61] This private legislation has led to some peculiar results.

Thus in *Re St. Dunstan's, Stepney*[62] Errington Ch. granted a faculty for the conversion of part of a disused burial ground, which was held by the London County Council as an open space, into a gymnasium or playground for children,[63] while in *Bermondsey Borough Council* v. *Mortimer*[64] Hansell Ch. granted a petition by the council for authority to erect a gardener's tool shed on a disused burial ground which was controlled by them as an open space, but refused a faculty for a urinal. He held that the one was necessary towards the user of the open space and that the other was not. In *Re St. Luke's, Chelsea*[65] it was held that this legislation did not justify the erection of a large obelisk and its plinth on a disused burial ground.

Section 3 of the D.B.G.A. 1884 provides primarily that "it shall not be lawful to erect any buildings upon any disused burial ground." Questions therefore arise, what are "buildings" and what is the meaning of "upon" a disused burial ground? These questions have respectively been the subject of consideration in the House of Lords and the Privy Council.

In *Paddington Corporation* v. *Attorney-General*[66] the object in question was a screen, erected on a disused burial ground, to

---

[61] [1976] Fam. 295 at 307, 308.
[62] [1937] P. 199.
[63] *Ibid.*, at 202 *et seq*. Errington Ch. commented critically on the lack of publicity for this private legislation eroding a public general Act.
[64] [1926] P. 87.
[65] [1976] Fam. 295.
[66] [1906] A.C. 1.

prevent the acquisition by neighbours of a right to the access of light across it. This erection was held not to be a "building" within section 3. In the Chancery Division[67] Buckley J. (whose judgment was restored by the House of Lords, having been reversed by the Court of Appeal) called attention to section 5 of the Metropolitan Open Spaces Act 1881[68] which provides that land is to be enjoyed "as an open space free from buildings"; he continued:

> "I think this means such buildings as would preclude or diminish its enjoyment in an open condition for exercise and recreation... In s.3 of the Act of 1884.... I think the word 'buildings' there means erections which would cover some part of the ground, as the enlargement of a church would do."[69]

In the House of Lords, the Earl of Halsbury said[70]:

> "I am of the opinion that it [section 3] meant what it said—that the space was to be unbuilt upon. It is to be disused as a burial ground, but it is not to be used as building ground—that is the meaning of it; and it appears to me that anything which approaches to the character of a building, whether temporary or permanent, is obviously within the prohibition."

And again:

> "I have to look at the word 'building' here with reference to this subject-matter and what the Act of Parliament was doing. It is very obvious, I think, that what was intended to be done was to keep this disused burial ground from being used as a building ground, to keep it as a place of exercise, ventilation, recreation and what not,—to prevent anything being done in the nature of building which will interfere with or restrict the free and open use of these spaces as constituted under the statute."[71]

---

[67] *Boyce v. Paddington Borough Council* [1903] 1 Ch. 109; see n. 58 above.
[68] The definitions in the Act of 1881 are incorporated in the D.B.G.A. 1884 by the amendments made under the Open Spaces Act 1887, s.4.
[69] [1903] 1 Ch. 109 at 117.
[70] *Paddington Borough Council v. Att.-Gen.* [1906] A.C. 1 at 3.
[71] *Ibid.*, at 4.

Whatever may have been the original context of the D.B.G.A. 1884, the amendments of the the Open Spaces Act 1887 place it among the open spaces legislation and Lord Halsbury's phrase "in the nature of building" is very wide, though, as the *Paddington* case itself showed, not wide enough to include a mere screen.

Thus in *Bermondsey Borough Council v. Mortimer*[72] Hansell Ch. held that a urinal was a building for the purposes of section 3 and also a gardener's tool shed (though the latter was legitimated by the Open Spaces Act 1906). In *Re St. John, Hampstead*[73] a columbarium was held to be a building. In *Re St. Luke's, Chelsea*,[74] the proposed structure was an obelisk of Nubian granite rising 17 feet, seven inches above the top of a podium of the same material seven feet square by seven feet, 10 inches high, the whole standing on a base of three steps of Portland stone, the lowest and largest of which was 19 feet, four inches in plan. Below was to be 1,200 cubic feet of reinforced concrete. This structure was held to be a building within section 3 on the ground that it would take up so much space.

On the other hand in *Re St. Peter the Great, Chichester*,[75] Buckle Ch. held that an electricity sub-station was not a "building": it was to consist of a rectangular metal cupboard four feet high, a transformer six feet high and some switch-gear in metal boxes. However the *Paddington* case had not been cited to him and his decision is difficult to reconcile with that case.

Following the *Paddington* case, it is conceived that a scaffold to facilitate the repair of the church, or indeed of buildings bordering a churchyard, cannot itself be a "building" and faculties are often granted for this purpose. A more doubtful case is that of a permanent fire escape fastened on the outside of an adjacent building and overhanging the churchyard. Further, it is to be noted that not even in *Re St. Mark's Church, Lincoln*[76] noted below, was it suggested that the wall of a churchyard, which must be "upon" the churchyard, would be a "building" for this purpose.

---

[72] [1926] P. 87.
[73] [1939] P. 281.
[74] [1976] Fam. 295.
[75] [1961] 1 W.L.R. 907.
[76] [1956] P. 336 at 343.

On the other hand, in *St. Nicholas Acons* v. *London County Council*[77] a brick-built structure with a roof of asphalt supported by wrought steel girders and reinforced concrete, for housing electrical equipment, was held to be a "building." It was also held to be "upon" the churchyard, notwithstanding that it as to be wholly subterranean, save for two ventilators, each nine inches high. The Privy Council expressed the view that as soon as the foundations were laid at whatever level the proposed structure would be a building and that the fact that it would not show above the surface would make no difference. This case differed from the *Paddington* case in that there could be no real doubt that the structure would be a building; in the *Paddington* case the status of the structure was dubious and it was therefore legitimate to look at the purposes of the Act to resolve the doubt.

While the structure in the *St. Nicholas Acons* case was below ground, that in *Re St. Mark's Church, Lincoln*[78] was a canopy, considerably above the surface, supported by columns that were not upon the disused burial ground at all. The canopy was intended to shelter from the rain persons waiting below it. It was held, as a whole, to be a building. Macmorran Ch. and the Court of Arches held that the part of such structure which was above the disused burial ground (and it was only a relatively small part) was still "upon" the burial ground and thus violated section 3 of the D.B.G.A. 1884. This is perhaps the most extreme application of the section and its logical consequences have caused much inconvenience. The subject-matter of *Re St. Botolph, Aldersgate Without*[79] was a churchyard wall with frescos on its inner side. The proposed structure was again a canopy, this time to protect from the weather the frescos and those who looked at them. Tristram Ch. held that this was not forbidden by section 3. It is difficult to see how this decision is reconcilable with that of the Court of Arches in *Re St. Mark's Church, Lincoln*, decided many years later. It is therefore

---

[77] [1928] P. 102; [1928] A.C. 469. The Privy Council disapproved *Re St. Nicholas Cole Abbey* [1893] P. 58 a decision of Tristram Ch.
[78] [1956] P. 336.
[79] [1900] P. 69.

doubtful whether the *St. Botolph's* case could properly be decided in the same way if it were to arise now.[80]

The exception expressed in D.B.G.A. 1884, s.3 is in favour of a building which is for the purpose of enlarging "a church, chapel, meeting house or other places of worship." In *Vicar and Churchwardens of St. James the Less, Bethnal Green v. Parishioners of Same*[81] there was a building, already on a disused burial ground, which was used for Sunday school and meetings. Tristram Ch. allowed it to be pulled down and a new and bigger building put up to replace it. The basis of his decision seems to have been that the existing building was a "meeting house" within the exception, and the whole operation substantially consisted of enlarging it.

The other reported cases on the exception have been about vestries, usually coupled with halls which were argued to be extensions of the church nearby. In *L.C.C. v. Dundas*,[82] the Court of Arches held that the proposed building was not an extension of the church. The case in its favour was not put on the ground that the hall was wanted as ancillary to worship: it was to be a much more general sort of parish meeting place. *L.C.C. v. Dundas* was evidently considered to inhibit developments, and in *Rector and Churchwardens of St. Margaret, Lothbury v. L.C.C.*[83] Tristram Ch. allowed vestries to be built on a disused churchyard but only after proposals for a much larger building, including a hall, were withdrawn. More recently, however, with the introduction of family services, it has been possible to re-open the subject and to argue that the block of buildings, vestries and a hall, which are so common in newly built churches, are ancillary to worship and are therefore proper parts of the church itself. This line of argument succeeded in *Re St. Mary's, Luton*,[84] where the Court of Arches upheld the judgment of the court below, distinguishing *L.C.C. v. Dundas* on the

---

[80] It is difficult to see what useful public purpose was served by disallowing the structures concerned in the *St. Nicholas Acons* or *Lincoln* cases. The *Paddington* case laid down an intelligible principle and it is unfortunate that in these two cases it could not be applied.
[81] [1899] P. 55.
[82] [1904] P. 1.
[83] [1909] P. 310.
[84] [1967] P. 151; [1968] P. 47.

facts. This liberating decision has been widely followed in unreported cases and in two reported ones, *Re St. Ann's Church, Kew*[85] and *Re St. Thomas, Lymington*.[86] As was done in the *Luton* case, the faculty should include conditions and undertakings to ensure that the proposed building shall at all times be used as part of the church and be under the control of the incumbent as such.[87]

The Open Spaces Act 1906

Where land is consecrated and set apart as a burial ground, the freehold (*i.e.* the life estate) is in the incumbent (if there is one), but the fee simple itself is in abeyance.[88] But by the combined effect of sections 6 and 20 of the Open Spaces Act 1906, the incumbent, though not having the fee simple, is nevertheless given a legal power to convey a disused burial ground in fee simple to the local authority for the purposes of that Act, or to create out of it a legal term of years or any lesser interest. The Act of 1906 repealed a number of earlier Acts designed to facilitate the provision of public open spaces, especially in towns.[89] A conveyance made under section 6 of the Act of 1906 does not in any way affect the status of the land conveyed as a consecrated burial ground under the control of the ordinary: therefore, a conveyance should be executed only under the authority of a faculty. Further, though the fee simple is called out of abeyance and vested in the local authority, it is held not only upon the continuing sacred uses imposed by the sentence of consecration, but also upon the statutory trusts of section 10 of the Act of 1906, which are in substance to maintain

---

[85] [1977] Fam. 12.
[86] [1980] Fam. 89.
[87] See p. 98. It should be remembered that the three other well-known cases about building on consecrated land were not concerned with *disused* burial grounds, *i.e. Corke* v. *Rainger* [1912] P. 69, *Re St. John's, Chelsea* [1962] 1 W.L.R. 706 and *Re St. Andrew's Church, Backwell* (1982); unreported, a case in the diocese of Bath and Wells.
[88] *Rector and Churchwardens of St. Gabriel, Fenchurch Street* v. *The City of London Real Property Ltd.* [1896] P. 95 at 101; *Re St. Paul's, Covent Garden* [1974] Fam. 1 at 4. The estate of the incumbent is in the nature of a life interest: see *per* Lord Selborne L.C., in *The Ecclesiastical Commissioner for England and Wales* v. *Rowe* (1880) 5 App.Cas. 736 at 744.
[89] For an example of the application of one of the repealed Acts, the Metropolitan Open Spaces Act 1881, see *Re St. Botolph Without Aldgate* [1892] P. 173.

and manage it "with a view to the enjoyment thereof as an open space within the meaning of this Act." But by section 11(1), the power of management conferred by section 10 is not to be exercised in relation to a consecrated burial ground unless and until the local authority is "authorised so to do by the licence or faculty of the bishop." Thus the disused burial ground remains as much under the control of the consistory court, through which the bishop acts, as if it was still vested in the incumbent.

There are, moreover, express provisions in section 11 reinforcing the control of the ordinary, namely that if games are to be permitted there must be a special faculty regulating them (sub-section (2)), and detailed requirements as to the notices and the like have to be complied with before there can be any interference with tombstones or monuments (sub-sections (3) and (4)).

Further, since all these provisions apply to disused burial grounds, section 3 of the D.B.G.A. 1884 continues to apply, though subject to any effects of the statutory trusts of section 10 of the Act of 1906 which *pro tanto* amends section 3 of the D.G.B.A. 1884. Thus in *Bermondsey Borough Council* v. *Mortimer*,[90] Hansell Ch. held that a shed for the gardener's tools was a necessary concomitant of an open space and was therefore authorised by section 10, notwithstanding that it was prima facie prohibited by section 3 of the D.G.B.A. 1884. Conversely, he held that a urinal was not necessary to an open space and was therefore still prohibited by section 3. Whatever may be thought of the conclusion of the learned chancellor on the particular evidence before him in regard to the urinal, the decision shows clearly how the mutual effects of the two sections are to be interpreted.[91] Under section 11(2) the court also imposed conditions upon the playing of organised games.

Again in *Re St. Luke's, Chelsea*[92] it was held that a massive obelisk would be a breach both of section 10 and of section 3. On the other hand, in the metropolis there is a private Act, promoted by the former London County Council in 1935,[93]

---

[90] [1926] P. 87.
[91] The urinal would since 1935 have been legitimated in the metropolis by the London County Council's private Act of that year: see below p. 163.
[92] [1976] Fam. 295.
[93] London County Council (General Powers) Act 1935, ss.42 and 51.

which allows extensive user for recreational purposes of disused burial grounds vested in local authorities under the Act of 1906 and authorises a number of sorts of building to be erected on them despite the provisions of any other statute, for example the D.B.G.A. 1884. In *Re St. Dunstan's, Stepney*[94] Errington Ch. held that this private legislation overrode, within the metropolitan area, the prohibition of section 3 of the D.G.B.A. 1884. The chancellor expressed some surprise that a public general statute should be overridden by a private Act in this way, but he had no hesitation in holding that that was the result. The private Act of 1935 was repealed on the occasion of the general reorganisation of local government in London in the 1960s, but its effects were carried forward in favour of the new local authorities by a jungle of special legislation which was exhaustively canvassed in *Re St. Luke's, Chelsea*.[95] Since these problems can arise only in the metropolitan consistory courts it would not be appropriate to discuss this local legislation more fully in a general book on faculties. But even in these dioceses the faculty jurisdiction is fully exercisable, as was made clear in *Re St. Luke's, Chelsea*, where a faculty was refused for certain proposals of the local authority.[96]

The Open Spaces Act 1906 is a useful piece of legislation in that it allows public money to be spent in maintaining disused burial grounds as open spaces available for the enjoyment of the public. But the areas in question remain consecrated land subject in full to the jurisdiction of the ordinary. Arrangements under this Act are common in the diocese of London; but most of the areas available to be dealt with in this way were so dealt with a long time ago; new cases of the kind are therefore somewhat infrequent.

Reservation of gravespaces and the burial of ashes

In the absence of other provision made by faculty, it is for the incumbent to choose where in a churchyard any given burial

---

[94] [1937] P. 199.
[95] [1976] Fam. 295, especially at 307 to 309.
[96] In the City of London there is another private Act, the City of London (Various Powers) Act 1952, s.4 of which enables the City Corporation to exercise powers of management over a disused burial ground without taking over the fee simple. Here too the faculty jurisdiction continues to apply.

shall take place. But two sorts of faculty are commonly granted in derogation of the right of the incumbent. Thus it is possible for a gravespace to be reserved by a faculty either for a parishioner or for a non-parishioner.[97] But, as Tristram Ch. pointed out,[98] such a faculty for a non-parishioner should not be granted save with the concurrence of the incumbent, and the court should be satisfied that the faculty can be granted "without serious risk of depriving parishioners, present or future, of their right of being buried there..." In practice faculties of this sort are not granted except after enquiry into the available space in the churchyard and with evidence that the incumbent and the P.C.C. (speaking for the parishioners) support the application.

The other class of faculty is for the reservation of an area for the burial of cremated remains. This arrangement is now very common and may be made either in respect of an open churchyard or a closed one. By encouraging cremation, it tends actually to benefit the parishioners in respect of their rights of burial, if the churchyard is open, since the burial of ashes takes up much less space than that of a body. The court should make regulations in the faculty as to the way of marking the places where ashes are buried: a great number of small plaques is not an embellishment to the churchyard and it is usually desirable to arrange that individual burials of ashes within the reserved plot shall not be marked at all, but that there shall either be a book of remembrance in the church or a collective monument in the burial plot on which individual names can be marked as burials occur. The details of such arrangements should always be discussed fully with the D.A.C. and the archdeacon.

It appears from the *Perivale* case[99] that at the beginning of the 20th century reservations of gravespaces were thought of as a legitimate source of fees for the incumbent and that at least some incumbents were in the habit of making many grants of reserved spaces. As Tristram Ch. pointed out, no such grant was valid without a confirmatory faculty. It is the better practice nowadays for the application to come forward by way of a petition for reservation and not by way of confirming a grant

---

[97] *Re Sargent* (1890) 15 P.D. 168 (in the Court of Arches) and *Re the Perivale faculty* [1906] P. 332.
[98] *Re the Perivale faculty* [1906] P. 332 at 336.
[99] *Ibid.*

already made by the incumbent. In the *Perivale* case, Tristram Ch. ordered the incumbent to refrain during the rest of his incumbency from making grants of this kind. It is not clear what power the court had to make this order; but it was at least an intimation that in future the court would not receive favourably any petitions for a faculty confirming one of that particular incumbent's grants.

Express provision is made by section 8 of the F.J.M. 1964 that any right for the exclusive use of any particular part of the churchyard, burial ground or other consecrated land for the purposes of sepulture, however granted or acquired and whether absolute or limited, shall cease 100 years after the passing of the Measure, *i.e.* on April 15, 2064, unless granted, enlarged or continued by a faculty issued after April 15, 1964. Further, no faculty granting such a right shall in future be issued for any period exceeding 100 years from the date of the faculty. These provisions do not apply to burial grounds provided under the Burial Acts 1852–1906 or the Public Health (Interments) Act 1879. It is often wise to impose a decidedly shorter limit than that, so that the control of the incumbent over the churchyard is not unnecessarily curtailed.

Since rights of sepulture are vested in private persons and the faculty is issued to such persons, considerable care should be taken by those who own the rights to ensure that the P.C.C. knows of the faculty and records it to save future controversy. The faculty itself should define closely the position and size of the plot with which it is concerned, and it is usually desirable to require the plot to be marked.

Exhumation

Once a body is buried in consecrated ground "the site is under the exclusive control of the Ecclesiastical Courts, and no body there buried can be removed from its place of interment without the sanction of a faculty to be granted upon the application of the executors or members of the family, for reasons approved by the Court, or upon the application of other parties upon the ground of necessity or of proved public convenience, and then only for re-interment in other consecrated ground."[1]

---

[1] *Per* Tristram Ch. in *Re Dixon* [1892] P. 386 at 393, 394.

This passage appears to mean that no human remains[2] can lawfully be removed from, or interfered with in, consecrated ground save under the authority of a faculty,[3] and that such faculty can be granted to the executors or members of the family for reasons approved by the court; faculties can also be granted to other persons "upon the ground of necessity or proved public convenience, and then only for re-interment in consecrated ground." Thus, in the case of a private application it is not absolutely necessary that the remains, when exhumed, shall be reinterred in consecrated ground, though the court must in all such cases approve the reasons for seeking the order and the matter is one for the discretion of the chancellor.[4] If the remains are not simply to be transferred to other consecrated ground, a licence from the Home Secretary is also required.[5]

Before acceding to a private application for exhumation, the court should make thorough enquiries to ensure that the executors and any surviving close relatives of the deceased are in agreement with the application. Such enquiries are especially necessary where the deceased had been divorced and more than one spouse or former spouse is still living. If the judge is satisfied that "any near relatives of the deceased person still living, and any other persons who in the opinion of the judge it is reasonable to regard as being concerned with the matter, are the petitioners or consent to the proposed faculty being granted"[6] he may dispense with citation and issue the faculty forthwith; and if these facts are not all present he may still dispense with the general citation and confine himself to ordering special citations to any persons who are not petitioners but who are near relatives or whom he thinks it is reasonable to regard as being concerned.

Orders are frequently made for exhumations incidental to such operations as extending or altering the church or for

---

[2] It is thought that the Ecclesiastical Courts protect ashes as much as corpses.
[3] It is an indictable offence to dig up a corpse unlawfully: see *R.* v. *Sharpe* (1845) Dea. & Bell C.C. 160 cited in *Williams* v. *Williams* (1882) 20 Ch.D. 659 at 663.
[4] *Re Matheson* [1958] 1 W.L.R. 246, where Steel Ch. allowed the exhumation of the remains of a deceased person so that they might be cremated and placed with those of his widow; the report does not state whether the latter were in consecrated ground. Conversely in *Re Dixon* [1892] P. 386 a similar order had been refused; *Re Matheson* appears to state the current practice.
[5] Burial Act 1857, s.25: and see *Re Talbot* [1901] P. 1.
[6] F.J.R. 1967, r. 5(6).

making alterations in the churchyard itself for the convenience of parishioners,[7] though, of course, the court always endeavours to keep the disturbance of human remains to the absolute minimum.[8] Any such remains as have to be disturbed must be re-buried reverently in consecrated ground under the directions of the court.[9]

In some cases persons extraneous to the family or parish ask for orders, on the ground of public convenience, which will incidentally involve the disturbance of human remains lying in consecrated ground. Occasionally such proposals are of so extreme a character that the chancellor will intimate at an early stage, when enquiries are made of his registrar before any petition is lodged, that he would prefer the public authority concerned to use any statutory powers which it may have to override the jurisdiction of the court, and thus to shoulder the whole criticism itself. But most cases of road widening and the like can better be dealt with by faculty, so that the court can ensure that all is done decently and in order.[10] In every such case, the remains disturbed should be ordered to be reinterred in consecrated land, and facilities should be given to the relatives of the individual deceased persons to say where that should be in each case. It is imperative that the fullest and most detailed public notice be given of proposals of this kind, in the citation and otherwise, to enable any relatives of the deceased persons whose remains would be disturbed to know what is proposed and to have an opportunity to state their views. Further, the case for the proposals must be proved conclusively and if the court is not completely satisfied the petition should be dismissed.[11] In all these cases, the paramount consideration to

---

[7] *Vicar and One of the Churchwardens of St. Botolph Without Aldgate v. Parishioners of Same* [1892] P. 161, per Tristram Ch. at 171.
[8] In the case of *Re St. Andrew's Church, Backwell* (1982); unreported, where a church extension was authorised in an open churchyard, none of the subjacent burials were disturbed because the building was supported by a ring of very slender piles driven from above.
[9] *Re St. Ann's Church, Kew* [1977] Fam. 12 at 17; *Re St. Thomas, Lymington* [1980] Fam. 89 at 95.
[10] For the jurisdiction see *Re St. John's Chelsea* [1962] 1 W.L.R. 706 at 710; for the grant of a faculty for road-widening, involving a very large number of exhumations, see *Re St. Mary The Virgin, Woodkirk* [1969] 1 W.L.R. 1867, in the appellate court in the Province of York.
[11] *Re Parish of Caister-on-Sea, Norfolk County Council v. Knights and Caister-on-Sea Joint Burial Committee* [1958] 1 W.L.R. 309.

be borne in mind by all concerned is that human remains, once interred in consecrated ground, are there under the protection of the ecclesiastical court of the diocese, and should not be interfered with in any way except for proved reasons of family or public convenience, and in the latter case always accompanied by re-interment in consecrated ground elsewhere.

The secular use of consecrated churchyards

Land consecrated by the bishop is set apart forever for sacred uses. Where a church is consecrated its sacred uses are for worship: where the consecration is as a burial ground, the sacred uses are for the purpose of the burial of the dead. Occasionally, land is consecrated for sacred uses, but without any specific purposes.[12] An ancient churchyard close to an ancient church is presumed to have been consecrated as a burial ground. Where consecration has occurred in the last 200 years, the actual sentence of consecration is usually to be found.[13] It is the best evidence of what was done and should be inspected if any question arises.

Two legal consequences follow from the imposition of sacred uses. "The fee of a church or churchyard is by law in perpetual abeyance, whilst the freehold of the... church and churchyard [is vested] in the incumbent; but in both cases for the use of the parishioners. The final control of the church ... and of the churchyard is vested in the chancellor, as ordinary for this purpose."[14] The position of the incumbent is analogous to that of a life tenant.[15]

It follows that no one may do anything to the consecrated land without the authority of the court, and that no legal or equitable right can be created by the incumbent in favour of a third party. Likewise, no highway can be dedicated to the public

---

[12] As in *Corke* v. *Rainger* [1912] P. 69.
[13] Though not necessarily in the Diocesan Registry of the diocese where the premises now are, owing to boundary changes. Further, a good many dioceses have arranged for their old documents to be lodged among the local archives kept by county council.
[14] *Vicar and One of the Churchwardens of St. Botolph Without Aldgate* v. *Parishioners of Same* [1892] P. 161, *per* Tristram Ch. at 167. See also *Rector and Churchwardens of St. Gabriel, Fenchurch Street* v. *The City of London Real Property Ltd.* [1896] P. 95 at 101.
[15] See *per* Lord Selborne L.C. in *The Ecclesiastical Commissioners for England and Wales* v. *Rowe* (1880) 5 App.Cas. 736 at 744.

over consecrated ground. The prohibition on sales, leases or other dispositions of a church or part of a church, imposed by this Pastoral Measure 1983, s.56(2) applies also to "consecrated land belonging or annexed to a church." But section 56(3) expressly allows the grant of a faculty authorising "a suitable use" of the consecrated land. Accordingly, the most that anyone can be given is a licence, so that what he does or what the public does is not a trespass. The licence can be given by the incumbent with the leave of the court. In the absence of an incumbent, or where the circumstances otherwise make it convenient, it can be given by the court itself.[16] Licences should usually be accompanied by a written agreement, enforceable in the secular courts, providing for the detailed terms on which the licence is granted, including money payments. The agreement should be made in every case by and with the P.C.C. as a perpetual body corporate and by the incumbent if there is one. Neither churchwardens, who constantly change and have no legal title to land, nor a priest-in-charge, who has no estate, should be contracting parties. Any money payments should be payable to the P.C.C. and not to the incumbent, since it will become taxable income in his hands and will usually not benefit him in practice owing to the modern arrangements about diocesan minimum stipends. Great care should be taken to ensure that neither the licence nor the agreement gives the appearance of creating a tenancy, lest it be argued that the Landlord and Tenant Act 1954 applies to it. A purported tenancy would in law be a nullity, owing to the consecrated status of the land, the abeyance of the fee simple and section 56 of the Pastoral Measure 1983. But the appearance of a tenancy would be misleading and would be calculated to give rise to secular litigation.

Licences of one sort or another over churchyards are extremely common, especially in the centre of towns where land is scarce and valuable: thus a licence can not only accommodate a neighbour but bring useful revenue to the church. The licence must never permit anything which conflicts with the sacred uses; further, if the land is a disused burial ground, it must not purport to authorise any infringement of section 3 of the D.B.G.A. 1884. Again, if the land is adjacent to a church, the

---

[16] As in *Re St. Paul, Covent Garden* [1974] Fam. 1.

licence or the agreement should contain careful provision to protect the fabric and quiet of the church. And finally it should include an adequate indemnity to the incumbent against claims in tort by persons taking advantage of the licence.

But, subject to these broad and overriding considerations, the licence may allow many sorts of activities. One very common kind is to allow persons in adjacent buildings to enter or leave them.[17] Sometimes a licence is granted for persons to leave a building adjacent to the churchyard in case only of fire or other emergency and to escape across the churchyard.[18] Licences for drainage or access are quite frequent, especially where a former parsonage near the churchyard is sold and the site developed. And in some cases a small strip of the churchyard is allowed to be treated as if it were part of the adjacent highway, usually though not always as a footpath.[19] Licences can be given for overhead wires though such cases may well be objectionable aesthetically,[20] or for small electricity sub-stations in churchyards that are still open[21]; or for underground electrical cables. In a churchyard that is still open, a temporary building may be allowed to be erected on an area not likely to be needed for burials during the period for which the building is to be there. But more permanent arrangements for underground wires, pipes and the like should be confined to edges and verges which will never be required for burial. Precautions should always be taken against the risk of persons being electrocuted by cutting with a spade near a buried electric cable.

The subject of licences for the secular use of churchyards was very fully discussed in *Re St. John's, Chelsea*,[22] which has been

---

[17] See *Rector and Churchwardens of St. Gabriel, Fenchurch Street* v. *The City of London Real Property Ltd.* [1896] P. 95.
[18] With redevelopment in the middle of towns, licences for emergency exits are often a necessary term of the planning permission and can thus be a source of considerable revenue to the church.
[19] See *Re Bideford Parish* [1900] P. 314 and *Re St. Mary The Virgin, Woodkirk* [1969] 1 W.L.R. 1867. These cases were both in the appellate courts. The churchyard in the former was a closed one; in the latter case it was open.
[20] In *Re Coleford Cemetery* [1984] 1 W.L.R. 1369 a licence was refused to the owner of a house adjacent to the consecrated public cemetery to introduce into that cemetery a line of posts carrying electric wires to supply the house.
[21] Such an installation was refused in respect of a *disused* burial ground in *Re St. Peter The Great, Chichester* [1961] 1 W.L.R. 907; this decision is open to some doubt.
[22] [1962] 1 W.L.R. 702.

approved by the appellate court of the Northern Province.[23] These cases are never easy and applications for a licence should always be supported by adequate professional evidence that the terms, including the payments, are adequate for the protection of the interests of the church, and the court must give meticulous care to the terms of the faculty and of the accompanying agreement. It is usually convenient to issue the citation at a fairly early stage and to arrange, if there is no opposition, for a hearing in chambers to settle the detailed documents, so as to ensure that nothing is allowed which conflicts with the main principles set out above. If there is opposition, the whole matter must of course be dealt with in open court.

One problem that deserves special attention is the length of the period for which the licence is granted and the conditions under which it can be terminated. Every case where the proposed licence is for period longer than a year should be the subject of consultation, often through the archdeacon, with the Diocesan Pastoral Committee, to ensure that, if there is any prospect of the land being declared redundant under the Pastoral Measure 1983 and so deconsecrated, no continuing licence will interfere with an advantageous sale. Generally speaking, the longer the proposed duration of a licence is to be, the more critical should be the approach of the court to it and in particular if money payments are concerned there should be provisions for them to be revised at frequent intervals.[24]

In general, almost any user which could be the subject-matter of an easement, either over the surface or above it or below it, if the land were not consecrated, can be the subject of a licence authorised by the court; but the power to grant it must be exercised with the greatest care so as to ensure that the consecrated land is neither abused nor improperly fettered. In every case where a licence over a churchyard is sought, the court should be satisfied that the proposed user does not conflict with the sacred uses and will not be detrimental to the adjacent church if there is one. Where a licence is to erect any form of

---

[23] *Re St. Mary The Virgin, Woodkirk* [1969] 1 W.L.R. 1867. *Re St. John, Chelsea* has not so far been considered by the Court of Arches, but is generally accepted as correct.

[24] Before 1971, a few licences were authorised in the diocese of London which conflict with this proposition and would not have been allowed at any later date.

building or permanent structure, the court must also be satisfied that the churchyard is not a disused burial ground and that no breach of section 3 of the D.B.G.A. 1884 is involved.

The petitioners in a petition for authority to grant a licence in respect of a churchyard should be the persons whose legal interests are affected that is to say the incumbent, if there is one, the P.C.C. or guild church council in some cases in the City of London and the proposed licensee. The churchwardens, as bishop's officers, are always competent parties and so is any priest-in-charge: but none of them is a necessary party.[25]

---

[25] See *Re St. Mary, Aldermary* [1985] Fam. 101 at 105D.

6. Unconsecrated Buildings and Land

Buildings

In previous chapters, we have been concerned with consecrated buildings, their contents, and consecrated land. These are the primary objects of the faculty jurisdiction. But sections 6 and 7 of the F.J.M 1964 extend the field.

Under section 6(1) the bishop has power by revocable order to direct that any building which he has licensed for public worship "shall be subject to the jurisdiction of the court of the diocese during such period as may be specified in the order." While such an order is in force the building in question shall "be subject, together with its furnishings and contents, to the jurisdiction of the court specified in the order as though it were a consecrated church" (s.6(2)). Any such order is to be registered in the Diocesan Registry (s.6(3)), but does not render invalid any act done before the making of the order (s.6(2)).

The purpose of such an order is to extend the control and the protection of the consistory court to the building to which the order applies and to all its furnishings and contents exactly as if the building had been consecrated. If that is not done, the person or body in whom the legal estate in the building happens to be vested could sell or otherwise dispose of it without reference to any ecclesiastical court. So far as the contents are concerned, the persons having title to them, or possession of them, could equally sell them without any ecclesiastical control. Moreover, those who happen to be running the building could introduce into it inappropriate contents.

It is submitted that, by virtue of the combined effect of section 6 and section 7,[1] the jurisdiction of the court applies not only to the building covered by the order but also to its curtilage.

---

[1] See at p. 175.

The control thus given to the consistory court is obviously intended to be exercised with some flexibility; the needs of a building merely licenced temporarily for public worship are obviously different from those of a church consecrated and set apart forever from all "profane and common uses." Although the building is made subject to the jurisdiction of the court by the order under section 6, as if it were consecrated, the freehold is not in abeyance; thus, in authorising dealings with such a building or the land on which it stands, the court can authorise transactions as comparatively freely as if it were dealing with unconsecrated churchyard.[2] There do not appear to be any reported decisions about section 6, and in practice it does not give rise to any special difficulties.

In each diocese it would be desirable for the chancellor soon after his coming to office, and then perhaps once in every 10 years, to call for a list of the buildings licensed for public worship and of the orders in force under section 6 and to consult with the bishop about the need for orders which are in force to continue or for new orders to be made. Apart from such a general review, archdeacons should be alert to call the attention of the bishop and the chancellor to any buildings within their archdeaconries which could usefully be made the subject of orders under section 6. On the whole, it seems that in a diocese all buildings which are for the time being used as churches in the popular sense should be subject to a uniform set of principles and practices.

Land

It appears that the consistory court has always had jurisdiction over unconsecrated land occupied with churches. It is now provided by section 7(1) of the F.J.M. 1964 as follows:

> "For the avoidance of doubt it is hereby declared that where unconsecrated land forms, or is part of, the curtilage of a church within the jurisdiction of a court that court has the same jurisdiction over such land as over the church."

The word "church" is not defined in the Measure, but is covered by section 3 of the Interpretation Measure 1925 as follows:

[2] See at p. 177.

"The expression 'church' means any church or chapel which has been consecrated for the purpose of public worship according to the rites and ceremonies of the Church of England."

Like all the provisions of section 3 this definition operates "unless the contrary intention appears."

Although section 7(1) of the 1964 Measure is expressed to be declaratory, section 7(2) provides that the section "shall not render unlawful any act done or proceedings taken in good faith before the passing of this Measure nor shall require the issue of faculties confirming such acts."

The effect of the provisions set out above is that since the passing of the F.J.M. 1964 the court has indubitably had jurisdiction over the curtilage of churches and also, it is submitted, over the curtilage of buildings covered by orders under section 6. There is, moreover, nothing in section 7 to take away any jurisdiction which the court may have had under the general law before 1964 over land surrounding and occupied with churches, even if such land is more extensive than "curtilage" necessarily connotes. Areas of this sort can conveniently be referred to as "unconsecrated churchyard", and the account given by Ellison Ch. of this part of the jurisdiction in *Re St. George's Oakdale*[3] may be accepted as correct. A typical way in which unconsecrated churchyard comes into being is when, usually after about 1815, land was bought for building a new church, a church was built on part of it, and then the church and the ground immediately under it alone were consecrated.[4] The adjacent land is still needed to give space to the church and to protect it against other buildings being put too close to it, in the same way as some land is generally held with a new house. Apart from the negative purpose of protection, the surrounding land can be cultivated as a garden and can make the church aesthetically more attractive. It is thus convenient for the protection and embellishment of the church that the surrounding land held with the church should be under the same jurisdiction as the church itself.

---

[3] [1976] Fam. 210 at 214D–H.
[4] See *Board of Works Plumstead District* v. *Ecclesiastical Commissioners for England* [1891] 2 Q.B. 361.

At an early date after the passing of the F.J.M. 1964 questions arose in connection with the land occupied with the then new church of *St. John's Church, Bishop's Hatfield*,[5] where the court had the advantage of a full argument by Dr. Wigglesworth, as to the meaning of "curtilage" in section 7 and as to how the jurisdiction declared by the section should be exercised. The judgment of the chancellor embodies and accepts these submissions. Thus, though the case was unopposed, it is submitted that it has a degree of authority on the meaning of "curtilage."

At the date of the *Hatfield* case, neither the chancellor nor counsel appear to have appreciated that the court has, and always has had, jurisdiction over unconsecrated churchyard as an area sometimes wider than the curtilage of the church.[6] In the course of investigating a case which raised a number of other issues,[7] Goodman Ch. discovered a much earlier case relating to churchyard at Christ Church, Chislehurst where, in 1897, Dr. Tristram, as Commissary-General of the diocese of Canterbury, authorised the sale of a piece of unconsecrated land at some distance from the church, being land vested in the incumbent and evidently treated as part of the churchyard. The whole text of the order of the court made by Dr. Tristram is now printed in the note to *Re St. Mary Magdalene, Paddington*.[8] The decision of Dr. Tristram is fully discussed in the judgment of the London consistory court in the *Paddington* case.

The total effect of these cases appears to be that the court has, and always has had, jurisdiction over unconsecrated churchyards and that, so far as such churchyards are within the more limited concept of "curtilage," that jurisdiction is expressly declared by section 7.

---

[5] [1967] P. 113.
[6] In *Re St. George's Oakdale* [1976] Fam. 210 at 214, Ellison Ch. referred to *Re St. John's, Chelsea* [1962] 1 W.L.R. 706 as showing that the court "assumed without question jurisdiction over the site of the former consecrated church as well as the unconsecrated churchyard adjacent to it." Examination of the report of the *Chelsea* case shows that the gravamen of that decision was about the *site* of the former church; however, both counsel agreed that the court should not differentiate between the church site and a small area of "curtilage" surrounding it: (at 708). This was before the F.J.M. 1964 was in force. There may well have been a fringe of unconsecrated land round the consecrated church site and occupied with it, but there was no argument or decision about the fringe as such.
[7] *Re Christ Church, Chislehurst* [1973] 1 W.L.R. 1317 at 1319F–G.
[8] [1980] Fam. 99 at 104.

The way in which this jurisdiction is to be exercised is, of course, governed by the fact that the land in question is, by definition, unconsecrated. Therefore it is neither subject to perpetual sacred uses nor is the fee simple in abeyance. Usually the fee simple is vested in the incumbent,[9] but cases occasionally arise where it is vested in another party, often the diocesan board of finance. Whoever has the legal estate, there is nothing to prevent that person, with the leave of the court and any other permissions which may be necessary,[10] conveying the legal estate away or creating another legal interest out of it. Thus in *Re St. Peter's, Bushey Heath*[11] the court granted a faculty for the creation of a legal easement. In the *Hatfield, Chislehurst* and *Paddington* cases the court allowed the incumbent to make a conveyance in fee simple. As was pointed out in the *Hatfield* case, the result of the buildings proposed to be erected on the land conveyed would have been that the land would cease to be curtilage of the church and that the court's jurisdiction was destroyed by the conveyance. It is doubtful, on the other hand, whether the land concerned in the *Paddington* case ceased to be curtilage of the church. For it was immediately adjacent to the church building and there was no proposal to build on it: it was wanted by the Westminster City Council as part of their canalside walk and so would remain open.[12] The broad principle as to the practical exercise of the jurisdiction over unconsecrated churchyards and church curtilages is that, while there is a wider latitude as to what can be done than there is in relation to consecrated churchyards, the court should act by analogy with the cases about consecrated land and must always ensure "that the church building itself will not be injured and that the services held therein will not be disturbed."[13] This will often necessitate the imposition of restrictive covenants binding the land conveyed as was done in the *Hatfield* and *Chislehurst* cases.

A curious controversy has arisen as to the form in which any conveyance authorised by the court should be made. In the

---

[9] As in *Re St. George's, Oakdale* [1976] Fam. 211 and *Re St. Mary Magdalene, Paddington* [1980] Fam. 99.
[10] As to which see further below p. 178.
[11] [1971] 1 W.L.R. 357.
[12] And in *Re St. John's Church, Bishop's Hatfield* [1967] P. 113 at 118 the court expressly said that one of the proposed buildings which would be linked to the church would continue to be in the curtilage of the church.
[13] *Re St. Peter's, Bushey Heath* [1971] 1 W.L.R. 357 at 360D–E.

Chislehurst case of 1897, Dr. Tristram simply authorised the incumbent, who had the legal estate, to convey the fee simple to a purchaser subject to covenants. A like order was made in the *Paddington* case in 1979, and the chancellor indicated that he would follow that practice whenever convenient. On the other hand in the *Hatfield* case and the *Chislehurst* case of 1973 the conveyances were made under the New Parishes Measure 1943 as amended by the Church Property (Miscellaneous Provisions) Measure 1960. In the *Paddington* case the court stated that the two methods were alternatives. But the practical disadvantage of the statutory procedure is that it brings in the bishop and the Church Commissioners whose consents are necessary and who thereby increase the expense without necessarily knowing anything about, or being interested in, the case.[14] Moreover, the purchase money has to be paid to the Church Commissioners and has to be applied by them "to such purposes, being purposes for the benefit of the ecclesiastical district in which the land is situate or charitable purposes relating to that district as may be agreed between the Commissioners and the Bishop after consultation with the owner." If the procedure adopted by Dr. Tristram is followed, no consents except that of the court are necessary and the court gives directions as to the application of the purchase money.

Quite apart from dealings with the title to the unconsecrated churchyard, faculties are needed for anything done on it; for example part of it may be used for the extension of the church, or for building a church hall. Such hall need not be physically attached to the church; the soil cannot be a disused burial ground and section 3 of the D.B.G.A. 1884 cannot apply. Again part may be set aside for the burial of cremated remains. In this last case, care must be taken to lay down in the faculty who is to decide where the remains of a given person may be interred (for the common law right to burial applies only to consecrated burial grounds) and on what principles, and also as to books of remembrance and the like. If part of the curtilage is wanted for road widening, it is possible for the court to allow the legal estate owner to dedicate it as a highway. All the same

---

[14] In *Re St. George's Oakdale* [1976] Fam. 210 at 222, Ellison Ch., as Vicar-General of the diocese, gave the consent of the bishop "to save troubling the Lord Bishop": This is an interesting application of the large and undefined powers of a diocesan Vicar-General.

precautions must of course be taken as in dealings with consecrated land in regard to making the P.C.C. a party if there are to be covenants and as to the disposition of any consideration money. In the *Bushey Heath* case[15] the court said that the money must go to the person who had the legal estate. Further, the court required that boundary marks should be affixed to show that the area over which the right of way was to be granted was still church property. In a case where an easement is granted to exhibit advertisements, covenants should be obtained to ensure their decency.

Since land is increasingly scarce and expensive, there is bound to be pressure on the church to use its unconsecrated churchyards. The number of cases under section 7 is therefore tending to increase. The jurisdiction is given for the protection of the church building, and the court should always have in mind in these cases its duty in that regard. If that is attended to, use of these areas to produce revenue or for public amenity is legitimate and desirable.

---

[15] [1971] 1 W.L.R. 357 at 360E.

7. Enforcement, Costs and Fees

Enforcement

At common law or in equity

In exercising the faculty jurisdiction, the consistory court either grants or withholds licences, called faculties, for the performing of acts which would be unlawful if not authorised by faculty. It follows that if any such act is done without applying for a faculty, or after a faculty has been refused, the person who does it acts unlawfully. Unlawful action has consequences in the general law, quite apart from any direct action which the consistory court may take to vindicate its authority. Thus if chattels appertaining to a church are purportedly sold by the churchwardens in whom they are vested without the authority of a faculty, the purchaser gets no title.[1] Accordingly, since churchwardens are a quasi-corporation for the purpose of holding title to church goods subsequent churchwardens could recover them at common law.[2] Moreover in those circumstances, an auctioneer is not likely to accept church treasures for sale without satisfying himself that sale has been authorised by faculty. At a more modest level, church goods are in fact sometimes sold without a faculty, and the author has personal experience in the diocese of Bath and Wells of a case in which the P.C.C. of a united parish decided to sell the organ from one of the churches and did so without a faculty. On the parishioners who frequented that church complaining, the archdeacon

---

[1] *Re St. Gregory's, Tredington* [1972] Fam. 236; see also *Re West Camel Church* [1979] Fam. 79 and *Re St. Mary's Barton-upon-Humber* [1987] Fam. 41.

[2] Blackstone, *Commentaries on the Laws of England*, Vol. 1, p. 394. The person in possession of the goods may have a defence under the Sale of Goods Act 1979, s.22 (market overt) or s.25(1) (innocent purchaser); but as to the latter see the decision of a majority of the Court of Appeal in *National Employers Mutual General Insurance Association* v. *Jones* [1987] 3 W.L.R. 901.

successfully traced the organ to the dealer who had it and compelled him to return it.

So far as concerns cases where work is done to the fabric of the church or in a churchyard without a faculty, the persons who enter and do the unauthorised work are trespassers and can be sued for damages at common law.[3] Moreover, while the work is not completed, the remedy could well be an injunction to stop it.[4] The ramifications of the entry being a trespass are extensive. Here again, there is an indirect assistance in that a grant-making body is likely to be chary of giving a grant for work which is unlawful, which may therefore be stopped by injunction and which the consistory court can require to be undone. Again, it is submitted that if any parishioner discovers that the P.C.C. is proposing to use its funds to pay for work to the church being done without a faculty and therefore unlawfully, he can sue the council in equity for breach of trust, damages and any injunction that is appropriate.

In the ecclesiastical courts

In the nineteenth century, when there was much controversy about ornaments illegally introduced into churches, it was not unknown for proceedings to be brought against an offending clergyman on the criminal side of the consistory court. In theory this remedy is still available, but it has fallen into disuse for half a century. The relevant powers of the consistory court are now on its civil side. Thus it can grant to any person who is qualified to be a litigant[5] a faculty authorising him to remove an offending object or to undo offending work.[6] Such an order is normally coupled with an order, under section 5 of the F.J.M. 1964, on the

---

[3] *Per* Garth Moore Ch. in *Re Woldingham Churchyard* [1957] 1 W.L.R. 811. Persons who, without a faculty, damage things in a church, such as an organ, may also be liable to prosecution under the Criminal Damage Act 1971: see *per* Garth Moore Ch. in *Re St. Mary's, Balham* [1978] 1 All E.R. 993 at 996e.
[4] Such an injunction could be sought by the archdeacon: see *per* Garth Moore Ch. in *Re St. Mary's, Balham* [1978] 1 All E.R. 993 at 997a.
[5] See pp. 43 *et seq.*
[6] A comparatively recent instance of this sort of case was *Re St. Mary, Tyne Dock* [1954] P. 369 and *Re St. Mary, Tyne Dock (No. 2)* [1958] P. 156. Such cases have seldom occurred since then in respect of ornaments in churches, but there was such an order on one minor point in *Re St. Michael and All Angels, Great Torrington* [1985] Fam. 81 at 91B–C.

person who introduced that object or did that work to pay all the expenses of removing or undoing it as the case may be. Under section 9 of the Measure the archdeacon is a qualified petitioner for such an order, and if he is unable or unwilling to act the bishop can appoint a substitute. Enforcement proceedings should normally be brought by the archdeacon, the incumbent and the P.C.C., or any one or more of them that is available.

The fullest modern authority on the form of remedy is *Re Woldingham Churchyard*.[7] In that case a monument had been introduced into a churchyard without authority being sought or granted. The stonemasons had given the customer an oral assurance that the necessary authority would be obtained, but had not obtained it. Just before erecting the monument, the stonemasons had approached the incumbent and had been told to apply for a faculty. By entering nevertheless and erecting the monument the stonemasons were guilty of what the court described as a "gross trespass," as well as a breach of contract to the customer. As the court said, for both of these actions they were liable in damages at common law. Later, the stonemasons and customer petitioned for confirmatory faculties, which were opposed by the incumbent and archdeacon. Out of consideration for the family of the deceased, the court said that it would grant a confirmatory faculty for part of the monument if the rest (kerbs and chippings) were first removed. The stonemasons were ordered to pay all the costs of removal and were authorised to remove them within one month. If that were not done, the customer was to have another month in which to remove them and so qualify for a confirmatory faculty for the rest of the monument. The stonemasons were ordered to pay the customer's expenses of removal. If neither was done, the incumbent would have a further month to remove them and after three months the order would go to the archdeacon. The stonemasons were ordered to pay all the expenses of removal by incumbent or archdeacon as well as all the costs of all parties to the suit. Finally, the court stated that if there was any repetition by the stonemasons of "this sort of behaviour they are likely to find themselves banned from

---

[7] [1957] 1 W.L.R. 811. There was a somewhat similar order in *Re St. Mary's Balham* [1978] 1 All E.R. 993.

carrying out any work in consecrated ground in this diocese."[8] This case was before the Measure of 1964, but the principles involved and the form of order still stand, reinforced by sections 5 and 9.

Proceedings of this sort have occurred before the author in unreported cases; but the mere threat of them, on more occasions, has been sufficient to ensure that the offending work was undone and usually at the stonemasons' expense.

It is not altogether clear whether in such a case the court may make a mandatory order. Before the Measure of 1964 it was held in *Re St. John-in-Bedwardine, Worcester*[9] that it could not; but it has been explained above[10] that the wording of seciton 5(1), appears to imply that such a power does now exist. It is, however, usually wise to hold this possibility in reserve; the author has no personal experience of making such an order, the *Woldingham* form of order, or the threat of it, being usually sufficient.

Contempt of court

If it is possible to make a mandatory order, the breach of it will be a contempt. Similarly, it is conceived that if a faculty is granted subject to a condition, and if the work is done and the condition is not observed, that would be a contempt. But the more practical use of proceedings for contempt is where a party to proceedings in the consistory court gives an undertaking to the court and fails to observe it. There are, indeed, many such undertakings, and if an undertaking is broken it is the very words of the contemnor himself, used in the undertaking, which he failed to observe. The contempt is thus easy to prove.

Under the Ecclesiastical Courts (Contempt) Act 1832, the consistory court had summary powers to deal with contempt; but that Act was repealed by the E.J.M. 1963, and the powers of the court are now embodied in section 81(2) of that Measure. It provides that "any act or omission in connection with proceedings ... [in the consistory court] ... which, if occurring in connection with proceedings in the High Court, would have

---

[8] [1957] 1 W.L.R. 811 at 813.
[9] [1962] P. 20.
[10] See pp. 78, 79.

been a contempt of the High Court shall be a contempt of [the consistory court]," for which proceedings "shall be brought in the High Court." (s.81(3)).

The practical way of enforcing a remedy for contempt is therefore by motion in the High Court for a writ of attachment. The present section appears not to go beyond the previously existing practice as to this sort of proceeding, the best known reported instance of which is R. v. *Editor of Daily Herald, ex p. the Bishop of Norwich*.[11]

Costs and fees

The consistory court has power to order the payment of costs by any party under the E.J.M. 1963, s.60, and provision is made in section 61 of that Measure for the person in whose favour such an order is made to enforce it, as if it were a contract debt, in the High Court or the county court. In such proceedings a certificate of the registrar of the consistory court as to the amount payable is to be conclusive evidence of the facts certified. Ancillary to this general power is a specific power under section 5 of the Measure of 1964 for the consistory court to make orders in respect of costs in proceedings for a faculty to put right something unlawfully done. There is a similar express power under section 10(*c*) of the same Measure to make an order against any other party to proceedings in which an archdeacon is engaged for payment of the "costs and expenses" of the archdeacon. Further, section 11 of the Measure provides that:

> "any sum payable by virtue of an order of the court in or consequent upon any proceedings for a faculty shall, if the county court so orders, be recoverable by execution issued from the county court or otherwise as if payable under an order of that court."

Section 61(2) of the E.J.M. 1963 makes the certificate of the registrar conclusive in proceedings under section 11 of the F.J.M. 1964, since it applies to "any proceedings in a civil court for recovery of costs."

The court fees in respect of faculty proceedings are regulated by the current Legal Officers' (Fees) Order formerly made under

---

[11] [1932] 2 K.B. 402.

the Ecclesiastical Fees Measure 1962, now made under Ecclesiastical Fees Measure 1986. Before the Order of 1980 there were many of such fees; but since that Order there are, in substance, only three sorts, i.e. lodgment fees, hearing fees and expenses, and the registrar's correspondence fee of a sum stated in the current fees Order or such larger amount as the chancellor may fix. All these fees are prima facie payable by the petitioner, but in some dioceses there are local arrangements under which the lodgment fees in most classes of case are either waived or are paid by the diocesan board of finance. These arrangements do not usually extend to hearing fees. Shortly, whatever is payable in respect of any of these fees falls on the petitioner; but in a proper case the court may make an order providing for them to be recouped wholly or partly in some other way as part of the petitioner's own costs. Where there has been a hearing, it is quite common for an order for such recoupment to be made against an unsuccessful party. In cases where the order leads to a fund coming into being, for example by way of proceeds of sale of a chattel or by way of revenue from a licence authorised by faculty, it is normal to provide for them to be recouped out of the fund.[12] Where there are judge's witnesses, or expenses incurred by the registrar in hiring a place for the court to sit, these expenses are treated as court expenses and are dealt with as part of the registrar's fees.

Beyond the court fees there are the parties' own costs of the proceedings. In the great majority of cases, such costs lie where they fall and there is no order in respect of them. But, depending on the conduct of the parties and the circumstances of the case, there may be an order for one party to pay the costs of one or more of the other parties. Thus in *Re St. John, Chelsea*,[13] where both the petition and the cross-petition failed, the petitioners were ordered to pay a third of the costs of the parties opponent. In *Re Woldingham Churchyard*,[14] the stonemasons were ordered to pay all the costs. In *Re St. George's, Birmingham*,[15] the successful petitioners were ordered to pay the

---

[12] For instance see *Re St. Mary's, Westwell* [1968] 1 W.L.R. 513, *Re St. Gregory's, Tredington* [1972] Fam. 236, *Re St. Mary's Gilston* [1967] P. 125 and *Re St. Mary le Bow* [1984] 1 W.L.R. 1363 at 1368–1369.
[13] [1962] 1 W.L.R. 706.
[14] [1957] 1 W.L.R. 811 and also *Re St. Mark's, Haydock* [1981] 1 W.L.R. 1164.
[15] [1960] 1 W.L.R. 1069.

costs of the archdeacon. In *Re All Saints', Leamington Priors*[16] the unsuccessful party opponent is stated in the report to have been "condemned in costs." In *Re St. Mary's, Luton*[17] the unsuccessful parties opponent were ordered to pay most of the costs of the petitioner. Apart from these cases there are several reported instances in which partial orders have been made, especially for splitting the court fees between the parties.[18] In the appellate courts, the costs of the appeal have prima facie followed the event,[19] but in special circumstances public authorities successful in the appeal have agreed to pay the costs of all parties.[20] In *Re St. Helen's, Brant Broughton*[21] there was no order for costs.

The foregoing analysis is sufficient to show that the practice in the consistory court is a good deal more flexible than that in the secular courts, where costs normally follow the event. The consistory courts are reluctant to make orders for costs of the parties to a suit. They will do so where the losing party is considered to have made unnecessary difficulties or, as in the case of orders for the removal of objects introduced without a faculty, has behaved illegally. But an unsuccessful party opponent who has put forward a reasonable case for having the matter investigated by the chancellor in public is seldom ordered to pay the full costs of the petitioner. When the court reserves judgment, as is very frequent when there has been a hearing, the best practice is for the reserved judgment to order the petitioner to pay all the court fees and to give all parties liberty to apply for such further or other order in respect of court fees and costs as they may be advised. Parties very seldom take

---

[16] [1963] 1 W.L.R. 806.
[17] [1968] P. 47. In *Re St. Andrew's Church, Backwell* (1982); unreported in the Bath and Wells diocese, a civil parish council which was an unsuccessful party opponent was ordered to pay half the costs of the petitioners and half the court fees.
[18] See *Re St. Mary, Tyne Dock (No. 2)* [1958] P. 156, *Re West Camel Church* [1979] Fam. 79.
[19] *Re St. Mary's, Luton* [1965] P. 47 and *Re St. Mary's, Fawkham* [1981] 1 W.L.R. 1171. In *Re St. Michael and All Angels, Torrington* [1985] Fam. 81 at 91 there was no order as to the costs of the appeal. In *Re St. Mary's, Banbury* [1987] Fam. 136 the Court of Arches left open the question of costs for later argument; and in *Re St. Stephen's, Walbrook* [1987] Fam. 146 the successful appellant undertook to pay all the costs of the archdeacon.
[20] *Re St. Edburga's, Abberton* [1962] P. 10 and *Re St. Mary the Virgin, Woodkirk* [1969] 1 W.L.R. 1867.
[21] [1974] Fam. 16. A benefactor paid all the costs.

advantage of this liberty, so that the effect is that the parties bear their own costs.

All orders for costs or court fees should provide for them to be taxed by the registrar of the consistory court except the registrar's own correspondence fee which under the Fees Orders the chancellor must himself fix. It is the registrar, who, as mentioned above, is empowered by section 61 of the E.J.M. 1963 to give a certificate as to the amount which will be conclusive in enforcement proceedings in the secular courts.

Appendix A

	Page
Faculty Jurisdiction Measure 1964	191
Faculty Jurisdiction Rules 1967 as amended by the Faculty Jurisdiction Rules 1987	204

Faculty Jurisdiction Measure 1964

(1964, No. 5)

ARRANGEMENT OF SECTIONS

Jurisdiction in faculty cases

SECT.
1. Vesting of privately owned parts of churches in the persons in whom the churches are vested.
2. Faculties for demolition of churches.
3. Faculties affecting monuments owned by persons withholding consent thereto.
4. Sale of books in parochial libraries under a faculty.
5. Payment of costs by party responsible for breach of law.
6. Licensed chapels may be made subject to faculty jurisdiction.
7. Curtilages of churches.

Rights of sepulture

8. Exclusive rights to burial spaces.

Parties and procedure in faculty cases

9. Archdeacons and non-resident electors to be deemed to have an interest in faculty cases.
10. Functions of archdeacons in faculty cases.
11. Mode of enforcing orders as to costs.

Archdeacon's certificate procedure

12. Archdeacons to issue certificates in certain cases.

Advisory committees

13. Diocesan Advisory Committees.

Miscellaneous

14. Rules.
15. Interpretation.

16. Repeal.
17. Extent and short title.

SCHEDULE.

A Measure passed by the National Assembly of the Church of England to enable ecclesiastical courts to vest privately owned parts of churches in the persons in whom the churches are vested; to amend the law relating to the issue of faculties out of such courts concerning the demolition of churches and works affecting monuments in private ownership; to empower bishops to make certain licensed chapels subject to the faculty jurisdiction of such courts; to declare the law relating to the jurisdiction of such courts over the curtilage of churches; to limit the duration of rights of sepulture; to make better provision for the enforcement of orders as to costs and expenses; to repeal and re-enact the Faculty Jurisdiction Measure, 1938, with amendments; and for other purposes connected therewith.   [15th April, 1964]

Jurisdiction in faculty cases

Vesting of privately owned parts of churches in the persons in whom the churches are vested

1.—(1) In this section "building" means any building or structure forming part of and physically connected with a church and "incumbent" means the incumbent of the benefice comprising the parish in which the church is situated.

(2) A court may in proceedings taken by an incumbent or parochial church council grant a faculty vesting any building in the person or body in whom the church is vested where the incumbent or parochial church council satisfies the court that:—

    (i) the person in whom the church is vested is not the owner entitled to possession of the building or that there is reasonable doubt as to the ownership or right to possession thereof; and

    (ii) the incumbent or parochial church council or some other person has taken all reasonable steps since, or shortly before, the commencement of the proceedings to communicate with all persons who may reasonably be supposed to have any rights of ownership or possession, whether absolute or limited, over the building; and

(iii) notwithstanding such reasonable steps there has been no communication with such person or persons or that all persons with whom communication has been made and who, on reasonable grounds, claim rights of ownership or possession over the building consent to the grant of a faculty under this section; and

(iv) no works of repair, redecoration or reconstruction have been executed upon the building by or on behalf of any person claiming any title thereto adverse to the title of the person in whom the church is vested during the seven years immediately preceding the commencement of the proceedings.

(3) In any proceedings for obtaining a faculty under this section the court may appoint a person being a solicitor to represent all persons other than those represented, known or unknown, who may have rights of ownership or possession over the building in question, and all proper costs of such solicitor in the proceedings shall be paid by the persons bringing the proceedings, unless otherwise ordered by the court.

(4) Where a faculty under this section is granted the building specified therein shall, by virtue of such faculty and without any further or other assurance or conveyance, vest in the person in whom the church is vested as part of the church for all purposes and any rights of property of any other person therein shall thereupon determine.

Faculties for demolition of churches

2.—(1) The court shall not grant a faculty for the demolition or partial demolition of a church except on the grounds specified in this section and shall not grant a faculty under sub-section (2) of this section nor under paragraph (i) of sub-section (3) of this section unless:—

(i) the person bringing proceedings for the faculty has, within the prescribed time, caused to be published in the "London Gazette" and in such other newspapers as the court may direct a notice stating the substance of the petition for the faculty; and

(ii) an officer of the court has given notice in writing to the Council and the advisory committee of the diocese in which the church is situated of the petition; and

(iii) the judge of the court has thereafter considered such advice as the advisory committee has tendered to the court; and

(iv) the judge has heard evidence in open court, after application for the purpose has been made to the court in the prescribed manner, from:—

(a) a member of the Council or some person, duly authorised by the Council; and

(b) any other person, unless in the opinion of the judge his application or the evidence which he gives is frivolous or vexatious.

(2) The court may grant a faculty for the demolition of the whole or part of a church if the court is satisfied that another church will be erected on the site or curtilage of the church in question or part thereof to take the place of that church.

(3) A court may grant a faculty for the demolition of part of a church if it is satisfied that:—

(i) the part of the church left standing will be used for the public worship of the Church of England for a substantial period after such demolition; or

(ii) such demolition is necessary for the purpose of the repair, alteration or reconstruction of the part to be demolished, or of the whole of the church.

Provided that a court shall not grant a faculty under paragraph (ii) of this sub-section unless an officer of the court has given notice in writing to the Council of the petition and the judge has considered any advice which the Council may tender to the court.

(4) A court may grant a faculty for the demolition or partial demolition of any church if, in respect of that church the following order has been made by a court of competent jurisdiction or any of the following notices has been served by the appropriate local authority:—

(i) an order under section [77 of the Building Act, 1984],[1] requiring execution of such work as may be necessary to obviate danger from the condition of that church;

(ii) a notice requiring the taking down, repair or securing of that church given under sub-section (2) of section sixty-two of the London Building Acts (Amendment) Act, 1939, or under the provisions of any other local Act empowering the council of a county, city, borough or district to give such a notice on the grounds that a building or structure is dangerous;

(iii) a notice that the local authority propose to take immediate action to deal with the church as a dangerous building under section [78 of the Building Act 1984];

(iv) a notice requiring the execution of works of repair or restoration to the church under section [79 of the Building Act, 1984].

(5) Nothing in this section shall be construed as prejudicing or affecting the provisions of the Ancient Monuments Acts, 1913 to 1953, or the Town and Country Planning Acts, 1947 to 1959.

Faculties affecting monuments owned by persons withholding consent thereto

3.—(1) This section shall apply to faculties for the moving, demolition, alteration or execution of other work to any monument erected, whether before or after the passing of this Measure, in or upon any church or other consecrated building or the curtilage thereof or upon consecrated ground other than consecrated burial grounds to which section eleven of the Open Spaces Act, 1906, applies or has been applied.

(2) Subject to the provisions of the succeeding sub-section a court may grant a faculty to which this section applies:—

(i) although the owner of the monument withholds his consent thereto or cannot be found after reasonable efforts to find him have been made; and

---

[1] The words in square brackets were substituted by the Building Act 1984, Sched. 6.

(ii) in respect of a monument erected under a faculty or affecting which any faculty has been granted, whatever the date of such faculty.

(3) No faculty to which this section applies shall be granted if the owner of the monument in question withholds his consent thereto but satisfies the court that he is, within a reasonable time, willing and able to remove the monument (or so much thereof as may be proved to be his property) and to execute such works as the court may require to repair any damage to the fabric of any building or to any land caused by such removal. The court may, upon a petition for a faculty to which this section applies, grant a faculty authorising such removal and for all purposes connected therewith and may make such orders as may be just as to the execution and cost of all necessary works.

(4) For the purposes of this section "monument" includes a tomb, gravestone or other memorial and any kerb or setting forming part thereof, and "owner" means the person who erected the monument in question and, after his death, the heir or heirs at law of the person or persons in whose memory the monument was erected and "property" shall be construed accordingly.

Sale of books in parochial libraries under a faculty

4.—(1) Notwithstanding anything to the contrary contained in section ten of the Parochial Libraries Act, 1708, any book in a parochial library appropriated to the use of the minister of any parish or place within the operation of that Act may be sold under the authority of a faculty, and in the case of every sale so authorised the proceeds of sale shall be applied for such of the ecclesiastical purposes of the parish as in such faculty may be directed. Before granting such a faculty the judge shall require the advisory committee to advise him thereon and shall consider such advice as the committee may tender to the court.

(2) Any question whether a library is within the said Act and is so appropriated shall be finally determined by the Charity Commissioners.

Payment of costs by party responsible for breach of law

5.—(1) If in any proceeding for a faculty, whether opposed or not, it appears to the court that any person being a party to the proceeding was responsible wholly or in part for the introduction into or removal from a church, churchyard or other consecrated ground of any articles without the necessary faculty, or for the execution of any work in a church, churchyard or other consecrated ground without the necessary faculty, the court may order the whole or any part of the costs and expenses of the proceeding or consequent thereon, including the cost of any works ordered by the court (so far as such costs, cost of works, and expenses have been occasioned by such introduction, removal or unlawful execution as the case may be), to be paid by such person.

(2) In any such proceeding the court may by way of special citation add as a further party to the proceeding any person alleged to be so responsible or partly responsible and not already a party and notwithstanding that such person resides out of the diocese.

Licensed chapels may be made subject to faculty jurisdiction

6.—(1) Where the bishop has licensed a building for public worship and he considers that circumstances have arisen which make it desirable that such building should be subject to the faculty jurisdiction he may by order direct that such building shall be subject to the jurisdiction of the court of the diocese during such period as may be specified in the order.

(2) Any building in respect of which an order is made under this section shall, during the period specified in the order, be subject, together with its furnishings and contents, to the jurisdiction of the court specified in the order as though it were a consecrated church; but an order shall not render unlawful any act done before the making of the order nor shall require the issue of faculties confirming such acts.

(3) The bishop shall send every order made under this section to the registrar of the diocese and the registrar shall register any order so made in the diocesan registry. There shall be payable to the diocesan registrar for registering such order, for permitting searches for and giving inspection and furnishing copies of any such order such fees as may from time to time be authorised by an order made under the Ecclesiastical Fees Measure, 1962.

(4) An order made under this section shall be revocable by the bishop at any time.

Curtilages of churches

7.—(1) For the avoidance of doubt it is hereby declared that where unconsecrated land forms, or is part of, the curtilage of a church within the jurisdiction of a court that court has the same jurisdiction over such land as over the church.

(2) This section shall not render unlawful any act done or proceedings taken in good faith before the passing of this Measure nor shall require the issue of faculties confirming such acts.

Rights of sepulture

Exclusive rights to burial spaces

8.—(1) Any right to the exclusive use of any particular part of a churchyard, burial ground or other consecrated land for the purposes of sepulture, whether absolute or limited and however granted or acquired, shall cease one hundred years after the passing of this Measure, unless granted, enlarged or continued by a faculty issued after the passing of this Measure:

Provided that the court shall not issue a faculty granting enlarging of continuing any such right for any period longer than one hundred years from the date of the faculty.

(2) This section shall not apply to burial grounds and cemeteries provided under the Burial Acts, 1852 to 1906, or the Public Health (Interments) Act, 1879.

Parties and procedure in faculty cases

Archdeacons and non-resident electors to be deemed to have an interest in faculty proceedings

9.—(1) For the purposes of any proceeding for obtaining a faculty the archdeacon of the archdeaconry in which the parish concerned is situate shall be deemed to have an interest as such, and any person whose name is entered on the electoral roll of the parish concerned but who does not reside therein shall be deemed to have an interest as though he were a parishioner of that parish.

(2) If the archdeaconry be vacant or the archdeacon be incapacitated by absence or illness from exercising or fulfilling the rights or duties conferred or imposed upon him by this Measure or is in the opinion of the bishop for any other reason unable or unwilling to act, such other person as the bishop shall appoint in that behalf in writing shall have power to act in the place of the archdeacon for the purposes of this Measure in any particular case.

(3) If the archdeacon or such other person as may be appointed under this section intervenes in any such proceeding all costs properly incurred by him or which he shall be ordered by the court to pay shall be paid by the board of finance of the diocese in which the parish concerned is situate:

Provided that a board shall not be liable for any sum by virtue of this section unless such intervention is approved by the board in writing and, if such approval is duly given, any order in such proceeding that the costs of the archdeacon or other appointed person be paid by any other party may be enforced by the board in the name of the archdeacon or other appointed person.

Functions of archdeacons in faculty cases

10. In any proceeding for obtaining a faculty the court may:—

   (*a*) decree the issue of a faculty, subject to a condition requiring the work authorised thereby or any part thereof to be carried out under the supervision of the archdeacon or of any other person nominated by the court in that behalf; and
   (*b*) direct that, in default of the incumbent and churchwardens carrying out the work so authorised or any part thereof, a faculty shall issue to the archdeacon authorising him to carry out the same; and
   (*c*) order that the costs and expenses of the archdeacon be paid by any other party to the proceeding.

Mode of enforcing orders as to costs and expenses

11. Any sum payable by virtue of an order of the court in or consequent upon any proceeding for a faculty shall, if the

county court so orders, be recoverable by execution issued from the county court or otherwise as if payable under an order of that court.

Archdeacon's certificate procedure

Archdeacons to issue certificates in certain cases

12.—(1) Every application received by the registrar of a diocese from the incumbent and churchwardens of a parish, supported by a resolution of the parochial church council, for authority to carry out:—

- (*a*) repairs to a church not involving substantial change in the structure of the building nor affecting its appearance either externally or internally; or
- (*b*) repairs to the contents of a church not materially affecting their nature or appearance; or
- (*c*) redecoration of a church or its contents; or
- (*d*) any alteration in an existing heating system not involving a substantial change in the appearance of the church either externally or internally;

shall, subject to the provision of this section, be referred by the registrar to the archdeacon of the archdeaconry in which the church is situate.

(2) The registrar shall not refer any such application to the archdeacon unless:—

- (i) he is satisfied that it is an application within the preceding subsection; and
- (ii) the application is supported by a certificate from the incumbent and churchwardens that notice of intention to make such an application has been given in the prescribed manner in the parish and that opportunity to object to the proposed works has been duly given to all having interest:

Provided that if the registrar is not satisfied that an application is within the preceding subsection he shall so inform the archdeacon and shall refer the application to the judge in the prescribed manner for directions thereon.

(3) If notice of objection to the proposed works is given to the registrar in the prescribed manner he shall not refer the application to the archdeacon but shall require the incumbent and churchwardens to apply to the court for a faculty in respect of the proposed works.

(4) The archdeacon shall consider any application referred to him under this section and shall: —

> (a) with the approval of the advisory committee, issue a certificate authorising the execution of the work proposed; or
>
> (b) direct that application should be made to the court for a faculty with regard thereto.

(5) A certificate issued by an archdeacon in pursuance of this section shall be a sufficient authority for the execution of the proposed work without a faculty.

(6) A copy of any certificate issued by an archdeacon under this section shall be transmitted by him to the registrar of the diocese and filed in the diocesan registry.

(7) The procedure laid down by this section may be followed at the discretion of the judge with regard to any other application which in his opinion is unlikely to give rise to any controversy or dissatisfaction in the parish concerned and is not of sufficient importance to justify the expense of proceedings for a faculty.

Advisory committees

Diocesan Advisory Committees

13.—(1) In every diocese there shall be an advisory committee for the care of churches, to be known as "the Diocesan Advisory Committee," consisting of the archdeacons of all the archdeaconries within the diocese and such other persons as the bishop may by writing appoint, whose term of office shall be five years. Members shall be eligible for re-appointment. The bishop may appoint one of the members of the advisory committee to be chairman.

(2) The advisory committee shall advise the archdeacon before the issue of a certificate under the preceding section and, if required to do so, shall advise: —

(a) the judge;
(b) intending applicants for faculties;
(c) persons building new churches or converting buildings for the purpose of churches or erecting buildings or converting existing buildings with the intention that they shall be licensed for public worship; and
(d) persons owning or responsible for the upkeep of unconsecrated buildings licensed for public worship.

Miscellaneous

Rules

14.—(1) A Rule Committee, constituted in manner laid down by the Schedule hereto, may make rules:—

(a) for regulating the practice of all courts in relation to applications for faculties and so that the power to make such rules shall extend to all matters of procedure and practice within the cognisance of the faculty jurisdiction of all courts;
(b) for regulating the manner in which the plans and specifications of any work for which a faculty is required shall be submitted to the advisory committee and the manner in which the report thereon of the advisory committee shall be submitted to the court;
(c) for regulating the procedure and practice where application is made for an archdeacon's certificate under section twelve of this Measure; and
(d) otherwise for carrying this Measure into effect.

(2) Upon the coming into operation of rules made under the preceding sub-section all rules of procedure in relation to applications for faculties of any court which are inconsistent therewith shall cease to have effect and no practice which is inconsistent with those rules shall thereafter prevail in any court.

(3) Every rule made in pursuance of this section shall be laid before the Church Assembly and shall not come into operation unless it has been approved by the Church Assembly.

(4) The Statutory Instruments Act, 1946, shall apply to any rule approved by the Church Assembly under the last foregoing

sub-section as if it were a statutory instrument and were made when so approved, and as if this Measure were an Act providing that any such rule should be subject to annulment in pursuance of a resolution of either House of Parliament.

Interpretation

15. In this Measure unless the context otherwise requires:—

"advisory committee" means the advisory committee for the care of churches of a diocese appointed under section thirteen of this Measure;
"bishop" means the bishop of the diocese concerned;
"council" means the Central Council of Diocesan Advisory Committees for the Care of Churches, as constituted in accordance with the resolution of the Church Assembly passed on the 18th June, 1958, or any body subsequently constituted to exercise the functions of the Council as so constituted;[2]
"court" means the ecclesiastical court of any province or diocese;
"judge" means the judge of any such court;
"prescribed" means prescribed by rules made under section fourteen of this Measure.

Repeal

16. The Faculty Jurisdiction Measure, 1938, is hereby repealed, but any rule made under the said Measure shall remain in force until replaced or otherwise revoked by rules made under this Measure.

Extent and short title

17.—(1) This Measure shall extend to the whole of the provinces of Canterbury and York, except the Channel Islands and the Isle of Man.

(2) This Measure may be cited as the Faculty Jurisdiction Measure, 1964.

---

[2] Now the Central Council for Churches.

Schedule

1. The Rule Committee shall consist of:—

   (a) A diocesan bishop nominated by the Archbishops of Canterbury and York;

   (b) The vicars-general of the provinces of Canterbury and York;
   The chancellor of the diocese of London;
   The registrars of the provinces of Canterbury and York;
   One diocesan registrar, not being a provincial registrar, nominated by the Archbishops of Canterbury and York.

   (c) Two persons, one clerical and one lay, nominated by the Council.

2. Any three members of the Rule Committee, two of them being persons holding offices mentioned in sub-paragraph (b) of the foregoing paragraph may exercise all the powers of the Rule Committee.

Faculty Jurisdiction Rules 1967[3]
(S.I. 1967 No. 1002)

Made (Approved by the Church Assembly)	4th July 1967
Laid before Parliament	11th July 1967
Coming into Operation	1st January 1968

In pursuance of section 14 of the Faculty Jurisdiction Measure 1964, the Rule Committee constituted in accordance with the Schedule to the said Measure hereby make the following Rules:—

Preliminary

1. These Rules may be cited as the Faculty Jurisdiction Rules 1967, and shall come into operation on the first day of January 1968.

---

[3] The Faculty Jurisdiction Rules 1967 were amended by the Faculty Jurisdiction (Amendment) Rules 1975 and the Faculty Jurisdiction Rules 1987, which came into operation on April 1, 1988, and revoked the 1975 Rules. The Rules of 1967 are here printed as amended by the Rules of 1987. The amendments are indicated by double square brackets.

2.—(1) In these Rules—

"The Measure" means the Faculty Jurisdiction Measure 1964;

"the judge" and "the registrar" mean, in relation to any proceedings, the chancellor and the registrar respectively of the diocese in which the church, churchyard or other place concerned is situated, and include any person appointed to act as the deputy of the chancellor or registrar, as the case may be;

"place of worship" means a building licensed for public worship and subject to the faculty jurisdiction by virtue of an order under section 6 of the Measure.

[["period of citation" means the period during which a citation issued under paragraph (1) of rule 5 is required to remain in position under that paragraph.

"statutory amenity society" means any of the following, the Ancient Monuments Society, the Council for British Archaeology, the Georgian Group, the Society for the Protection of Ancient Buildings, the Victorian Society, and such other body as may be designated by the Dean of the Arches as a statutory amenity society either generally or for the purpose of any class of application for faculty.]]

(2) The Interpretation Measure 1925 shall apply for the interpretation of these Rules as it applies for the interpretation of Church Assembly Measures.

Application for archdeacon's certificate

3.—(1) An application under section 12 of the Measure by the incumbent and churchwardens of a parish for authority to carry out the works mentioned in subsection (1) of that section or, subject to the exercise of the judge's discretion under subsection (7), other works or purposes, shall be in the form set out in the Appendix, and shall be lodged at the diocesan registry.

(2) Any necessary designs, plans or other documents giving particulars of the proposed works or purposes shall accompany the application.

(3) If the advice of the Diocesan Advisory Committee has been sought, their recommendation of the proposals (which may be endorsed in accordance with Rule 10 on the designs, plans or other documents) or their report thereon shall accompany the application.

(4) The notice of intention to make the application, which is required by section 12(2) of the Measure, shall be in the form set out in the Appendix, [[and, for a continuous period of not less than 10 clear days including two Sundays, shall be displayed—

(a) In the case of application relating to a parish church—
  (i) on a notice board or in some other prominent position inside that church, and
  (ii) on a notice board outside that church,
(b) In the case of an application relating to a church or place of worship which is not a parish church—
  (i) on a notice board or in some other prominent position inside that church or place of worship, inside the parish church or parish churches in the parish concerned and inside any other church or place of worship in that parish as the registrar may direct, and
  (ii) on a notice board outside the church or place of worship to which the application relates, outside the parish church or parish churches in the parish concerned and outside any other church or place of worship in that parish as the registrar may direct;

and if there is no notice board within the grounds of any building mentioned in sub-paragraph (a)(ii) or (b)(ii) above, the notice required to be displayed outside that building under those sub-paragraphs shall be displayed on the outside of the principal door of that building.]]

(5) The certificate required by the said section 12(2) of the Measure that notice of intention to make such an application and opportunity to object has been duly given shall be in the form set out in the Appendix, and shall be endorsed on a copy of the notice of intention.

(6) If the registrar is not satisfied that the application is within section 12(1) of the Measure, he shall refer it to the judge by submitting the application and supporting documents with his observations thereon, and the judge may, if he also is not satisfied as aforesaid, exercise his discretion under section 12(7) and allow the procedure under the section to be followed accordingly.

(7) A notice of objection to the proposed works or purposes under section 12(3) of the Measure shall be in the form set out in the Appendix and shall be lodged at the diocesan registry not more than 14 days after the notice of intention was first affixed, and the registrar shall not refer the application to the archdeacon until after the expiration of that period.

(8) The approval of the Diocesan Advisory Committee required by section 12(4) of the Measure for the issue of the archdeacon's certificate shall be in writing and signed by the chairman or secretary, and a recommendation of the proposed works or purposes endorsed on the designs, plans or other documents giving particulars thereof and signed as aforesaid shall be a sufficient approval.

(9) The archdeacon's certificate shall be in the form set out in the Appendix.

Petition for faculty

4.—(1) A petition for a faculty for any works or purposes other than the demolition or partial demolition of a church shall be in the form set out in the Appendix.

(2) A petition for a faculty for the demolition or partial demolition of a church shall include all such statements and information, so far as relevant, as are required by Form No. 6 and shall also state which of the grounds specified in section 2 of the Measure are relied on, and shall give full particulars of those grounds and of the circumstances giving rise to the petition, and of the arrangements proposed to be made to meet the situation arising from the demolition or partial demolition of the church, including arrangements for the disposal of the fittings and contents of the church, and shall give information on any other matters on which the judge should be informed.

(3) Any necessary designs, plans or other documents giving particulars of the proposed works or purposes for which the faculty is required shall accompany the petition.

(4) If the advice of the Diocesan Advisory Committee has been sought, their recommendation of the proposals (which may be endorsed in accordance with Rule 10 on the designs, plans or other documents) or their report thereon shall accompany the petition.

(5) The petition and accompanying documents shall be lodged at the diocesan registry and, in the case of proceedings for the demolition or partial demolition of a church, an additional copy of the petition and documents shall be lodged.

[[*Requirements as to notice of petition*

5.—(1) The registrar shall lay every petition for a faculty and its supporting documents before the judge who if he considers it a fit case shall direct that a general citation shall issue in Form No. 7A set out in the Appendix, and shall require a copy of the citation to be displayed for a continuous period of not less than 10 days including two Sundays or such other longer period as the judge may direct—

- (*a*) In the case of a petition relating to a parish church—
    - (i) on a notice board or in some other prominent position inside that church, and
    - (ii) on a notice board outside that church,
- (*b*) in the case of a petition relating to a church or place of worship which is not a parish church—
    - (i) on a notice board or in some other prominent position inside that church or place of worship, inside the parish church or parish churches in the parish concerned and inside any other church or place of worship in that parish as the registrar may direct, and
    - (ii) on a notice board outside the church or place of worship to which the application relates, outside the parish church or parish churches in the parish concerned and outside any other church or place of worship in that parish as the registrar may direct;

and if there is no notice board within the grounds of any building mentioned in sub-paragraph (a)(ii) or (b)(ii) above, the notice required to be displayed outside that building under those sub-paragraphs shall be displayed on the outside of the principal door of that building.

(2) The judge, if he considers it desirable and practicable so to do, may require a copy of the citation to be posted in some prominent position elsewhere in the parish concerned (whether

inside or outside a building) where it will be clearly visible to the public.

(3) If the judge directs or the law otherwise requires any person to be specially cited the registrar shall serve on him a copy of the citation.

(4) The judge if he thinks fit may order that notice of the citation be published in such newspapers or other publications as he directs and in such form as he directs.

(5) Upon the expiry of the period of citation the citation or a copy thereof shall be returned to the registrar with a certificate of execution duly completed thereon in accordance with Form No. 7A in the Appendix.

(6) Notwithstanding anything in paragraph (1) of this rule, in the case of a petition for a faculty for the exhumation of any human remains, the judge shall have the following powers that is to say:

  (a) if he is satisfied that any near relatives of the deceased person still living and any other persons who in the opinion of the judge it is reasonable to regard as being concerned with the matter are the petitioners or that they consent to the proposed faculty being granted, he may dispense with the issue of a citation and decree the issue of the faculty forthwith;
  (b) in any other case he may dispense with the issue of a general citation and may direct that any of the persons referred to in sub-paragraph (a) above who are not the petitioners shall be specially cited.

(7) Where the petition is for a faculty for the demolition or partial demolition of a church the notice stating the substance of the petition (which is required by section 2(1)(i) of the Measure to be published by the petitioners in the London Gazette and in such other newspaper as the court may direct) shall be published:

  (a) in the case of the London Gazette not more than four weeks after the petition was lodged at the registry,
  (b) in the case of such other newspapers within such period as the judge shall direct or, if no period is directed, within 14 days of the giving of the direction.

(8)(i) Where the petition is for a faculty for the disposal of an article which in the opinion of the judge is or may be an article of historic or artistic interest, he may direct the registrar to serve notice in writing of the petition on the Council for the Care of Churches[4]; and where the judge gives such a direction, he shall direct the petitioner to serve on that Council a copy of the petition and of the accompanying documents which were lodged in the diocesan registry under rule 4(5).

(ii) in this rule "article" may include not only an ornament or moveable object but also a part of a building, any thing affixed to land or a building and any part of an article.]]

[[*Objections to petition*

5A.—(1) Any interested person who wishes to object to a proposed faculty being granted shall at any time during the period of citation or within seven days after the expiry of the said period send to the registry and to the petitioners a written notice of objection containing the information required by Form No. 7A in the Appendix and he shall thereupon be treated as a party opponent for all purposes including any order for costs which may be made by the judge pursuant to section 60 of the Ecclesiastical Jurisdiction Measure 1963.

(2) In this Rule "interested person," in relation to a petition for a faculty, means—

- (*a*) any person who is resident in the parish concerned and any person whose name is entered on the electoral roll of the parish concerned but who does not reside therein;
- (*b*) the archdeacon of the archdeaconry in which the parish concerned is situated;
- (*c*) the local planning authority for the area in which the church or place of worship is situated;
- (*d*) any statutory amenity society;
- (*e*) any other body designated by the judge for the purpose of the petition; and
- (*f*) any other person appearing to the registrar to have a lawful interest in the subject matter of the petition.

---

[4] Now the Central Council for Churches.

(3) Where any interested person has given notice of objection, the registrar shall direct him to lodge at the registry written Particulars of Objection setting out in detail the grounds of his objection on Form No. 7B in the Appendix and shall require him to serve a copy of his Particulars of Objection on the petitioners not more than 21 days from the date of the registrar's direction.

(4) In a case where either no notice of objection has been given under paragraph (1) above or, if such notice of objection has been given, no Particulars of Objection have been lodged within the time allowed, or where the judge is satisfied that all the parties concerned consent to the grant of a faculty, the judge may, subject to the production of such evidence (if any) as he may require, and subject to the requirements of section 2(1) or section 4 of the Measure, grant the faculty.

(5) Where Particulars of Objection have been lodged at the registry the petitioners may not more than 14 days after the lodging of those Particulars lodge at the registry an Answer thereto and shall serve a copy thereof on each of the parties opponent.

(6) If any party objects to any pleading of an opposing party, or to any part of any such pleading as being irrelevant, embarrassing, or bad in law he may, not more than 14 days after it has been sent to him, lodge at the registry a notice in writing setting out his reasons for objecting thereto and he shall at the same time serve a copy of the said notice on the parties opponent; and a party whose pleading is so objected to may not more than 14 days after the lodging of the said notice lodge in the registry and serve on the opposing party an amended pleading.

(7) Where objection has been taken to any pleading (including an amended pleading) under the last foregoing paragraph and no amended pleading has been lodged in respect of that objection wihin the time allowed the registrar shall lay the pleading before the judge, who shall either appoint a day to decide as a preliminary issue the matters raised by the objection or reserve them for decision at the general hearing of the case.

(8) If any issue raised by the pleading remains outstanding after the pleadings are closed the judge or the registrar if ordered by the judge shall give such directions to the parties as he may think fit in relation to discovery of documents, the number of expert witnesses to be called on behalf of any party,

the exchange of reports of expert witnesses and any other matter which he considers will facilitate the hearing of the case.]]

[[*The hearing*

6.—(1) Where the period of 28 days from the time given for compliance with any directions given under paragraph (7) of Rule 5A above has expired or where the case is one to which section (2)(1)(iv) of the Measure applies, the registrar shall lay all the documents lodged at the registry before the judge, who shall appoint a time and place for the hearing of the case.

(2) In addition to notifying the parties the registrar shall send to the archdeacon and, if it has considered the case the Diocesan Advisory Committee, written notice of the time and place of the hearing.

(3) The evidence at the hearing of any proceedings for a faculty shall be given orally save that the judge upon application by a party or of his own motion may by order direct;

 (*a*) that all or any part of the evidence may be given before an examiner appointed by him or by affidavit, and

 (*b*) subject of paragraphs (4) and (5) below, that a written statement may be given in evidence without the attendance of the maker of the statement.

(4) An application to submit a written statement in evidence at the hearing may be made by or on behalf of any person who is not a party to the proceedings and the judge may, if he thinks fit, give leave for a written statement to be admitted in evidence without the attendance of the maker of the statement provided that a copy of the written statement is lodged at the registry and that a copy is delivered by that person to the parties not less than 21 days before the date of the hearing.

(5) Notwithstanding anything in paragraph (3) above, the judge shall be entitled on receiving a copy of a written statement to require the attendance at the hearing of the maker of the statement for cross-examination by the parties, and if any party on receiving a copy of the statement applies to the judge for an order requiring the attendance of the maker of the statement at the hearing for cross-examinaton, the judge may make an order accordingly; and in the event of the failure of the maker of the

statement to attend the hearing when required to do so under this paragraph, his written statement shall not be admitted in evidence save in exceptional circumstances with the leave of the judge.

(6) An application to give evidence made by a member of the Council for the Care of Churches or other person by virtue of section 2(1)(iv) of the Measure shall be made to the registrar and shall

(a) if made by a member of the Council or a person authorised by the Council, be in Form No. 8 in the Appendix and be lodged at the diocesan registry not more than six weeks after the Council has received notice in writing of the petition under section 2(1)(ii) of the Measure;

(b) if made by any other person, be in Form No. 9 in the Appendix and be lodged at the registry not more than four weeks after the date of the last publication in accordance with Rule 5(7) of the notice stating the substance of the petition.

(7) Where notice in writing of a petition has been served on the Council for the Care of Churches under rule 5(8) —

(a) a report by the Council on the matter to which the petition relates may be made and sent to the judge within six weeks after the date on which the Council received notice of the petition; or

(b) an application to give evidence in the proceedings may be made by a member of the Council or a person authorised by the Council, and any such application shall be in Form No. 9A set out in the Appendix and shall be lodged at the diocesan registry not more than six weeks after the said date.

(8) The judge may of his own motion direct the summoning of a member of the Diocesan Advisory Committee or any other person to give evidence at the hearing of any petition for a faculty, if he considers that the person summoned may be able to give relevant evidence and is willing to give it.

(9) Where any person has applied in accordance with paragraph (6) or (7) of this rule, or has been summoned under paragraph (8) thereof, to give evidence in proceedings for a

faculty, the registrar shall give to the parties to the proceedings not less than seven clear days' notice in writing that the evidence is to be given and of the name and address of the proposed witness and, in the case of a witness summoned under paragraph (8) of this rule, of the nature of the evidence required of him.

(10) Evidence given by any such person as is referred to in paragraph (9) of this rule shall be subject to cross-examination by the party or parties concerned.

(11) The substance of any report made to the judge by the Council for the Care of Churches under paragraph (7) of this rule shall be disclosed to the parties to the proceedings.]]

[[*Disposal of proceedings by written representations*

6A.—(1) Except in any case in which the judge is required to hear evidence in open court under section 2(1) of the Measure, the judge, if he considers it expedient to do so and is satisfied that all the parties to the proceedings have agreed in writing, may order that the proceedings shall be determined upon consideration of written representations instead of by a hearing in court.

(2) Where an order has been made by the judge under paragraph (1) above, the registrar shall give notice—

    (i) that the petitioners shall lodge at the registry and serve on each of the parties opponent within 21 days of the direction a written statement in support of their case including the documentary or other evidence upon which they wish to rely;

    (ii) that each of the parties opponent shall not more than twenty-one days after the lodging of the petitioners' statement lodge at the registry and serve on the petitioners a written statement in reply to the petitioners' statement and in support of his case including any documentary or other evidence upon which he wishes to rely;

    (iii) that the petitioners may not more than 14 days after the lodging of the statement of an opposing party lodge at the registry and serve on such opposing party a written statement in response thereto.

(3) If any party does not comply with any such direction, the judge may declare him to be in default and may thereafter proceed to dispose of the case without any further reference to such party.

(4) Any party against whom an order declaring him to be in default is made may at any time apply to the court to revoke that order, and the judge may in his discretion revoke the order on such terms as to costs or otherwise as may be just.

(5) Notwithstanding the existence of an order that the proceedings shall be dealt with by written representations, the judge may if he thinks fit at any stage revoke the order and direct that the proceedings shall be determined at an oral hearing and he shall thereupon give directions for the future conduct of the proceedings.

(6) If no order has been made under paragraph (5), the judge shall determine the proceedings upon the pleadings and the written statements and evidence submitted to him under this rule, and his decision thereon shall be as valid and binding on all parties as if it had been made after an oral hearing.

(7) The judge or the registrar (if so authorised by the judge) may give such other directions as to him appear just and convenient for the expeditious despatch of proceedings under this rule.]]

7.—(1) Where a faculty is granted authorising works or purposes other than the demolition or partial demolition of a church, and the case is one in which no objections have been taken to the granting thereof, the faculty shall be in the form set out in the Appendix.

(2) Unless the judge otherwise directs there shall be included in every faculty authorising works a provision requiring the works to be completed within such period as the judge may direct and requiring their completion to be certified by such persons as the judge may direct and the certificate to be lodged at the diocesan registry within that period.

(3) There shall be issued with every faculty containing such a provision as aforesaid a certificate in the form set out in the Appendix to be completed in accordance with that provision and, if the faculty is issued subject to a condition requiring the works or any part thereof to be carried out under the supervision of the archdeacon or any other person (as provided

in section 10(*a*) of the Measure), the certificate shall also certify that that condition has been complied with.

Interchangeability of certificate and faculty procedures

8.—(1) If, as a result of directions of the judge or the archdeacon or the giving of a notice of objection, an application under section 12 of the Measure is not granted and a faculty is required, the judge or (subject to any directions of the judge) the registrar may, if the applicants so desire, direct that the application shall be treated as a petition for a faculty, and Rules 4 to 7 shall apply thereto, so far as applicable, subject to the following provisions:—

(*a*) the judge may direct that the general citation shall be dispensed with and that any notice of objection given under section 12(3) of the Measure and Rule 3(7) shall be treated as an entry of appearance to the petition;

(*b*) if no such notice of objection has been given, the judge may proceed under Rule 5(6)[5] as in the case of a petition to which no appearance has been entered.

(2) Where a direction is given under paragraph (1)(*a*) of this Rule and any notice of objection has been given as aforesaid, the registrar shall notify the person or each of the persons giving the notice of the effect of the direction, and that, if it is desired to contest the proceedings for a faculty, a statement in writing setting out his objections in detail must be lodged not more than 14 days after the registrar's notification has been received.

9. If it appears to the registrar or judge that the petitioners for a faculty, being the incumbent and churchwardens of a parish, could more appropriately have made an application under section 12 of the Measure, he may, if the petitioners so desire, direct that a notice of intention to make such an application in respect of the works or purposes concerned may be given and certified under Rule 3(4) and (5), and that, on receipt of the certificate by the registrar, the petition shall be treated as an application under section 12.

---

[5] The reference is to r.5(6) in the unamended Rules of 1967, which has been revoked. It should be to the present r.5A(4).

Diocesan Advisory Committees and Council for the Care of Churches[6]

10.—(1) Where the advice of a Diocesan Advisory Committee is required by intending applicants under section 12 of the Measure or by intending petitioners for a faculty, they shall submit to the Committee all necessary designs, plans or other documents giving particulars of the proposed works or other purposes, and if the Committee decide to recommend the works or purposes, their recommendation may be endorsed on the said documents and signed by the chairman or secretary of the Committee; and if no such endorsement is made, they shall make a separate report to the intending applicants or petitioners, which may be in the form of a copy of the relevant minutes of the Committee signed as aforesaid.

(2) Without prejudice to the requirements of sections 2 and 4 of the Measure in relation to the faculties therein mentioned, the judge may at any stage of the proceedings for a faculty require the advice of the Diocesan Advisory Committee, and may refer any report of the Committee to the Council for the Care of Churches for further consideration and advice; and the substance of any report made to the judge by the Committee or Council shall be disclosed to the parties.

(3) A Diocesan Advisory Committee may make its own rules of procedure, and may adopt any general regulations as to procedure made by the said Council.

Appointment of person to act for archdeacon

11.—(1) In making an appointment under section 9(2) of the Measure of a person to act in place of an archdeacon on the ground of incapacity, the bishop may act on such evidence of the incapacity of the archdeacon as he shall think sufficient, and a statement of the fact of his incapacity in the instrument of appointment shall be conclusive.

(2) An instrument of appointment under section 9(2) shall be in the form set out in the Appendix.

[[*Appointment of person to sit as clerk of the court in place of registrar*

11A. If the judge by whom any proceedings for a faculty are to

---

[6] Now the Central Council for Churches.

be heard is of opinion that by reason of the fact that the registrar has acted for any of the parties or has otherwise been personally connected with the proceedings he ought not to sit as clerk of the court at the hearing, he shall appoint another practising solicitor to sit as such clerk in place of the registrar.]]

General provisions

12.—(1) Service of any document may be effected—

   (a) by leaving the document at the proper address of the person to be served, or
   (b) by sending it by the recorded delivery service to that address, or
   (c) in such other manner as the judge or registrar may direct.

(2) For the purpose of this Rule, and of section 26 of the Interpretation Act 1889 (as applied by the Interpretation Measure 1925) in its application to this Rule, the proper address of any person on whom a document is to be served under this Rule shall be—

   (a) his usual or last known address, or
   (b) the business address of the solicitor (if any) who is acting for him in the proceedings.

(3) Any document required by these Rules to be lodged at the diocesan registry may be lodged by delivering the document at the registry, or by sending it by post properly addressed to the registrar at the registry.

13.—(1) Where anything is required by these Rules to be done not more than a specified number of days or weeks after a specified act or event, the day on which the act or event occurred shall not be counted.

(2) The registrar or judge may, on an application made by the person concerned, extend the time within which anything is required to be done by these Rules, and the application may be made notwithstanding that the time has expired.

(3) The registrar or judge may exercise the said power on an ex parte application, or may give directions for the giving of notice thereof and for a hearing.

(4) Any such application may be granted on such terms as the registrar or judge may think just.

14. Non-compliance with any of these Rules shall not render any proceedings void unless the judge so directs, but the proceedings may be set aside, either wholly or in part, as irregular, or may be amended or otherwise dealt with in such manner and upon such terms as the judge thinks fit.

15. Where any of these Rules requires a document to be in a form set out in the Appendix, and that form is not in all respects appropriate, the Rules shall be construed as requiring a form of the like character, with such variations as circumstances may require, to be used.

16. Nothing in these Rules shall prejudice any powers or rights reserved to the Bishop of a diocese by the instrument appointing the Chancellor of the diocese.

17. The Faculty Jurisdiction Rules 1964 and all diocesan Rules relating to faculty proceedings are hereby revoked.

Henry Willink.
Robert Exon.
S. I. A. Evans.
D. M. M. Carey.
Innes N. Ware.
J. S. Widdows.
W. S. Wigglesworth.

Dated the ninth day of July 1967.

Approved by the Church Assembly the fourth day of July 1967.

John Guillum Scott,
Secretary.

Appendix

FORMS

No. 1

Application for archdeacon's certificate

Diocese of
Parish of

1. We, A.B., incumbent of the parish of   and C.D., of   and E.F., of   churchwardens of that parish, hereby apply under section 12 of the Faculty Jurisdiction Measure 1964 for authority to carry out the works or purposes described in the Schedule hereto. (*See note at end of form on the matters appropriate for this procedure.*)

2. The particulars of the said works or purposes are correctly shown on the designs, plans or other documents accompanying this application. (*Such documents may not always be necessary. They should be initialled by one of the applicants.*)

3. The Diocesan Advisory Committee has been consulted and [their recommendation is endorsed on the said accompanying documents] [their report accompanies this application].

4. The estimated cost of carrying out the pro-posed works or purposes is £   , of which sum £   has already been promised or paid and the balance will be defrayed by

5. A resolution of the parochial church council approving the proposed works or purposes was carried [unanimously] [by   votes to   of the members present and voting] at a meeting held on the   day of   19   , and a copy of the resolution signed by the [chairman] [secretary] accompanies this application.

6. Notice of intention to make this application was affixed on or near the principal door of the parish church [and of the church or place of worship of   ] during the period from   to   inclusive, and a copy of the notice and the certificate endorsed thereon signed by the applicants accompanies this applica- tion. (*This notice must be affixed for a continuous period of at least 10 clear days including 2 Sundays.*)

Dated the   day of   19

Signature of applicants.

Schedule

Description of works or purposes

(Here describe concisely but accurately the works or purposes proposed.)

Questions

(To be answered by the Applicants. Some questions may be irrelevant, especially if the application is for purposes other than works; they may be left blank or answered with a simple negative.)

1. What is the approximate age of the church or building?

2. Is an architect employed or to be employed? If so, state his name and enclose any report made by him as to the present condition of the church or building and as to the proposed work.

3. Give the name and address of any builder, organ builder, worker in stained glass, bell-founder, or other artist, craftsman or contractor to be employed.

4. Has the approval of the office in which the church or building is insured against fire been sought? If so, a copy of their approval or reply should accompany the application.

   Note: An answer is required only when alterations to heating or lighting are involved (including installation of organ blowers).

5. State the period estimated for the completion of the proposed work.

6. Has any previous faculty or licence or certificate been issued or sought affecting the proposed work or purposes? If so, give particulars of the faculty, licence or certificate.

7. If there is a lay rector, has his consent been obtained?
   Note: An answer is required only when the work affects the chancel, and any consent should accompany this application.

8. Are any private rights in seats affected? If so, describe them and state whether the persons entitled consent and in what terms.

9. Will any graves, monuments, or inscriptions be interfered with? State how they will be dealt with. Have the owners or relatives been found? If so, state whether they consent and in what terms. If they have not been found, state what efforts have been made to find them.

10. Will any carved work in wood or stone, stained glass windows or ornamental work in metal or other material or ancient windows, doorway or other specimen of ancient architecture be interfered with?

11. Will Divine Service be interrupted? If so, state what arrangements are proposed.

12. If the disposal of any church property is contemplated, give particulars.

13. Are there any other circumstances connected with the application on which the Archdeacon should be informed?

Signatures of applicants.

NOTE

An application may be made under section 12(1) of the Measure by the incumbent and churchwardens of a parish for an archdeacon's certificate in respect of the following works:—

(a) repairs to a church not involving substantial change in the structure of the building nor affecting its appearance either externally or internally; or
(b) repairs to the contents of a church not materially affecting their nature or appearance; or
(c) redecoration of a church or its contents; or
(d) any alteration in an existing heating system not involving a substantial change in the appearance of the church either externally or internally.

In addition, under section 12(7), the judge has a discretion to allow the archdeacon's certificate procedure to be followed in the case of any other application which in his opinion is unlikely to give rise to any controversy or dissatisfaction in the parish concerned and is not of sufficient importance to justify the expense of proceedings for a faculty.

No. 2

Notice of intention to make application under section 12

Diocese of

Parish of

Take notice that the incumbent and churchwardens of this parish intend to make an application under section 12 of the Faculty Jurisdiction Measure 1964 (subject to the discretion of the judge, if required, under section 12(7)) for authority to carry out the following works or purposes:—
(*Here describe the proposed works or purposes.*)

If any parishioner or person whose name is entered on the electoral roll of the parish or other person having an interest in the proposed works or purposes wishes to object thereto, he should state his objection in writing on a form obtainable from the Diocesan Registry at (*State address of registry.*)

and deliver or send it to the Diocesan Registrar at the Diocesan Registry, so as to reach him not later than (*Specify date 14 days after notice was first affixed.*)

Affixed this   day of   19

                              Signatures of incumbent and
                              churchwardens.

No. 3

Certificate of notice of intention under section 12

We certify that this Notice was affixed on or near to the principal door of the parish church of

[and of   ] during the period from
                    to
inclusive.

All persons having an interest have therefore been given an opportunity to object to the proposed works or purposes in accordance with the said Notice.

Dated this   day of   19

                              Signatures of incumbent and
                              churchwardens

No. 4

Notice of objection given to registrar under section 12(3)

To the Registrar of the Diocese of
 I,   of

hereby give notice of objection under section 12(3) of the Faculty Jurisdiction Measure 1964 to the proposed works or purposes specified in the Notice of Intention given by the incumbent and churchwardens of the parish of
dated

I am [a parishioner of the said parish] [a person whose name is entered on the electoral roll of the said parish] [a person having an interest in the proposed works or purposes by reason that

                                                           ]

Dated this   day of   19

                              Signature of objector.

No. 5

Archdeacon's certificate

Diocese of

Parish of

In pursuance of section 12 of the Faculty Jurisdiction Measure 1964 I, archdeacon of
with the approval of the Diocesan Advisory Committee, hereby authorise the carrying out in the [parish church or churchyard] [church or churchyard of   ] [place of worship of
           ] of the works or purposes proposed in an application dated the   day of   19
and made by the incumbent and churchwardens of the said parish.

The works as authorised shall be completed within
months from the date hereof, and their completion shall be certified to the registrar by the incumbent and churchwardens of the parish.

Dated this   day of   19

                              Signature of Archdeacon.

No. 6

Petition for faculty

In the Consistory Court of the Diocese of

Parish of

To the Worshipful Chancellor of the diocese of   and Official Principal of the Consistory Court of that diocese.

The petition of the undersigned (*Here state the full names and the residential address and description of each petitioner.*)

Sheweth as follows:—

1. It is desired to obtain the grant of a Faculty authorising the works or purposes described in the Schedule hereto.

2. The particulars of the said works or purposes are correctly shown on the designs, plans or other documents accompanying this petition. (*The documents should be initialled by one of the petitioners.*)

3. The Diocesan Advisory Committee has been consulted and [their recommendation is endorsed on the said accompanying documents] [their report accompanies this application].

4. The estimated cost of carrying out the proposed works or purposes is £   of which sum £   has already been promised or paid and the balance will be defrayed by

5. A resolution of the parochial church council relating to the proposed works or purposes was carried [unanimously) [by votes to   of the members present and voting] at a meeting held on the   day of   19   and a copy of the resolution signed by the [chairman] [secretary] accompanies this application.

Your Petitioners therefore pray that you will decree a Faculty authorising the works or purposes aforesaid.

Dated the   day of   19

Signatures of Petitioners.

SCHEDULE

Description of works or purposes

(Here describe concisely but accurately the works or purposes proposed. Reference to a plan is not a sufficient description.)

(The subject and position of any window tablet or other memorial and the wording and style of any inscription should be included.)

QUESTIONS

(To be answered by the Petitioners. Some questions may be irrelevant, especially if the application is for purposes other than works; they may be left blank or answered with a simple negative).

1. What is the approximate age of the church or building?

2. Is an architect employed or to be employed? If so, state his name and enclose any report made by him as to the present condition of the church or building and as to the proposed work.

3. Give the name and address of any builder, organ builder, worker in stained glass, bell-founder, or other artist, craftsman or contractor to be employed.

4. Has the approval of the office in which the church or building is insured against fire been sought? If so, a copy of their approval or reply should accompany the application.

   Note: An answer is required only when alterations to heating or lighting are involved (including installation of organ blowers).

5. State the period estimated for the completion of the proposed work.

6. Has any previous faculty or licence or certificate been issued or sought affecting the proposed work or purposes? If so, give particulars of the faculty, licence or certificate.

7. If there is a lay rector, has his consent been obtained?

   Note: An answer is required only when the work affects the chancel, and any consent should accompany this petition.

8. Are any private rights in seats, affected? If so, describe them and state whether the persons entitled consent and in what terms.

9. Will any graves, monuments, or inscriptions be interfered with? State how they will be dealt with. Have the owners or relatives been found? If so, state whether they consent and in what terms. If they have not been found, state what efforts have been made to find them.

10. Will any carved work in wood or stone, stained glass windows or ornamental work in metal or other material or ancient windows, doorway or other speciment of ancient architecture be interfered with?

11. Will Divine Service be interrupted? If so, state what arrangements are proposed.

12. If the disposal of any church property is contemplated, give particulars.

13. Are there any other circumstances connected with the petition on which the Court should be informed?

Signatures of Petitioners.

[[No. 7A

General citation and notice of objection

A.B., Chancellor of the diocese of   , To the incumbent and churchwardens of the parish of   . Whereas a Petition has been lodged in the registry of the Consistory Court of the diocese by X.Y. praying for a Faculty to issue authorising the following works or purposes, that is to say:—

By this citation all persons having or claiming to have a lawful interest in the subject matter of the petition are hereby required, if they or any of them wish to object to the grant of a Faculty for the works or purposes stated above, to deliver or send to the Diocesan Registrar at   a written notice of objection using the form of words set out below so as to reach him not later than *(Incumbent or Churchwarden to specify date 17 days after copy of Citation is first affixed.)*

And take notice that if no valid notice of objection has been given to the Diocesan Registrar within the time prescribed above a Faculty may be granted for the works or purposes aforesaid or otherwise as the Consistory Court of this diocese may think fit.

Dated this   day of   19

                                                  Signature of Registrar

Notice of objection

I   of

wish to object to the grant of a Faculty authorising the proposed works or purposes to be carried out.
(Note: copy and use whichever of the following is applicable):—

"I have an interest in the subject matter of the petition as [a parishioner(s) of the said parish]
[a person whose name is entered on the electoral roll of the said parish]
[an officer of the local planning authority in whose area the church (place of worship) lies]
[an officer of a statutory amenity society, namely the   society]
[a   (state any other interest not in preceding examples)]

Dated this   day of   19

                                                  Signature of objector

(Note: on receipt of your notice of objection the Diocesan Registrar will send you a form upon which you will be required to give full particulars of the grounds of your objection).

Appendix A

Directions to incumbent and churchwardens

We require you to affix a copy of this citation for a continuous period of not less than 10 days including two Sundays in each of the following places:

(i) on a notice board or in some other prominent position inside the parish church of [and of the church or place of worship of]

(ii) on a notice board outside but within the grounds of the said parish church or, if there is no such notice board then on the outside of the door of the said parish church [and of the church or place of worship of]

(iii) on a notice board or in some other prominent position (whether inside or outside a building) elsewhere in the parish where it will be clearly visible to the public.

Certificate of execution[1]

I, the undersigned hereby certify that a copy of this citation was affixed during the period from   to   inclusive

(i) on a notice board [on a   ] in the parish church of [and of the church or place or worship of]

(ii) outside the said parish church on [a notice board] [church door] [and outside the church or place of worship of on [a notice board] [the door]]

(iii) on the notice board [on a   ] elsewhere in the parish,[2] namely at

Dated this   day of   19

Signature of Incumbent
or Churchwarden

[1] The certificate of execution must be completed in full by making appropriate entries in the banks and deleting inappropriate words.
[2] Complete (iii) only where citation elsewhere in the parish has been directed.

No. 7B

Particulars of objection to petition for faculty

To the Registrar of the Diocese of

In the matter of a Petition relating to the church of   in the Parish of

seeking a faculty for (*State generally works or purposes.*)

I have previously given notice of objection. My objection relates to the whole [part] of the proposed works. (*Delete whichever is inapplicable.*)

The part(s) of the proposed works or purposes to which I object are:

(A)

(B)

The grounds for my objection are:

(*Here set out concisely the points which you rely upon in support of your objection.*)

(1)

(2)

(3)

(*If necessary continue with numbered paragraphs on a separate sheet.*)

Dated this   day   of 19

Signature of objector (or counsel or solicitor).

Directions

1. This form must be completed and returned to the Registrar at   if you wish to continue to be treated as an objector.

2. If you do not return the form within 21 days from the date of this direction it will be assumed you no longer wish to object and you will have to apply to the Consistory Court for leave to continue with your objection out of time.

3. You must deliver or send a copy of these Particulars of Objection to the Petitioners not later than 21 days from the date of this direction.

Dated this   day of   19

Signature of Registrar

I certify that I have sent a copy of these Particulars of Objection to the Petitioners today.

(Signature of objector or solicitor)

Dated this   day of   19

No. 8

Application by member of Council for Care of Churches[7] or person authorised by Council to give evidence under section 2(1)(iv)

Diocese of

I,   of

, hereby apply under section 2(1)(iv) of the Faculty Jurisdiction Measure 1964, to give evidence in open court in the proceedings for a faculty to demolish [a part of] the church or place of worship of   in the parish of

[7] Now Central Council for Churches.

I am a member of [a person duly authorised by] the Council for the Care of Churches [to give evidence in the said proceedings]. [A copy of my authority is annexed hereto).

Dated this   day of   19

Signature of applicant.

No. 9

Application by person other than member of or person authorised by Council to give evidence under section 2(1)(iv)

Diocese of

I,   of
                    , hereby apply under section 2(1)(iv) of the Faculty Jurisdiction Measure 1964 to give evidence in open court in the proceedings for a faculty to demolish [a part of] the church of
in the parish of

I am interested in the said proceedings by reason that (*Here state the reason e.g. that the applicant is a parishioner, but the reason need not necessarily disclose an interest in the legal sense. State also the matters on which the applicant proposes to give evidence.*)

Dated this   day of   19

Signature of applicant.

[[No. 9A

Application by member of Council for the Care of Churches or person authorised by Council to give evidence under rule 6(7).

Diocese of

I,   of
hereby apply under rule 6(7) of the Faculty Jurisdiction Rules 1967, as amended, to give evidence in open court in the proceedings for a faculty to dispose of

Appendix A

I am a member of [a person duly authorised by] the Council for the Care of Churches [to give evidence in the said proceedings]. [A copy of my authority is annexed hereto.]

Dated this   day of   19   ]]

No. 10

Form of faculty in unopposed proceedings

A.B., Chancellor of the Diocese of   and
Official Principal of the Consistory Court of that diocese

To C.D.,   and E.F.,
(*State names and descriptions of petitioners.*)

Whereas a petition presented by you has been filed in the registry of our said Court together with designs, plans or other documents, praying for a Faculty to issue authorising the works or purposes specified in the said petition and documents and described in the Schedule hereto.

And whereas by our direction a Citation was duly issued and executed citing all persons interested to show cause why a Faculty should not issue, and no objections have been taken to the granting thereof.

We now grant our Faculty authorising you to carry out the said works or purposes in accordance with the said designs, plans or other documents.

Provided that the said works shall be completed within   months from the date hereof or such further period as we may allow [and shall be carried out under the supervision of

of   ] and their completion shall be

certified by   of

, and the certificate lodged at the diocesan registry within the period allowed. (*Only applicable to works.*)

In testimony whereof we have caused our Seal to be affixed to these Presents.

Dated this   day of   19

Signature of Registrar.

SCHEDULE

Description of works or purposes

No. 11

Certificate of completion of works authorised by faculty

Parish of

We, A.B. of   and C.D. of

hereby certify that the works authorised by the faculty dated the
          day of   19   have been carried out in
accordance with the designs or plans and specifications filed in the registry.
 [the work was carried out under the supervision of
                              of   ].

Dated this   day of   19

Signature of persons required
to certify

Counter-signature by person (if any)
directed to supervise the work.

No. 12

Instrument of appointment under section 9 of person to act for archdeacon

To   of

I, A   Bishop of

in pursuance of section 9(2) of the Faculty Jurisdiction Measure 1964 hereby appoint you to act in the place of the archdeacon of [the archdeaconry being vacant] [the archdeacon being incapacitated] [the archdeacon being in my opinion unable or unwilling to act] in the matter of (*Here specify the case in which the person appointed is required to act.*)

Dated this   day of   19

Signature of Bishop.

Appendix B

	Page
Instrument of Delegation to Archdeacons (General)	239
Form of Authority to be given by an Archdeacon	240
Instrument of Delegation to Archdeacons (Churchyards)	241
Instrument of Delegation (Incumbents)	242

Instrument of Delegation to Archdeacons (General)

In the Consistory Court of
the Diocese of

1. I hereby authorise each and every Archdeacon in the Diocese to grant to the Incumbent, Curate-in-Charge, Parochial Church Council, or some or one of them, of any Church within his own Archdeaconry, permission to execute works of repair, maintenance or alteration to the fabric of a Church or to the chattels, fixtures, fittings or other contents (not being organ) of such Church.
Provided that an Archdeacon shall before exercising the power hereby conferred upon him satisfy himself

   (a) by consultation with the Chairman or Secretary of the Diocesan Advisory Committee or the relevant expert who is a member of the Committee in a case of urgency, or with that Committee itself in any other case, that the work proposed is aesthetically or technically appropriate to be done; and
   (b) by enquiries made by himself that the said works have the unanimous support of the Parochial Church Council and that there is no reason to suppose that they are opposed by any significant body of opinion in the Parish outside such Council.

2.   (i) An Archdeacon may authorise temporary re-arrangements of the furnishings in a Church within his Archdeaconry with a view to seeing whether it is appropriate for the furnishings of the Church to be re-ordered.
   (ii) An Archdeacon in giving authority under this paragraph shall specify for how long such authority shall continue in force.

   Provided that:
   (i) no such authority shall be in force for more than 12 months; and

(ii) that permanent re-ordering shall not be authorised except by faculty.

3. Save as provided in paragraph 2 this Instrument does not authorise an Archdeacon to permit the introduction of new furnishings or other contents into a Church and save as provided in paragraph 5(ii) nothing herein confers upon an Archdeacon power to permit things belonging to a Church to be sold or otherwise disposed of.

4. Nothing in this Instrument affects the requirement that work to an organ may be authorised only by faculty.

5. Nothing in this Instrument
  (i) authorises an Archdeacon to permit work to be done which involves the expenditure of more than £4,000 exclusive of fees and Value Added Tax, or such greater sum as I may hereafter specify in writing; or
  (ii) takes away or abridges the power of an Archdeacon to authorise informally work or acts which are minimal and of an uncontroversial or routine character; or
  (iii) authorises an Archdeacon to permit, authorise, ratify or confirm any work which has already been done when he acts.

6. Any permission or authority given by an Archdeacon under this Instrument shall be given in writing in duplicate.

Form of Authority to be given by an Archdeacon

Diocese of

In exercise of the powers which the Chancellor of the Diocese has conferred on me and being satisfied:—
  (a) after consultation with the Diocesan Advisory Committee that the works proposed are aesthetically or technically appropriate to be done, and
  (b) by my own inquiries that the works have the unanimous support of the Parochial Church Council and that there is no reason to suppose that they are

opposed by any significant body of opinion in the parish outside such Council,

I HEREBY AUTHORISE you to carry out the works as specified in the documents set down in the Schedule hereto
And you are to report to the Diocesan Registry not later than the   day of   198 the action taken under this authorisation.

The Schedule

To the Incumbent and Parochial Church Council of

A copy of this authority has been lodged with the Diocesan Registry by
the Archdeacon

Instrument of Delegation to Archdeacons
(Churchyards)

In the Consistory Court of the
Diocese of

1. In relation to any churchyard within his own Archdeaconry, I hereby authorise each and every Archdeacon in the Diocese to grant to any applicant permission to introduce into the churchyard a tombstone or monument of any description provided:

>   (i) That an Archdeacon shall before exercising the power hereby conferred satisfy himself by enquiries made by himself that the introduction of the proposed tombstone or monument has the unanimous support of the Parochial Church Council and that there is no reason to suppose that such introduction is opposed by any significant body of opinion in the parish outside such council, and

(ii) No such permission shall be granted except after the proposal to grant it has been approved by the Diocesan Advisory Committee.

2. I hereby further authorise any Archdeacon (subject to the conditions and provisos contained in paragraph (1) to make, in respect of any particular churchyard within his own Archdeaconry, a scheme under which a ledger stone or stones of dimensions less than 4 feet (1200mm) by 2 feet (600mm) may be introduced into such churchyard under permission granted by the Incumbent (or in the absence of an Incumbent the Curate in charge or Team Vicar, if there is one, or the Rural Dean, if there is not).

3. Every permission or Scheme given or made by an Archdeacon under this Instrument shall be given or made in writing in duplicate and one copy thereof shall forthwith be delivered to the Diocesan Registrar.

4. The powers delegated to an Archdeacon under this Instrument shall be in addition to the powers delegated to him by the Instrument of Delegation which I executed on [date] and any subsequent amendment thereof or addition thereto.

5. This Instrument shall be cited as "the Instrument of Delegation to Archdeacons (Churchyards) [date]."

6. This Instrument shall come into force on [date].

Chancellor of the Diocese [signed] ....

Instrument of Delegation (Incumbents)

In the Consistory Court of the
Diocese of

In exercise of the powers vested in me as Chancellor of the Diocese of   I declare and decree as follows:

Instrument of Delegation 243

1. I delegate to the incumbent of every parish in the Diocese power on my behalf to grant permission for the introduction into any churchyard in his parish of any monument conforming exactly with the conditions set out in Schedule A hereto.

2. Where a benefice has no incumbent, the curate in charge or team vicar (if there is one) shall have the powers hereby conferred on the incumbent. If in any benefice there is no incumbent and no curate in charge or team vicar, the said powers may be exercised by the Rural Dean.

3. It is expressly declared that no such powers are conferred on sequestrators as such.

4. No permission granted under the foregoing powers shall be valid unless it is given in writing in duplicate in the prescribed form and is given before any work pursuant to it is begun. The "prescribed form" means the form set out in Schedule B hereto or such other form as I may from time to time in writing prescribe.

5. Save as aforesaid, no permission shall be given for the introduction of any monument into a churchyard except by a faculty granted out of this Court or by myself in writing under my hand or by an Archdeacon under the Instrument of Delegation to Archdeacons of even date herewith or any subsequent Instrument replacing or amending it.

6. In this instrument the word "churchyard" includes any land consecrated for the interment of the remains of the dead, whether adjacent to a church or not.

7. This instrument shall be cited as "The Instrument of Delegation to Incumbents [date]."

8. This instrument shall come into operation on [date].

Schedule A

Monuments or tomb stones conforming exactly with the following provisions may be introduced into a churchyard with the written permission of the Incumbent (or Curate in Charge, Team Vicar or Rural Dean where the Benefice is vacant).

(i) A headstone shall be no more than 4 feet (1200mm) high, 3 feet (900mm) wide and 6 inches (150mm) thick and no less than 2 feet 6 inches (750mm) high, 1 foot 8 inches (500mm) wide and 3 inches (75mm) thick, and shall not be erected within 4 feet (1200mm) of the outer wall of the church.

(ii) A base forming an integral part of the design of a headstone may be permitted provided it does not project more than 2 inches (50mm) beyond the headstone in any direction provided

> (a) that where the headstone is more than 3 feet high the projection of the base may be increased to 4 inches (100mm)
> (b) that the headstone shall in all cases be fixed on a foundation slab (not necessarily of quarried stone) which is itself fixed flush with the turf and extends to between 3 and 5 inches (75 to 125mm) all round, so that a mower may pass freely over it.

(iii) Horizontal ledgers shall either be flush with the turf or raised not more than 9 inches (225mm) above a base, which shall be flush with the turf and shall extend not less than 3 inches (75mm) all round the ledger. The inclusive measurements of a ledger shall be not more than 7 feet (2100mm) by 3 feet (900mm) nor less than 4 feet (1200mm) by 2 feet (600mm) provided however that stones of smaller dimensions may be introduced pursuant to a Scheme made for a particular churchyard by the Archdeacon in whose Archdeaconry the churchyard lies.

(iv) Vases shall not be more than 12 inches × 8 inches × 8 inches in size (300 × 200 × 200mm).

(v) Where a part of the churchyard has been set aside for the burial of cremated remains no monument or vase shall be introduced into that area except in accordance with the terms of the Faculty setting the area apart.

(vi) Except as stated in (vii) below, monuments may be of natural wood or natural stone. Stones traditionally used in local buildings or closely similar to them in colour and texture are to be preferred. The stone shall not be mirror polished in any way so as to reflect.

(vii) A monument shall not be of black granite nor of pearl granite nor of all polished granite of whatever colour, nor of white marble, synthetic stone or plastic.

(viii) A monument shall not include any raised kerb, railings, stone or other chippings, picture or photograph, built-in vase container, statuary or bird bath. Every monument shall be simple in shape.

(ix) No advertisement or trade-mark shall be inscribed in the monument, but the name of the mason may be incised at the side or on the reverse of a headstone in unpainted and unleaded letters no more than half an inch (13mm) in height.

Schedule B

Diocese of

Application to Incumbent for Permission to Introduce a Memorial into a Churchyard

The Chancellor of the Diocese has delegated to Incumbents and Curates-in-Charge or Team Vicars (or in the case of a vacancy in the benefice the Rural Dean, but not to Churchwardens or Sequestrators) authority to permit, in writing but without a faculty, the introduction of
monuments into churchyards so long as they comply with certain specifications. Such specifications appear in the printed Churchyard Rules which have been circulated to Incumbents and to Stonemasons and ordered to be placed on all Church notice-boards. Applications outside this authority delegated by the Chancellor of the Diocese should be made through the Incumbent/Curate-in-Charge/Team Vicar/
Rural Dean to the Archdeacon of the appropriate Archdeaconry.

For full details please see the current edition of the Churchyard Rules.

Name of churchyard

Name of applicant
Address

Name of monumental mason
Address

Description of memorial

Size of memorial

Type of stone or wood to be used

Surface finish

Description of any carving or decoration

Appendix B

Wording of inscription

Type of lettering

Size of lettering

Colour of lettering

Full sketch of memorial showing ground level

(Where this is an application to the Archdeacon, there should be given the fullest possible particulars (including a clear plan) of the situation in the Churchyard in which the applicant proposes to place the tombstone or monument).

1. I have read the current edition of the Churchyard Rules issued by the Chancellor of the Diocese.
2. (a) I claim that under the terms of such Rules the Incumbent has power to permit the introduction into his churchyard of the monument described herein or
   (b) I accept that the Incumbent has no power to permit the introduction into his churchyard of the monument described herein but this application is submitted for approval by him and his Parochial Church Council and for onward transmission to the Archdeacon of his Archdeaconry.

(Please delete the alternative which does not apply).

3. I apply to the Incumbent or Archdeacon to grant permission accordingly.
4. I undertake that if permission is granted by the Incumbent or Archdeacon the monument will be erected in exact conformity with its description in this application.
5. I further undertake to indemnify the Incumbent or Archdeacon against all costs and expenses to which he may be put in respect of any deviation from the undertaking numbered 4 above.

6. I do not object to the Stonemason's name being incised upon the memorial (provided such incision meets the requirements of the Churchyard Rules).

Date　　　　　　　　Signed
　　　　　　　　　　　　　　　　　　　Applicant

We undertake to observe and be bound by the above.

Date　　　　　　　　Signed
　　　　　　　　　　　　　　　　　　　Monumental Mason

For use by the Incumbent or Archdeacon

The Incumbent or Archdeacon will indicate by his signature below that he authorises the introduction into the Churchyard of the monument described herein and, having signed the forms, will return one copy to the applicant and retain the other himself.

Date　　　　　　　　Signature
　　　　　　　　　　　　　　　　　Incumbent or Archdeacon

The Incumbent hereby acknowledges receipt of the fee of £

Date　　　　　　　　Signature
(*Where alternatives are provided, please delete whichever does not apply.*)

Appendix C

	Page
The Ecclesiastical Exemption	251

The Ecclesiastical Exemption

So far as concerns cases arising under the faculty jurisdiction, the substance of the ecclesiastical exemption is that an ecclesiastical building which is for the time being used for ecclesiastical purposes is exempt from listed building control and the ancient monuments legislation. The most authoritative account of the relevant legislation is set forth in the speech of Lord Cross of Chelsea in *Att.-Gen.* v. *Howard Church Trustees*.[1] It may, however, be convenient to summarise the essential provisions here.

Under the Town and Country Planning Act 1971, s.54(1), the Secretary of State is required to make lists of buildings "of special architectural or historic interest." A building included in such a list is called a "listed building,"[2] and by the same subsection "any object or structure fixed to a building, or forming part of the land and comprised within the curtilage of a building" is to be "treated as part of the building." Thus more is comprised in the listing than the primary building itself, and in particular all the equipment fixed inside the primary building is covered by the listing.

By section 55(1) a person commits an offence if he

> "executes or causes to be executed any works for the demolition of a listed building or for its alteration or extension in any manner which would affect its character as a building of special architectural or historic interest and the works are not authorised under this Part of this Act"

Then follow provisions for the granting of such authority by the written consent of the Secretary of State or of the local planning authority. The written consent is referred to as "listed building consent."

By section 58(1) a building which is not a listed building but which appears to the local planning authority to be of special architectural or historic interest and to be in danger of

---

[1] [1976] A.C. 363 at 370 to 374.
[2] s.54(9). This section has been amended and extended by the Housing and Planning Act 1986, Sched. 9, para. 1(1); see at p. 253.

"demolition or of alteration in such a way as to affect its character as such" may be the subject of a temporary notice called a "building preservation notice." The effect of the notice, while it is in force, is that the building is to be treated as if it were a listed building.

The exemption is created by section 56(1) which provides that section 55 is not to apply to works "for the demolition, alteration or extension of an ecclesiastical building which is for the time being used for ecclesiastical purposes or would be so used but for the works..." It is also provided that a building used or available for use of a minister of religion as a residence is not to be treated as an ecclesiastical building. In section 58(1) there is a corresponding exemption from liability in respect of a building preservation notice.

So far as concerns the ancient monuments legislation, section 61(8) of the Ancient Monuments and Archaeological Areas Act 1979 excepts "any ecclesiastical building for the time being used for ecclesiastical purposes" from the definition of "monument" in section 61(7).

In *Att.-Gen.* v. *Howard Church Trustees*[3] there was extensive discussion of what an "ecclesiastical building" is. But it was clear in that case that the building in question was on any view an ecclesiastical building, so that question needed no decision. But the ecclesiastical building in question had ceased to be used for ecclesiastical purposes because those who were responsible for it had decided, for reasons which seemed good to them, to close it. Subsequently it was demolished. The demolition therefore required listed building consent. It had been argued that the building was closed because it was being demolished and that therefore listed building consent was unnecessary on the ground that it would have been in ecclesiastical use but for the demolition. This view of what had happened did not find favour with the House of Lords.

The foregoing statutory arrangements have recently been made subject to alteration by ministerial order under the Housing and Planning Act 1986. Section 40 provides:

> "the enactments relating to listed buildings... are amended in accordance with Part I of Schedule 9 with respect to the following matters—

[3] [1976] A.C. 363.

(a) the treatment of free-standing objects and structures within the curtilage of a listed building; . . .
(e) the extent of the exemption accorded to ecclesiastical buildings."

Schedule 9, Part I, paragraph 1 provides that section 54(9) of the Town and Country Planning Act 1971 shall be amended by substituting for the words "and for the purposes" to the end of the subsection:

"and for the purposes of the provisions of this Act relating to listed buildings and building preservation notices the following shall be treated as part of the listed building—
(a) any object or structure affixed to the building
(b) any object or structure within the curtilage of the building which, although not fixed to the building, forms part of the land and has done so since before 1st July 1948."

By paragraph 5 of Part I of Schedule 9, a new section, 58AA, has been inserted into the Act of 1971. Subsection (1) of the new section enables the Secretary of State by order to provide "for restricting or excluding in such cases as may be specified in the order the operation in relation to ecclesiastical buildings of sections 56(1) and 58(2) of this Act (buildings excepted from provisions relating to listed buildings and building preservation notices)." Then follows subsection (2) which provides that "an order under this section may:

(a) make provision for buildings generally, for descriptions of buildings or for particular buildings;
(b) make different provision for buildings in different areas, for buildings of different religious faiths or denominations or according to the use made of the buildings;
(c) make such provision in relation to a part of a building (including, in particular, an object or structure falling to be treated as part of the building by virtue of section 54(9) of this Act) as may be made in relation to a building and may make different provision for different parts of the same building;
(d) make different provisions with respect to works of different descriptions or according to the extent of the works;

(e) make such consequential adaptations or modifications of the operation of any provision of this Act or of any instrument made under this Act as appears to the Secretary of State to be appropriate."

These provisions are sweeping and enable the Minister to make one or more orders destroying the exemption altogether or to make a series of partial orders without any limit upon their numbers.

Finally, subsection (3) of section 58AA amends section 287 of the 1971 Act by providing that an order under section 58AA: "shall be subject to annulment in pursuance of a resolution of either House of Parliament." This is the procedure known as "negative resolution." It cannot be very likely that the House of Commons, in which the Government of the day normally has a majority, will ever pass a resolution annulling an order made by the Government. But the possibility of a negative resolution in the House of Lords is a safeguard of some substance.

The consequence of the amendments made by the Act of 1986 is to make the future of the ecclesiastical exemption precarious. The new power has not, so far, been exercised.

Where a controversial faculty is sought in relation to a listed building, it is necessary for the consistory court to consider this legislation. The degree of weight which ought to be given to the fact of listing is the subject of an unfortunate conflict of judicial opinion,[4] but the absolute minimum appears to have been stated aptly by Boydell Ch. in *Re St. Mary's Banbury*[5]:

"This is a grade A listed building; and any proposal to alter the structure of such a building must be approached with the same care and be subject to the same detailed consideration as would be necessary if churches were to lose their ecclesiastical immunity and if, therefore, this were an application for listed building consent pursuant to the provisions of the Town and Country Planning Act 1971."

It will therefore be necessary in such a case for the court to consider section 56(3) of that Act which is as follows:

---

[4] See Chapter 3.
[5] [1985] 2 All E.R. 611 at 618 f–g; unfortunately this passage does not appear in the Law Reports, [1986] Fam. 24.

"In considering whether to grant planning permission for development which consists in or includes work for the alteration or extension of a listed building, and in considering whether to grant listed building consent for any works, the local planning authority or the Secretary of State, as the case may be, shall have special regard to the desirability of preserving the building or any features of special architectural or historic interest which it possesses."

The consistory court should therefore ascertain whether the building is listed, and in what grade, what its features of special architectural or historic interest are and whether the works proposed will affect them adversely. The court is not bound to refuse a faculty if there would be such adverse effects, but they are an important element in the exercise of its discretion. Further, the Secretary of State has from time to time issued circulars for the guidance of local planning authorities.[6] In a controversial case the consistory court would be wise to give consideration to this material.

---

[6] See Circular No. 23/77, Listed Buildings in Conservation Areas; and Circular No. 12/81, Historic and Building Conservation Areas.

Index

Access,
  rights of, 168, 170
Alms box, 113
Altar. *See* Holy table.
Altar frontals, 117
Alternative Service Book, 133
Amenity societies. *See* Parties.
Apparitor, 12
Appeals, 19, 81
  as to doctrine, etc., 76, 77, 81, 111
Archaeology, 38
Archdeacon, 38
  annual visitations, 24, 84, 125
  certificate of, 21, 31, 200, 205, 216, 220
  commissary of, 24
  costs and expenses of. *See* Costs.
  decision of, 22, 31
  delegation to, 21–22, 30–31, 239–242
  deputy, 25, 27, 84, 103, 182, 199, 217, 235
  enforcement by, 26, 96
  in faculty proceedings. *See* Parties.
  informal approach to, 25
  member of D.A.C. *See* D.A.C.
  parish meeting under, 29, 120
  permission for experiments, 121
  preliminary visit by, 35
  remedial faculty to. *See* Faculty.
  repairs by, 84
  supervision of faculty, 28, 80, 199, 215
  tenure and general duties, 23
  vacancy of post. *See* Deputy.
Arches Court of Canterbury. *See* Appeals.
Architect. *See* Church; D.A.C.
Armorial bearings, 134–135
Armour, 137
Ashes, 134, 145, 163–165
Aumbry, 79, 115. *See also* Sacrament.

Baptism, 116
Bells, 38, 106–108, 113, 124

Bells—*cont.*
  sanctuary bell, 107, 115
Bible, 113
Bishop,
  legal secretary of, 13, 45
  litigant, as, 14
Bones. *See* Human remains.
Book of Remembrance, 164
Books. *See* Library; Register books.
Boundary, 179
Building,
  meaning of, 98, 156
  subterranean, 97, 159
  temporary, 170
  unconsecrated, 1, 23, 173
Burial grounds and churchyards, 139–172, 173–179. *See also* Churchyard.
  building on, 57, 62, 79, 92, 95, 153–163
  burial rights. *See* Burial rights.
  closed, 140, 145
  consecrated, 139, 168
  deconsecrated, 95, 141, 171
  disused, 139, 153–163, 172
  faculty jurisdiction, 139, 161
  licence of, 100, 140, 169
  maintenance of, 144
  no sale or tenancy of, 100, 140, 168
  open space, as, 98, 161–163
  ownership of, 2, 48, 140, 168, 177
  reordering of, 145–149
  tombstones in. *See* Tombstones.
  unconsecrated, 1, 48, 95, 134, 173, 198
Burial in church, 133–134
Burial rights, 75, 143–145, 163–165, 198

Candles,
  electric, 113, 129
Candlesticks, 115, 117
Canopy, 159
Car park, 148

257

Index

Carpets, 38, 116
Cathedral Treasury. *See* Chattels, loans.
C.C.C.: Central Council for Churches, 42, 62, 67, 70, 104, 123, 203, 213, 217, 232, 233
Ceremonial. *See* Appeals.
Chairs. *See* Pews.
Chalice, 117
Chancellor, 7–14, 205
   delegation. *See* **Archdeacon; Incumbent**
   deputy and vacancy, 10
   judicial discretion of, 73
   mode of address, 12
   Official Principal, as, 10
   precedence and mace and seal of, 7, 12
   qualifications and tenure, 7
   Vicar General, as, 9
Chancery Court of York. *See* Appeals.
Chapel, licensed, 1, 23, 33, 173, 197
Charity, licence to, 101
Chattels, 103–138
   citation as to, 62
   doctrinal significance, 113–119
   gifts, 116
   illegal, 57, 115, 181
   insurance of. *See* **P.C.C.**
   loans to museums, etc., 127
   moveable, 112–120
   redundant church, of, 117
   ownership of, 2, 16
   proceeds of sale, 48, 123
   recovery of, 180
   repairs to. *See* **Repairs**.
   sale of, 53, 56, 85, 117, 121–125
   title to. *See* **Churchwardens**.
   unwanted, 116
Church, 83–138, 205
   architect, 5, 34, 36, 39, 83, 85
   burial in. *See* **Burial**.
   curtilage of, 174, 198
   dangerous or vandalised, 90–92
   extension of, 92–98, 160, 178
   fabric of, 83–103
   hall. *See* **Hall**.
   interior, 38
   meaning of, 87, 175
   memorial tablets in, 135
   neglected, 85
   new, 33
   ownership of, 2
   part demolition. *See* **Demolition**.
   private ownership of parts, 192

Church—*cont.*
   redundancy of, 85
   reordering, 38, 39, 99, 118–121
   repairs. *See* **Repairs**.
   secular use of, 99
Churchwardens, 2, 16. *See also* **Parties**.
   Consistory Court duties, 67
   duties of, 84
   evidence of, 40
   owners of bells, 106
   owners of chattels, 122
   pews and seating by, 109
   sale by. *See* **Chattels**.
Churchyard wall, 158
Churchyards, 139–172, 174, 243
   See also **Burial grounds and churchyards**.
Citation, 49, 58–63, 146, 208
   certificate of, 209, 230
   form of, 59, 63, 228
   period, 205, 208
   special, 197
Columbarium, 134, 158
Commissary, archdeacon, of, 24
Commissary Court, 7
Commissary General, 7
Commission of Review, appeals to, 19
Communion linen, 113, 121
Communion plate. *See* **Plate**.
Confessional, 115
Consecration, 1, 102
   infringement of, 58, 96
Conservation, 119. *See also* **Parties**.
Consistory Court, 7, 203
   chambers, 3, 59, 67
   contempt of. *See* **Contempt**.
   costs in. *See* **Costs**.
   fees, 70, 184
   judicial review of, 20
   open court, 3, 41, 53, 59, 67
   parties, archdeacon or deputy, 26
   place of hearing, 11
   power to grant licence, 100
   procedure in. *See* **Faculty proceedings**.
   secular courts, relation to, 19
   task of, 5, 98
   undertakings to, 47, 96, 161, 183
Contempt, 11, 67, 183
Contents of church. *See* **Chattels**.
Costs, 81, 184–187
   Archdeacon, of, 27, 29, 184, 186, 199, 210
   against objectors, 48, 186, 197
   against party in breach, 182, 196

Costs—*cont.*
  enforcement of, 184, 199
  taxation of, 187
Court of Ecclesiastical Causes Reserved. *See* **Appeals.**
Cross, stations of, 115
Crucifix, 114
Crypt never leased, 100, 101

Decorations. *See* **Chattels.**
Demolition, 53, 57, 62, 67, 87–92, 193
D.A.C.: Diocesan Advisory Committee, 5, 32–43
  archdeacon's certificate, 41, 207
  archdeacon's position in, 25
  agendas of, 49
  appointments to, 34, 38
  delay of, 42
  duties of, 201
  expenses of members, 39
  functions of, 32–33
  members of, 37, 104, 106, 201
  organs subcommittee, 104
  party and evidence. *See* **Parties.**
  recommendations, 37, 40, 41, 207, 217
  secretariat of, 35–37
  stamp of, 41
  standing committee of, 36, 37–38
  views of, 90, 103, 106, 123, 125
  witnesses. *See* **Witnesses.**
D.B.F.: Diocesan Board of Finance. *See* **Chattels,** sale of.
Diocesan registrar. *See* **Registrar.**
  secretary. *See* **D.A.C.,** secretariat.
Doctrine, etc. *See* **Appeals.**
Drainage, rights of, 170

Ecclesiastical exemption, 4–6, 251–255. *See also* **Listed building.**
Ecclesiastical building, 96
Electrical equipment, 38
Electricity substation, 158, 170
Electricity wires, 170
Embroidery. *See also* **Chattels.**
Enforcement. *See* **Faculty; Costs.**
English Heritage, 86
Exhumation. *See* **Human remains.**
Experiments, permission for, 21
Fabric. *See* **Church.**
Faculty,
  completion certificate, 215, 235
  conditional, 28, 80, 161, 199, 215
  confirmatory, 8, 53, 56
  demolition for. *See* **Demolition.**

Faculty—*cont.*
  enforcement of, 180–184
  form of, 215
  interlocutory, 53, 58
  mandatory, 78, 183
  material alteration, for, 2, 3, 16
  nisi, 58
  occupation by charity, for, 101
  order, 77
  preliminary consideration of, 57
  remedial, 26, 29, 78, 181, 197, 199
  supervision of. *See* **Archdeacon.**
  temporary, 58
  time limit for works, 59, 215
  until further order, 79
  urgent. *See* **Faculty proceedings.**
  vesting private part of church, 192
Faculty jurisdiction, 1, 15–19. *See also* **Burial grounds.**
  Measure and Rules, 191–236
  cases nearly *de minimis,* 31
  de minimis exception, 20, 114
  essential features, 17
Faculty Jurisdiction Commission, 5
Faculty proceedings,
  See also **Consistory Court; Faculty.**
  citation. *See* **Citation.**
  consultation before, 52, 120
  controversial, 61
  costs, 120. *See also* **Costs.**
  disclosure of documents, 211
  evidence, 68, 70, 212–214
  fees, 54
  forms, 54, 207, 225–236
  hearing,
    notice of, 214
    procedure at, 68
    time for, 66, 212
  irregular, 219
  judgment reserved, 186
  notice of objection 48, 63, 210, 229
  onus of proof, 73–77
  opposed, 59
  order, 77. *See also* **Faculty.**
  parish meeting before, 29, 120
  parish opinion, 71, 74
  particulars of objection, 64, 211, 231
  parties. *See* **Parties.**
  petition, 54
    form, 54–57, 225–228
    lodging of, 57, 208
    notice of. *See* **Citation.**
    preparation before, 55
  petitions, 71
  pleadings, 65, 211

Index

Faculty proceedings—*cont.*
  pleadings, bad, 211
    default of, 66
  procedure, 52–82
  remedial faculty, 26
  rules, 52, 202, 204–236
  service of documents, 218
  summons for directions, 65, 72
  time, enlargement of, 64, 218
  types of faculty. *See* **Faculty**.
  uncontentious, 40, 64, 72, 211, 215, 234
  urgent, 53, 58. *See also* **Faculty**.
  viewing *locus in quo*, 71
  witnesses. *See* **Witnesses**.
  written representations, 41, 72–73, 214
Fire escape, 158, 170
Fixtures. *See* **Bells, Church, Chattels.** *See also* **Holy table, Organs, Pews.**
Flagon. *See* **Silver.**
Font, 113
Furniture, 38. *See* **Chattels.**

Gifts, 116–117
Glass, stained, 41
Goods. *See* **Chattels.**
Grant, DoE, from, 55
Grave spaces. *See* **Burial rights.**
  position of, 143, 163
Gutters, 85

Hall, 160, 178
Heating, 38, 39, 128–130, 200
Helmet. *See* **Armour.**
Heraldry. *See* **Armorial bearings.**
High Court, 184
Highway, 168, 178
Historic Buildings Council, 94
Holy table, 110–112, 113, 115, 119
Holy water stoup, 115
Human remains, 16, 44, 57, 61, 96, 165–168

Incumbent. *See also* **Parties.**
  delegation to. *See* **Tombstones.**
  property title of, 2, 100, 140
Injunction, 181
Inscription, 138, 151
Insurance. *See* **P.C.C.**
Interior. *See* **Church.**

Judge. *See* **Chancellor.**

Kerbstones, 144, 244. *See also* **Tombstones.**

Land,
  consecrated, 23
  illegitimate use of, 27
  unconsecrated. *See* **Chapels; Churchyard.**
Lay Rector. *See* **Rector.**
Leasing, no power of, 100, 101.
Lectern, 113
Ledger stones, 242, 244. *See* **Tombstones.**
Library, 1, 16, 125–127, 186
Licence documents, 101
Lighting, 128–130. *See also* **Candles.**
Listed building, 75
Local authority, notices by, 90
Loudspeakers, 129

Marriage licences, 9
Mausoleum, 148. *See also* **Tombstones.**
Memorial. *See* **Petitions.**
Memorials, 135–138. *See also* **Tombstones.**
Monument collective, 164
Monuments, 196. *See also* **Tombstones.**
Mortuary, 44
Moveables, 112–130. *See also* **Chattels.**
Museums. *See* **Chattels.**

Noise, 101

Obelisk, 44, 158
Objections. *See* **Faculty proceedings.**
Offices. *See* **Church,** extensions.
Official Principal. *See* **Chancellor.**
Oil cruet, 115
Open space. *See* **Burial grounds.**
Organs, 38, 103–122, 180
Ornaments. *See* **Chattels; Plate.**
Ownership. *See* **Title.**

Parochial library. *See* **Library.**
Parties, 43–51, 210
  acting archdeacon. *See* **Archdeacon.**
  archdeacon, 26, 27, 47, 50, 64, 94, 102, 122, 198, 210
  amenity society, 49, 93, 205, 210
  churchwardens, 45, 47
  close relatives, 46
  costs liability for. *See* **Costs.**
  C.C.C., 50
  D.A.C., 27, 47, 50, 213
  designated person, 210

Parties—*cont.*
  donor, 44
  electoral roll, on, 47, 48, 198, 210
  freeholders, 44
  government minister, 46
  incumbent, 44, 54
  interested person, 43, 63, 210
  local authority, 44
  local planning authority, 48, 210
  ornaments as to, 44
  other designated bodies, 50
  parish council (civil), 45
  P.C.C., 45, 47, 54
  rateable occupier, 45
  residents, 48, 210
Pastoral need, 40
P.C.C.: Parochial Church Council. *See also* **Parties.**
  duty for repairs, 83
  insurance by, 83, 127
  not liable for illegal work, 80
  request for parish meeting by, 30
  undertakings. *See* **Consistory Court.**
Petition. *See* **Faculty proceedings.**
Petitions, 71
Pews, 3, 75, 108–110, 118, 124
Photographers. *See also* **Contempt.**
Pictures, 38, 244. *See also* **Chattels.**
Place of worship, 205
Planning permission, 93, 95
Plans and specifications, 36, 37, 39, 85, 207, 217
Plaque, 138. *See also* **Memorials.**
Plate, 113. *See also* **Chattels; Silver.**
Plate of redundant church, 118
Prayer book, 113
Privy Council. *See* **Appeals.**
Pulpit, 113
Pyx, hanging, 116. *See also* **Sacrament.**

Quinquennial Review, 18, 34. *See also* **Repairs.**

Reading desk, 113
Recreational facilities, 156, 161–163
Rector. *See* **Incumbent.**
  lay, rights of, 56, 84, 140
Redecoration. *See* **Repairs.**
Register books, 113
Registrar, 2, 15, 205
  bishop's legal adviser, 14
  bishop's legal secretary, 13
  deputy, 13, 218
  duties of, 15
Repairs, 39, 83–87, 200

Repairs—*cont.*
  responsibility for, 47
Restrictive covenants, 177
Reverence, superstitious, 115
Ritual. *See* **Appeals.**
Road widening, 140, 167
Royal Fine Arts Commission, 94. *See also* **Parties.**
Rural Dean, 84

Sacrament, reservation of, 130–133
Safe, 132
Sale of church items. *See* **Chattels.**
Sanctuary,
  bell. *See* **Bells.**
  gong, 115
  lamp, 129. *See also* **Candles.**
Scaffold, 156
Sepulture. *See* **Burial rights.**
Silver, 26, 38. *See also* **Chattels; Plate.**
Sketch, 11
Stained glass, 38, 138
Surplices, 113

Tabernacle, 115. *See also* **Sacrament.**
Tapestries, 117
Thurible, 115
Title. *See* **Incumbent; Rector.**
  to chattels. *See* **Churchwardens.**
  to churchyard. *See* **Churchyard.**
  to memorials. *See* **Memorials.**
  to tombstones. *See* **Tombstones.**
Tombstones, 38, 56, 96, 143, 192. *See also* **Burial grounds.**
  archdeacon's powers, 30, 241
  incumbent's powers, 20, 149, 242
  inscriptions on, 151, 244
  materials of, 150, 244
  ownership, 46, 97, 146, 185, 196
  permission for, 245
  regulations, 144, 149, 152
  removal, 144, 145–149, 182, 196
  scheme for, 243
  unauthorised, 182
Treasures. *See* **Chattels; Silver.**
Trespass, 181

Undertaking. *See* **Consistory Court.**

Valuables. *See* **Chattels.**
Vases, 244
Vault, family, 44
Vestry, 160
Vicar. *See* **Incumbent.**
Vicar General. *See* **Chancellor.**

Witnesses,
   expert, 65, 74, 120, 211
   judge's, 69, 185
   statutory, 69
   subpoena of, 68

Words and phrases,
   "fiat", 58
   "pass the seal", 12